Affordable Elegant Meals

SUSAN LAMMERS
Editor

CYNTHIA SCHEER
Writer and Food Stylist

LINDA HINRICHS
CAROL KRAMER
Designers

FRED LYON
Major Photographer

SARA SLAVIN
Photographic Stylist

ELLEN BLONDER
EDITH ALLGOOD
Illustrators

CALIFORNIA
CULINARY
ACADEMY

Ortho Books

Publisher
Robert L. Iacopi

Editorial Director
Min S. Yee

Managing Editors
Jim Beley
Anne Coolman
Susan Lammers
Michael D. Smith
Sally W. Smith

Production Director
Ernie S. Tasaki

Editors
Richard H. Bond
Alice E. Mace

System Manager
Christopher Banks

System Consultant
Mark Zielinski

Asst. System Managers
Linda Bouchard
William F. Yusavage

Photographic Director
Alan Copeland

Photographers
Laurie A. Black
Richard A. Christman

Asst. Production Manager
Darcie S. Furlan

Production Editors
Jill Fox
Don Mosley
Anne Pederson

Chief Copy Editor
Rebecca Pepper

Photo Editors
Kate O'Keeffe
Pam Peirce

National Sales Manager
Charles H. Aydelotte

Sales Associate
Susan B. Boyle

Operations Assistant
Gail L. Davis

Administrative Assistant
Georgiann Wright

Address all inquiries to:
Ortho Books
Chevron Chemical Company
Consumer Products Division
575 Market Street
San Francisco, CA 94105

Copyright © 1985
Chevron Chemical Company
All rights reserved under
international and Pan-American
copyright conventions.

First Printing in July, 1985

1 2 3 4 5 6 7 8 9
85 86 87 88 89 90

ISBN 0-89721-052-2

Library of Congress Catalog Card
Number 85-070882

Chevron Chemical Company
575 Market Street, San Francisco, CA 94105

Danielle Walker *(left)* is chairman of the board and founder of the California Culinary Academy. **Cynthia Scheer** *(right)* is a food writer and home economist. She has been a food editor of *Sunset Magazine* and has written 15 cookbooks on a variety of subjects. Other books by Cynthia Scheer in the California Culinary Academy Series include *Breads, Breakfasts & Brunches, Salads,* and *Soups & Stews.* A resident of the San Francisco Bay Area, she has traveled extensively throughout the United States, Mexico, and Europe to explore and experience the foods of many regions.

The California Culinary Academy Among the forefront of American institutions leading the culinary renaissance in this country, the California Culinary Academy in San Francisco has gained a reputation as one of the most outstanding professional chef training schools in the world. With a teaching staff recruited from the best restaurants of Western Europe, the California Culinary Academy educates students from around the world in the preparation of classical cuisine. The recipes in this book were created in consultation with the chefs of the California Culinary Academy.

Acknowledgments

Manuscript Reviewer
Charlotte Walker

Copyediting and Proofreading
Naomi Steinfeld, copyeditor
Janine Hannel, proofreader
Teresa Castle, proofreader

Photographers
Laurie Black, Academy photography
Alan Copeland, page 30, 80
Fischella, photograph of Danielle
  Walker
Michael Lamotte, front cover,
  back cover

*Food Styling for Front Cover,
Back Cover*
Amy Nathan

Food Styling at the Academy
Jeff Van Hanswyk

Color Separations
Color Tech Corporation

Calligraphy
Chuck Wertman

Editorial Assistants
Anne Ardillo
Bil Lawrence

Cover Photo: Pot au Feu (page 86) is just one of the many affordable, elegant meals featured in this book. This is a classic dish made with beef brisket and an array of fresh vegetables.

Back Cover Photos:
Upper left: Leeks, carrots, potatoes, onions, garlic, and herbs are just some of the ingredients that go into a rich veal stock. This stock can later be used in a variety of ways for everything from soup to sauces.

Upper right: Two trouts garnished with lemon and parsley are ready to enter the fish poacher, where they will be simmered in white wine and herbs.

Lower left: Four Cornish game hens are arranged artfully on a platter with baby carrots and green beans. Chefs know that the way food is presented is just as important as how it tastes. You can learn to present food with flair at home.

Lower right: Rosettes of whipped cream are piped onto a cake with a pastry bag and an open-star tip. As a finishing touch, they add a professional look that makes this chocolate cake something special.

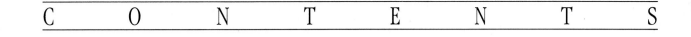

INTRODUCING INEXPENSIVE MEATS 5

Economy cuts are more plentiful and varied than you might suppose. Transform them into elegant meals.

ELEGANT WHOLE-MEAL SOUPS 59

Meals from the soup kettle offer economy, make-ahead convenience, and wonderful flavor.

AFFORDABLE ROASTS 15

For inexpensive elegance from the oven, discover the less costly cuts of beef, pork, lamb, veal, and poultry. They make wonderful roasts perfect for family and guests.

STEWS FOR SPECIAL MEALS 81

Slow cooking brings out a wealth of flavor and tenderness in the humblest meats and poultry.

THIRTY-MINUTE MEATS 31

The cook in a hurry need not fall back on the costliest cuts. Thrifty meals can also be quickly cooked.

MAKE-AHEAD CASSEROLES & MEAT PIES 103

Advance planning makes both elegance and economy possible with these dishes and menu ideas.

Traditional meat dealer Anthony Iacopi of San Francisco knows the value of less expensive cuts of meat. With a little effort you too can learn about meat values.

Introducing Inexpensive Meats

Serving an elegant, affordable meal does not require a sacrifice in quality, flavor, or satisfaction. In fact, many of the most famous and elegant dishes of the world do not demand the use of expensive and exotic ingredients. As the recipes in this book will show you, there are many inexpensive cuts of meat that can be used to create a wide variety of delicious and hearty meals.

GETTING THE MOST FROM YOUR MEAT DOLLAR

The choicest cuts of beef, pork, and lamb are taken from the loin and rib sections (which account for only a small part of the available meat). Because the loin and rib cuts are familiar and dependably tender, they are in the greatest demand; therefore, they command the highest prices. Yet an amazing variety of less costly cuts can be found at any supermarket meat counter. When prepared properly, they'll yield a rewarding variety of tender, delicious meat dishes.

The less expensive cuts of meat are generally tougher (although they are just as nutritious as the tenderest of cuts). These cuts of meat are tough because they are taken from those muscles that receive much more exercise. When a muscle is used often, its fibers toughen, and connective tissue develops within the muscle to strengthen and support it. Muscles that are rarely used remain tender and develop very little connective tissue. For example, the tender loin muscle right in the middle of the back does very little work, while the hard-working muscles of the legs and neck can be downright tough.

The best buys at the meat counter are usually the less tender cuts. But with some know-how, you can get the most from the meat you purchase.

The two basic methods of cooking meat involve either *dry heat* or *moist heat.* Dry-heat cooking includes roasting, broiling, pan-broiling, frying, grilling, and barbecuing. Dry heat should be used to cook only the very tender cuts, because it tends to toughen meat fibers. Less tender cuts require moist-heat methods, such as stewing, braising, simmering, and other methods of cooking in liquid.

Moist heat helps tenderize the meat; the long, slow process of cooking in liquid breaks down the tough connective tissue, eventually turning it to gelatin. Some of the tougher cuts of meat (although not *the* toughest) can be tenderized before cooking, then cooked with dry heat. Marinades, pounding and cubing, and commercial tenderizers are common ways of tenderizing meat. Each chapter in this book is based on a different method of cooking. Each method features appropriate cuts of meat. Some of these choices may surprise you—they depart from tradition and reveal more versatility than you might suspect.

THE VARIOUS CUTS OF MEAT

There are hundreds of names for cuts of meat. Many of these names are regional adaptations: A *New York steak* in one area might be called a *club steak* or a *top sirloin* in another. Some of these names are actually recipe names rather than names of retail cuts: *London broil*—a name commonly seen at the meat counter—is actually the name of a recipe, not a retail cut of beef. In fact, the cut of beef used to make London broil is *flank steak*, and it sells for a lower price when labelled as such. You'll find it easier to identify cuts of meat and to sniff out their potential as main dishes that your family and guests will enjoy if you familiarize yourself with the basic retail and wholesale cuts (illustrated on page 8).

There are nine wholesale (or primal) cuts on a side of beef; similar divisions are made for other types of meat. The *short loin, sirloin,* and *rib* primal cuts contain the tenderest meat; cuts from these areas—whether beef, pork, veal, or lamb—are usually the most costly. From this area come the expensive steaks, beef fillet, pork tenderloin, standing rib roast, rack of lamb, and center-cut pork chops.

Most of the recipes in this cookbook are for the cuts of meat from in front of, behind, and below the rib and loin, where the bargains are. Some of the consistently lowest-priced meats are from the *chuck* cuts—shoulder and blade from beef, and blade and Boston butt from pork. Below this area are the front leg cuts. In beef these include the *foreshank* (the source of beef shanks) and in pork they include the *picnic shoulder* (providing picnic shoulder roast). Immediately behind the foreshank is the breast area, or *brisket* of beef, notable for the corned beef it produces. The breast also yields pork spareribs and veal and lamb breast. In pork, the boneless meat from this section is cured and smoked to make bacon. The *short plate*, which is behind the breast area, is the source of short ribs. The most important cut taken from the *flank*, just below the short loin, is the flank steak. Behind the loin is the leg or round. In beef it contains the familiar round steak, which has three quite different portions (each with its own fascinating potential) as well as rump roasts, the sirloin tip, and, of course, oxtails. In pork the leg is smoked for ham; in lamb the entire leg may be sold as leg of lamb.

Of course a low price per pound on meat doesn't necessarily guarantee economy. Keep in mind the amount of cooked lean meat the cut will provide, as well. From cuts with little or no fat or bone, you can expect three or four servings per pound. Cuts with a medium amount of bone (poultry falls into this category, as do many chops and steaks) provide two to three servings per pound. From cuts with a high proportion of fat and bone—such as spareribs, beef and lamb shanks, short ribs, and premium steaks (such as porterhouse and T-bone)—you will get just one to two servings per pound.

Reading a Meat Label

All meat sold in the United States is checked by federal or state and city inspectors for wholesomeness. Such inspection guarantees that the meat is suitable for consumption. In addition, most meat is graded by the United States Department of Agriculture (USDA) for quality. "Quality" is determined by such characteristics as tenderness, juiciness, and flavor, which contribute to the palatability of the meat. The top grades in beef are USDA Prime, USDA Choice, and USDA Good.

Most of the beef graded "Prime" is found in restaurants and specialty meat markets. The grade most widely sold at retail markets is "Choice." The next level on this quality scale is "Good"-grade beef. This is relatively tender and somewhat leaner than the higher grades, but lacking some of their juiciness and flavor. It is sold by many supermarket chains under their own quality designation rather than a USDA grade name.

Beef that passes federal inspection for wholesomeness is stamped with a round, purple mark made with an edible vegetable dye. The number inside the mark is the official number assigned to the establishment where the animal was processed (see illustration). State-inspected beef will have a different-shaped inspection mark, depending on the state. The inspection mark is placed only once on wholesale cuts, so you are likely to see it only on large cuts of beef.

Prime The top or highest grade of meat, containing the greatest degree of marbling. Generally it is sold to finer restaurants and select meat stores. It is always sold at higher prices because it's produced in very limited quantities.

Economical cuts of beef, combined with a variety of fresh vegetables and seasonings, offer infinite possibilities for elegant and delicious dishes.

BEEF CHART

RETAIL CUTS OF BEEF AND WHERE THEY COME FROM

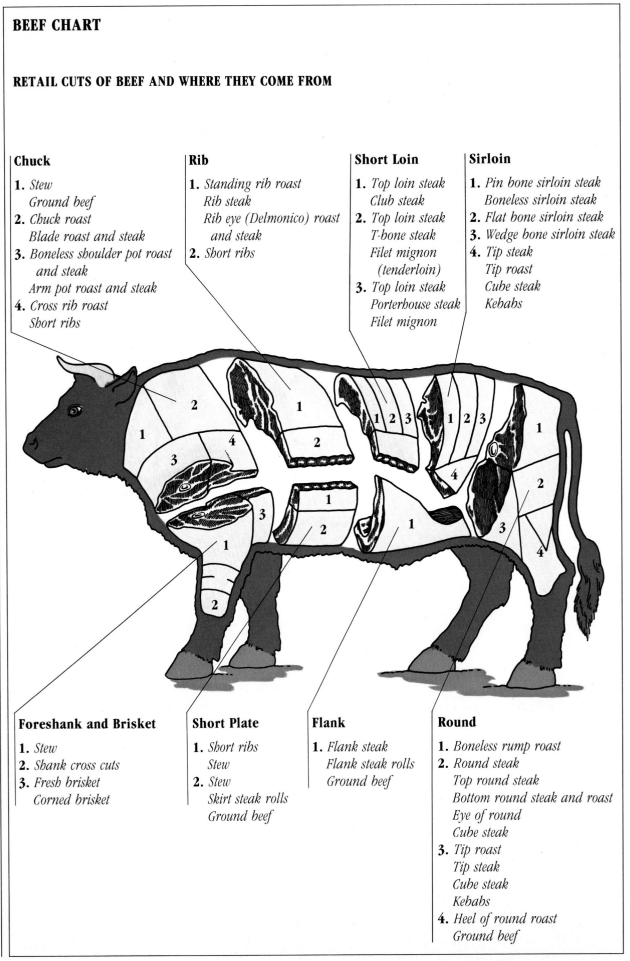

Chuck

1. *Stew*
   Ground beef
2. *Chuck roast*
   Blade roast and steak
3. *Boneless shoulder pot roast*
   and steak
   Arm pot roast and steak
4. *Cross rib roast*
   Short ribs

Rib

1. *Standing rib roast*
   Rib steak
   Rib eye (Delmonico) roast
   and steak
2. *Short ribs*

Short Loin

1. *Top loin steak*
   Club steak
2. *Top loin steak*
   T-bone steak
   Filet mignon
   (tenderloin)
3. *Top loin steak*
   Porterhouse steak
   Filet mignon

Sirloin

1. *Pin bone sirloin steak*
   Boneless sirloin steak
2. *Flat bone sirloin steak*
3. *Wedge bone sirloin steak*
4. *Tip steak*
   Tip roast
   Cube steak
   Kebabs

Foreshank and Brisket

1. *Stew*
2. *Shank cross cuts*
3. *Fresh brisket*
   Corned brisket

Short Plate

1. *Short ribs*
   Stew
2. *Stew*
   Skirt steak rolls
   Ground beef

Flank

1. *Flank steak*
   Flank steak rolls
   Ground beef

Round

1. *Boneless rump roast*
2. *Round steak*
   Top round steak
   Bottom round steak and roast
   Eye of round
   Cube steak
3. *Tip roast*
   Tip steak
   Cube steak
   Kebabs
4. *Heel of round roast*
   Ground beef

Choice The grade generally sold at retail stores. It's preferred because it contains sufficient marbling for taste and tenderness, but is less costly than U.S. Prime.

Good Lower-priced grade of meat with less marbling than U.S. Choice. It's good eating and is as nutritious as the other grades, although it is not as tender.

Since the mid-1970s, the National Livestock and Meat Board has adopted guidelines to standardize meat cuts. A labelling program for all red meat has been adopted by many retail stores. The kind of meat (beef, pork, lamb, or veal), the primal cut, and the retail cut are all included on the label. Because this information tells you exactly which sections of the animal the cut has been taken from, you can better determine the characteristics of the meat, which will help you tailor your cooking methods to it.

Selecting Meat

When selecting red meat, check its appearance carefully. Inspect the color, marbling, and fat cover.

The color of the lean should be bright to deep red (unless the meat has been cured, aged, or smoked). The younger the animal, the brighter the red will be. You may notice that when you slice open a piece of meat or break open ground beef, the interior is purplish. This deeper color is normal. The bright red color on the outside develops as a result of exposure to oxygen in the air.

The tiny flecks of fat throughout the lean are the meat's *marbling*. This internal fat contributes to the meat's flavor, tenderness, and juiciness. Many cuts of meat are surrounded by a layer of fat called the *fat cover*. It doesn't directly add to the meat's flavor, but helps to keep it from drying out before it is cooked.

It also helps to retain juices during cooking. The fat cover surrounding roasts serves to baste them while they cook. When selecting steaks and roasts, look for a fat cover about ½ inch thick.

Exploring Some Standard Meat-Counter Specials

Discovering the hidden values of meat can be exciting. Using some of the meats featured as supermarket specials, you can perform masterful culinary tricks any week of the year.

Chuck Roast A blade-cut chuck roast takes its name from the knife-shaped blade bone that bisects the top third from left to right.

There are really three distinct meaty parts. The flatiron muscle, the portion at the left in the chuck roast illustration, is tender enough to stir-fry quickly or to use for a speedy sauté, such as Beef Stroganoff on page 42. The center part is the least tender; it requires long, slow cooking in a liquid. A good use is the Burgundy Beef Stew on page 83.

In the remaining third of this roast is a hidden but very tender steak, actually an extension of the rib eye. Cutting a 5-pound blade-cut chuck roast horizontally will give you two steaks. You can cook them in many elegant ways, all as quick as they are delicious (see page 44 for Steak With Tangy Herb Butter, as well as Mustard and Pepper Steak on page 45, Steak and Onions for Two on page 42, and Gypsy-Style Steak on page 43).

When you see this chuck roast at a special price, buy two. At home, divide them along the natural boundaries, as shown in the illustrations.

After separating the meat from the bones, save the bones. You can use them to make a meaty soup stock to use for flavoring gravies and sauces (see page 28).

Package and label the different sections from the roast, and freeze any meat you can't use within three or four days.

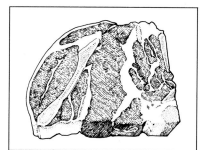

Thrifty blade-cut chuck roast.

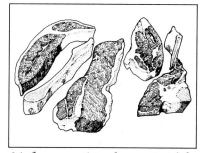

Stir-fry or sauté tender meat at left, stew center section, cut rib eye into two steaks; save bones for soup.

Round Steak Boneless or bone-in, full-cut round steak is another beef cut that's frequently priced as a very good buy. This cut has three quite obvious divisions, each of which is usually sold separately at a much higher price per pound. Clearly, then, it is well worth the slight effort of separating them yourself.

Two of the three muscles in the round, the eye and the bottom round, are fairly compact. Although the eye of round is a good cut of meat, it is the least tender part of the round. Handled cleverly, it makes a steak to cook quickly (as in the Elegant Eye of Round Steaks, page 45) or to braise in a savory liquid (Braised Eye of Round Steaks, page 86).

The bottom round, especially, is coarse and requires long, slow cooking in liquid to become tender. This is the portion of the round that gives the cut its Swiss steak associations. But for two more unusual treatments, try Round Steak and Kidney Beans or Sauerbraten-Style Steak Strips (pages 95 and 84).

The top round is the most tender, and also the largest portion. Thick cuts, particularly if graded "Choice," can be broiled to the rare or medium-rare stage very satisfactorily. If you find that top round usually isn't tender enough when broiled or cooked by other dry-heat methods (grilling, pan-frying, or barbecuing), use a marinade or an unseasoned meat tenderizer. Some specific suggestions for lean, reasonably priced, and versatile top round include Shish Kebab Sauté and Beef Fondue (pages 52 and 48).

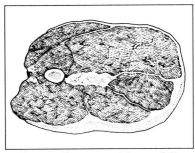

With or without round bone, full-cut round steak is usually a good buy.

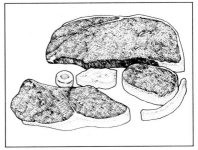

Separated into its three muscles, from most tender to least tender: top round, bottom round, and eye of round. Each requires a different cooking method.

Pork Two gold-mine pork buys are the (hind) *leg* and *picnic shoulder* (front leg). Both contain cuts that, if purchased separately, would cost more per pound. A 10-pound leg provides steaks or chops (from the tip and top leg muscles), roasts, stew or kebab cubes, crackling (from the skin), hocks, and strips of fat for flavoring.

When you cut up a leg, first remove the hock—the end bone that was attached to the pig's foot. Cut through the space between the joint and the leg bone to separate the hock from the rest of the leg. Next, remove the skin by cutting under it through the fat layer. Leave on some of the fat to keep the meat moist.

Now separate the four leg muscles: Cut along the natural seams of the tip muscle down to the bone, around the bone, then along the seam to remove the entire muscle. Then remove the top muscle by cutting along the bone to loosen it. Cut along the seam that connects it to the bottom and eye muscles. Leave the remaining muscles together, or divide them along their natural seams. The shoulder also yields excellent cuts of meat. A six-pound shoulder provides cutlets, chops, kebab, and stew cubes, a hock, bones, meat for grinding, skin for crackling, and a roast that will feed four.

Cutting up the shoulder is similar to cutting up the leg. Cut the hock off first, just as you did with the leg. Then remove the arm bone. Trim off the skin. Leave the shoulder intact for a huge roast, or separate it along the muscles' natural seams.

Whole Chicken and Turkey Even when chicken doesn't have a special price tag, whole birds are less expensive than those that have been cut up. When you buy chicken in this form, you also have a choice of ways to use it. Depending on the size, you can roast it whole, with or without

stuffing; cut it in halves to bake, broil, or barbecue; quarter it for neat, meaty, one-serving portions; or cut it into conventional pieces.

What's more, you'll also have giblets and some bones, such as the neck and backbone, which you can save in the freezer for making broth later on. Freeze the livers until you have enough to make a luscious hors d'oeuvre spread.

A boneless chicken breast is another choice cut that is always more expensive when bought separately. However, just a little practice will enable you to bone it yourself for some very impressive dishes.

There are so many ways to cut up the versatile and economical whole frying chicken—halves, quarters, pieces, or elegant boneless breasts. It's easy when you follow the step-by-step instructions, *How to Cut Up a Chicken*, on page 11.

When shopping for chicken, avoid birds with skin that is dry, hard, purplish or bruised, broken, or scaly. Watch for "freezer burn"—brownish patches that indicate dehydration or long and improper storage of frozen birds. Always cook poultry thoroughly.

Another excellent buy is whole frozen turkey. A large turkey can provide enough meat to feed a small family for days, and the carcass, neck, giblets, and wing tips are great for soup and stock. Although turkey is substantially larger than chicken, the procedure for cutting it up is similar. Thaw a whole frozen turkey in the refrigerator until it is still frosty but not frozen solid. As soon as you've cut up the bird, place the pieces (properly packaged) back in the freezer.

HOW TO CUT UP A CHICKEN

Buying whole chickens and cutting them yourself is an easy way to save money. Freezer-stored cut-up chickens—wrapped, packed, and frozen in halves, quarters, and pieces—are a boon to the busy cook. Keep poultry frozen no more than 6 to 8 months.

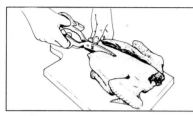

1. *Place the chicken breast-down on a board. Use a knife or kitchen scissors to remove the backbone; cut along both sides.*

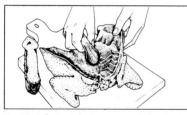

2. *Reach inside to remove the keel bone that separates the two sides of the breast. Loosen the dark hard part and the flexible white portion with your fingers or a small knife; pull it out in one or two pieces. Save the bones for broth (see page 13).*

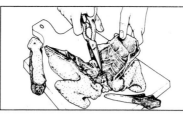

3. *For chicken halves, cut between the breasts where the keel bone was removed. Each half of a small bird (2½ pounds or less) makes a generous single serving to bake, broil, or barbecue (see* Piquant Roast Chicken Halves, *page 28).*

4. *To cut chicken quarters, lift up on rib bones of breast section to see where it divides from the leg-thigh part (that meat is a little darker). Cut from side to side below the bottom rib bones. Quarters from 3-pound (and larger) chickens can be baked, broiled, barbecued, or cooked in delicious sauces.*

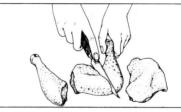

5. *You now have two leg-thigh quarters and two breast-wing quarters. Wiggle the drumstick to find the joint, then cut through it (between the bones, if you can find the right spot) to separate the legs from the thighs. Finally you will be left with chicken breasts with wings attached. Often, in preparing elegant continental entrées, you can remove the two smaller wing joints and bone the breast, leaving just the large wing joint with the bone in. But for day-to-day family dishes, you will probably proceed from here by simply cutting off the entire wing at the joint where it is attached to the breast.*

HOW TO BONE A CHICKEN BREAST

Every time you cut up a thrifty whole chicken, you get two plump breast pieces to use in some of the most elegant dishes of all. This is the way to bone them. Use a small sharp boning knife.

1. *First remove the rib bones from each breast half. Insert the tip of a small sharp knife under the long, bottom rib bone. Work it under the bone and cut it away from the meat (pull up on the bones; push and scrape the meat downward and free). Keep cutting around the outer edge of the breast to, and then through, the shoulder joint to remove the entire rib cage.*

2. *Working from the ends, scrape the meat away from each side of the wishbone; cut and lift it out. Turn the meat over and pull away the skin with your fingers. Reserve the bones and skin for broth.*

Storing the Meat You Buy

Because meat and poultry are perishable foods, buy only what you can store and use efficiently while the meats are in the refrigerator or freezer.

Meats keep better if they are allowed to dry out a little on the surface, so keep refrigerator wrappings loose. You can use foil, waxed paper, or the original supermarket packaging.

For best quality, your freezer should freeze meat fast and keep it with a minimum of temperature fluctuation at 0° F or colder. Otherwise, large ice crystals form, rupturing the meat fibers and allowing the juices to escape when the meat is thawed.

To ensure freshness and top quality during storage, freeze meat as soon as possible. Frozen meats are most useful when they are "ready to cook," so trim excess fat and remove bones, if practical, or cover sharp, protruding bones with folded freezer wrap or foil so that they will not pierce the outer wrapper. Divide large cuts into meal-sized pieces and wrap them individually. Shape ground beef into patties. Cube cuts that you plan to use for stew. Do not season meat before freezing—it will shorten freezer life.

Before freezing, package meat and poultry in moisture/vapor-proof wrapping materials, such as specially coated freezer paper. You can freeze prepackaged meat just as it comes from the supermarket meat counter for up to two weeks without rewrapping. For longer freezer storage, repackage the meat in coated freezer paper. Uncoated butcher paper, however, is not suitable for freezing.

To freeze fresh poultry, first rinse and dry the bird. Poultry that is commercially frozen is already packaged for freezer storage and needs no

MAXIMUM STORAGE-TIME RECOMMENDATIONS FOR FRESH, PROCESSED, AND COOKED BEEF		
Type of Meat	Refrigerator 36°–40° F or 2°–4° C	Freezer 18° F or 0° C
Fresh Beef		
Roasts, steaks	2-4 days	6-12 months
Beef for stew	2 days	6-8 months
Ground beef	1-2 days	3-4 months
Beef variety meats	1-2 days	3-4 months
Fresh Veal		
Roasts, chops, cutlets	2-4 days	6-9 months
Ground veal	1-2 days	3-4 months
Cured and/or Smoked and Ready-to-Serve Beef Products:		
Corned beef	1 week	2 weeks
Frankfurters	4-5 days	1 month
Luncheon meat	1 week	Not recommended
Sausage—smoked	3-7 days	1 month
dry and semidry (unsliced)	2-3 weeks	Not recommended
Cooked beef products	4-5 days	2-3 months

additional wrapping. Freeze poultry unstuffed; stuffing can develop harmful bacteria if frozen inside the bird. Package the giblets and liver separately; they develop an "off" flavor when packaged with the bird.

Wrapping Techniques

Package meat, using either the butcher- or drugstore-wrap method. A convenient way to freeze meatballs, beef cubes, chops, or ground meat patties is to tray-freeze them, then package them in freezer-weight plastic bags. To tray-freeze, spread the unwrapped portions of meat on a baking sheet and freeze just until they are firm. This allows you to remove only as many as you need. Also, they will thaw quickly.

Drugstore Wrap for flat- or rectangular-shaped foods such as steaks or chops: Cut off enough wrapping material to wrap around the food about 1½ times. Place the food in the center of the wrap and bring opposite edges of the wrap together over the top so that they meet. Repeatedly crease and fold the edges together until the fold lies against the food.

Press the fold down across the food, squeezing out the air. Fold one end of the packaging material in; then fold that end once and bring it up against the food. Repeat with the other end. Seal with freezer tape.

Butcher Wrap for bulky items such as roasts: Use enough wrapping material to wrap around the food twice. Place the food at one corner of the wrap and turn it and the paper over at the same time. Tuck the side edges up around the food and roll the food toward the opposite corner. Bring up the end and seal with freezer tape.

Thawing Frozen Meat

To retain optimum quality and texture, the safest and best way to thaw meat is in the refrigerator. Although meat takes substantially longer to thaw inside the refrigerator than it does at room temperature, it will retain its original flavor and moistness, and there will be less chance of spoilage. Allow 4 to 6 hours per pound for thawing.

12

Most cuts of meat and poultry can be cooked without thawing; however, large cuts like roasts may dry out, lose more juices, and overcook on the outside before the center is done. A frozen roast will take 1⅓ to 1½ times the usual cooking period. Frozen ground meat, chops, and steaks take 1½ to 2 times longer to cook. Frozen cuts cooked by moist heat need little additional cooking time, if any.

Meats that are to be shaped, stuffed, coated with flour or crumbs, dipped in batter, or deep-fried should be completely thawed first.

Stocking Your Freezer With a Side of Beef

If you have a capacious freezer, one economical way to buy beef is to purchase it a side (a half) or a quarter at a time, packaged, labeled, and frozen. You can work with the meat dealer to get just the cuts you want. A cooperative butcher will divide the chuck or round into the various muscles, according to their tenderness (this is shown on a smaller scale on page 10).

The price per pound is based on the hanging weight of the entire side or quarter. Due to loss of moisture, bone, and trimmed fat, there is about a 27 to 28 percent weight loss by the time the beef is broken down into the retail cuts you specify.

The hindquarter, which includes the loin section, is usually more costly than a forequarter (mostly rib and chuck). From a 300- to 320-pound side of beef, figure on about 17 percent loin cuts, 9 percent rib cuts, 22 percent round, 26 percent chuck, and the remaining 26 percent flank, plate, shanks, and suet.

Save the Bones—and the Chicken Livers

When you bring home meat or poultry containing bones, save the bones in a sturdy plastic bag in the freezer until enough have accumulated to make a rich, full-flavored broth.

It can be used: as liquid in stews, spaghetti sauce, and gravy; for cooking rice when you make a pilaf; and as the starter for a full-meal soup. Although a good broth needs to cook for a long time, it doesn't require your attention; you can spend those hours doing something else.

RICH BEEF BROTH OR CONCENTRATE

Bones from several chuck roasts are especially fine for making this flavorful beef broth. If you wish, you can cook it down further to make a concentrated meat jelly; French chefs call it *glace de viande* and use it devotedly to enrich sauces for meat.

    10 pounds (approximately) meaty beef bones
     3 medium carrots
     3 large onions
     2 stalks celery, with leaves, chopped
     1 can (1 lb) tomatoes, coarsely chopped, liquid reserved

1. Preheat oven to 450° F. Place bones in a single layer in a large, open roasting pan. Sprinkle with one of the carrots, sliced, and one of the onions, thickly sliced. Bake, uncovered, until meat and bones are well browned (about 30 minutes).

2. Transfer the mixture to a deep kettle (at least 12-quart size). Chop remaining carrots and onions and add them along with celery and tomatoes and their liquid. Add water to cover bones. Bring to a boil, cover, reduce heat, and simmer 18 to 24 hours.

3. Strain the soup to remove bones and vegetables. Return the broth to pot. Simmer, uncovered, until it is reduced by about half. Pour the broth through several thicknesses of dampened cheesecloth or a clean muslin or linen kitchen towel into a large bowl. Cover and chill.

4. *For beef broth:* Remove and discard fat. Reheat and season lightly with salt. Freeze for long-term storage.

5. *For beef concentrate:* Place the broth in a 3- to 4-quart saucepan after it has been chilled and the fat removed (broth will be firm and gelatinous at this stage). Bring to a gentle boil and cook, uncovered, stirring occasionally until it is thick enough to make a syrupy-looking coating on the spoon and boils all over in large shiny bubbles. Cool, then pour into several small jars and refrigerate (for up to 2 or 3 weeks) or freeze. Use about 2 teaspoons per cup of water to make regular-strength beef broth.

Makes 2½ to 3 quarts rich broth or 2 cups concentrate.

GOLDEN CHICKEN BROTH

The flavor and richness of homemade chicken broth is incomparable to the store-bought version.

     5 pounds bony chicken pieces (backs, necks, and/or wings)
     1 medium onion, chopped
     1 carrot, sliced
     1 stalk celery, with leaves, chopped
     3 sprigs parsley
     ¼ teaspoon dried thyme
        Half a bay leaf
        Dash dried marjoram
     9 cups cold water
        Salt

1. In a deep kettle (8- to 10-quart size), place chicken pieces, vegetables, parsley, thyme, bay leaf, marjoram, and cold water. Bring the liquid to a boil, then reduce heat and simmer, covered, until the broth has a rich chicken flavor (3½ to 4 hours).

2. Strain the broth, discarding bones and vegetables. Return the broth to the kettle and simmer, uncovered, until reduced to about 8 cups (about 1 hour). Salt to taste.

3. If possible, chill the broth overnight, then skim off and discard fat. Freeze; or chill and use within 3 to 4 days.

Makes about 8 cups.

Pork spareribs, like short ribs of beef, can be roasted very easily. These succulent Cider-Glazed Spareribs Flamed in Bourbon make an elegant presentation.

Affordable Roasts

Roasting, one of the oldest and most appreciated cooking methods, is a traditional way of cooking for big family gatherings, elegant dinners, and festive occasions. For inexpensive elegance from the oven, explore the less costly cuts of beef, pork, lamb, veal, and poultry. In addition to being delicious, their slow cooking time gives you the freedom to enjoy the company of your guests. You can turn these meats into impressive family feasts and dinners for guests without overextending your food budget.

AFFORDABLE ROASTS

First of all, what *is* a roast? It is a cut of meat or poultry cooked uncovered in the oven by dry heat (without the addition of moisture). Most roasts are cooked in a shallow pan to permit good air circulation; the result is even heat penetration. A roast is usually placed fat side up, which lets the fat that melts during cooking baste the meat as it drains. A rack or trivet in the bottom of the pan holds the meat out of its drippings.

For most roasts, a constant, moderate oven temperature—usually 325° F—produces the juiciest meat with the least shrinkage. At this setting, heat penetrates all the way to the center of even a large roast before the outside becomes dry or burned. You may have been told to sear meat at a high temperature "to seal in the juices." Actually, repeated tests have shown that, on the contrary, meat cooked this way is *less* juicy. The drippings may produce a browner gravy, but it also produces drier meat and a spattered oven.

An absolutely basic piece of equipment for roasting is a meat thermometer, preferably a mercury one. Inserted so that the bulb is in the center of the largest muscle without touching fat or bone, it shows the temperature of the thickest part of the roast—the only reliable indicator that the meat has cooked to the degree of doneness you prefer.

Roasting timetables like the one on page 18 can help you estimate how long to cook a roast in the oven. But if you've ever agonized over a gray beef roast that should have been pink, or a seemingly glorious holiday turkey that resisted the carver's best efforts, you will appreciate the usefulness of an accurate meat thermometer.

SOY AND SESAME ROAST

Because a boneless rump roast is both lean and compact, standard dry-heat methods will do for roasting it to tender juiciness. For extra tenderness, however, marinate it first, then cook it to a rare 130° F to 135° F.

  ⅔ cup soy sauce
  2 tablespoons honey
  ½ teaspoon ground ginger
  2 cloves garlic, minced or pressed
  ⅓ cup dry sherry
  1 boneless rolled rump roast (4 to 4½ lbs)
  2 tablespoons sesame seed

1. Preheat oven to 325° F. Gradually stir soy sauce into honey in a small bowl. Blend in ginger, garlic, and sherry. Place roast in a bowl or deep casserole just large enough to hold it comfortably. Pour on marinade. Cover and refrigerate for 8 hours or overnight, turning meat occasionally.

2. Toast sesame seeds by spreading them in a shallow pan and baking in a 350° F oven, stirring occasionally, until lightly browned (8 to 10 minutes).

3. Remove meat, reserving marinade. Place roast on a rack, fat side up, in a shallow roasting pan. Sprinkle with toasted sesame seeds. Roast uncovered, drizzling occasionally with marinade, until meat thermometer registers 130° F to 135° F (rare), 1½ to 2 hours.

4. Slice thinly and serve.
Serves 6 to 8.

HERB-CRUSTED CROSS RIB ROAST

The boneless rolled chuck roast specified here and on page 17 is also known by other names—X-rib roast and Diamond Jim roast. In this recipe, a rare beef roast is seasoned with herbs and mustard and served with a nippy horseradish sauce.

  1 teaspoon each *dry mustard and coarsely crushed whole black pepper*
  ½ teaspoon each *dried rosemary and summer savory*
  1 clove garlic, minced or pressed
  1 teaspoon olive oil or salad oil
  1 boneless rolled cross rib roast (4½ to 5 lbs)

Horseradish Sauce

  1 cup whipping cream
  1 teapoon sugar
  Dash salt
  1 teaspoon lemon juice
  3 tablespoons prepared horseradish

1. Preheat oven to 325° F. In a small bowl mix dry mustard, pepper, rosemary, savory, garlic, and olive oil into a paste. Press onto outside surfaces of the roast. Place roast, fat side up, on a rack in a shallow roasting pan.

2. Roast, uncovered, until meat thermometer registers 135° F (rare) to 145° F (medium-rare to medium), 1½ to 2 hours.

3. Let stand for a few minutes, then carve into thin slices. Serve with Horseradish Sauce.
Serves 8 to 10.

Horseradish Sauce In chilled bowl combine whipping cream, sugar, salt, and lemon juice. Beat with chilled beaters until stiff. Fold in horseradish. Chill for 1 to 2 hours to blend flavors.
Makes 2 cups sauce.

ITALIAN-STYLE ROAST BEEF WITH BAKED VEGETABLES

A cross rib roast, also called a shoulder clod roast—a fairly lean, yet juicy boneless rolled roast from the shoulder or chuck—often carries a merely moderate price tag. For the most tender results, cook it to a rare 135° F to 145° F. Baked with onions, carrots, and new potatoes and accompanied by a salad and dessert, it provides a satisfying meal for family or guests.

⅓ cup olive oil or salad oil
¼ teaspoon dried oregano
2 cloves garlic, slivered
2 pounds small new potatoes
3 medium onions, cut in eighths
6 large carrots, cut
    lengthwise in quarters
1 boneless rolled cross rib
    roast (4½ to 5 lbs)
    Coarsely ground pepper
    Chopped parsley and lemon
    wedges, for garnish

1. Preheat oven to 325° F. In a shallow roasting pan about 10 by 15 inches, mix oil, oregano, and garlic. Peel potatoes completely, if you wish, or peel a 1-inch-wide strip around center of each. Add potatoes, onions, and carrots to oil mixture, stirring to coat well. Move vegetables to both ends of pan.

2. Place roast, fat side up, in center of pan. Sprinkle with pepper. Roast uncovered for about 1½ to 2 hours, turning potatoes once, until vegetables are tender and meat thermometer inserted in center of thickest part of roast registers 135° F (rare) to 145° F (medium-rare to medium).

3. Slice meat, spoon pan juices over slices, and serve with parsley-sprinkled vegetables and lemon wedges to squeeze over each serving.

Serves 8 to 10.

Italian-style cross rib roast baked with carrots, onions, and potatoes makes a splendid dinner for family or friends. To make the dinner extra-special, serve it with a hearty red wine such as Cabernet Sauvignon, or an Italian red wine such as a Barbera.

ROASTING TIMETABLE

	Weight (Pounds)	Oven Temperature	Internal Meat Temperature	Cooking Time (Minutes per Pound)
Beef				
Rib	6 to 8	300°–325° F	140° F (rare)	23 to 25
(Ribs that measure 6			160° F (medium)	27 to 30
to 7 inches from chine			170° F (well)	32 to 35
bone to tip of rib)	4 to 6	300°–325° F	140° F (rare)	26 to 32
			160° F (medium)	34 to 38
			170° F (well)	40 to 42
Rolled rib	5 to 7	300°–325° F	140° F (rare)	32
			160° F (medium)	38
			170° F (well)	48
Rib eye (Delmonico)	4 to 6	350° F	140° F (rare)	18 to 20
			160° F (medium)	20 to 22
			170° F (well)	22 to 24
Tenderloin, whole	4 to 6	425° F	140° F (rare)	45 to 60 (total)
Tenderloin, half	2 to 3	425° F	140° F (rare)	45 to 60 (total)
Boneless rolled rump	4 to 6	300°–325° F	150°–170° F	25 to 30
Tip	3½ to 4	300°–325° F	140°–170° F	35 to 40
	4 to 6	300°–325° F	140°–170° F	30 to 35
Veal				
Leg	5 to 8	300°–325° F	170° F	25 to 35
Loin	4 to 6	300°–325° F	170° F	30 to 35
Rib (rack)	3 to 5	300°–325° F	170° F	35 to 40
Boneless shoulder	4 to 6	300°–325° F	170° F	40 to 45
Pork, Fresh				
Loin				
Center	3 to 5	325°–350° F	170° F	30 to 35
Half	5 to 7	325°–350° F	170° F	35 to 40
Blade loin or sirloin	3 to 4	325°–350° F	170° F	40 to 45
Boneless double	3 to 5	325°–350° F	170° F	35 to 45
Arm picnic shoulder	5 to 8	325°–350° F	170° F	30 to 35
Boneless	3 to 5	325°–350° F	170° F	35 to 40
Cushion	3 to 5	325°–350° F	170° F	30 to 35
Blade Boston shoulder	4 to 6	325°–350° F	170° F	40 to 45
Leg (fresh ham)				
Whole (bone in)	12 to 16	325°–350° F	170° F	22 to 26
Whole (boneless)	10 to 14	325°–350° F	170° F	24 to 28
Half (bone in)	5 to 8	325°–350° F	170° F	35 to 40
Spareribs		325°–350° F	Well done	1½ to 2½ hrs (total)
Pork, Smoked				
Ham (cook-before-eating)				
Whole	10 to 14	300°–325° F	160° F	18 to 20
Half	5 to 7	300°–325° F	160° F	22 to 25
Shank or rump portion	3 to 4	300°–325° F	160° F	35 to 40
Ham (fully cooked)	10 to 14	325° F	140° F	15
Halff	5 to 7	325° F	140° F	18 to 24
Arm picnic shoulder	5 to 8	300°–325° F	170° F	35
Shoulder roll	2 to 3	300°–325° F	170° F	35 to 40
Canadian-style bacon	2 to 4	325° F	160° F	35 to 40
Lamb				
Leg	5 to 8	300°–325° F	175°–180° F	30 to 35
Shoulder	4 to 6	300°–325° F	175°–180° F	30 to 35
Boneless	3 to 5	300°–325° F	175°–180° F	40 to 45
Cushion	3 to 5	300°–325° F	175°–180° F	30 to 35
Rib	1½ to 3	375° F	170°–180° F	35 to 45
Turkey	6	325° F	180°–185° F	3 hours
	8	325° F	180°–185° F	3½ hours*
	12	325° F	180°–185° F	4½ hours*
	16	325° F	180°–185° F	5½ hours*
	20	325° F	180°–185° F	6½ hours*

*Unstuffed turkeys require about ½ hour less roasting time.

	Weight (Pounds)	Oven Temperature	Time per pound (Without Stuffing)	Cooking Time*
Chicken	1½	400° F	40 min	1 hour
	2	400° F	35 min	1 hr 10 min
	2½	375° F	30 min	1 hr 15 min
	3	375° F	30 min	1 hr 30 min
	3½	375° F	30 min	1 hr 45 min
	4	375° F	30 min	2 hours
	4½	375° F	30 min	2 hrs 15 min
	5	375° F	30 min	2 hrs 30 min

*Increase roasting time by 15 minutes when chicken is stuffed.

MUSHROOM-STUFFED MEAT LOAF

This is no plain-and-ordinary meat loaf; stuffed with seasoned chopped mushrooms, it is special enough for a company meal.

  2 tablespoons butter or margarine
  ¾ pound mushrooms, chopped
  1 medium onion, finely chopped
  1 teaspoon lemon juice
  2 cups soft bread crumbs
  ½ teaspoon garlic salt
  ¼ teaspoon dried thyme
  ¼ cup chopped parsley
  2 eggs
  ¼ cup catsup
  2 teaspoons prepared mustard
  1 teaspoon Worcestershire sauce
  1½ teaspoons salt
  2 pounds ground beef

1. Preheat oven to 350° F. Heat butter in a large frying pan. Cook chopped mushrooms with onion until lightly browned. Remove from heat and lightly mix in lemon juice, then ½ cup of the bread crumbs, garlic salt, thyme, and parsley.

2. Beat eggs with catsup, mustard, Worcestershire sauce, and salt. Lightly mix in remaining bread crumbs and the ground beef.

3. Pat half the ground beef mixture into a 9- by 5-inch loaf pan. Cover with mushroom stuffing. Top with remaining meat mixture. Bake uncovered until browned (about 1 hour and 15 minutes). Let stand for a few minutes. Remove from pan to slice. *Serves 6 to 8.*

CHUCK ROAST MARINATED IN BEER

A marinade containing some form of acid—lemon juice, vinegar, or wine—can tenderize as well as flavor some of the less tender cuts of meat. Prove it to yourself by giving this lemon-beer marinated chuck roast a try—but *only* if you like rare meat; if cooked beyond the rare stage, this roast won't be tender.

Most roasts are cooked in a 325° F oven, but this dish is an exception. Because this type of chuck roast is much broader than it is thick, a hotter oven does a better job of browning the outside of the meat while keeping the inside rare and juicy.

> 1 blade-cut or seven-bone chuck roast (4½ to 5 lbs), trimmed of fat
> 1 cup beer
> ½ cup salad oil
> 2 tablespoons lemon juice
> 1 clove garlic, minced or pressed
> 1 bay leaf
> ¾ teaspoon salt
> ½ teaspoon each *pepper, dry mustard, rosemary, oregano, and thyme*

1. Place roast in a shallow baking dish. Thoroughly combine beer, oil, lemon juice, garlic, bay leaf, salt, pepper, mustard, rosemary, oregano, and thyme; pour over roast. Cover and refrigerate for 4 to 6 hours or overnight, turning meat occasionally.

2. Preheat oven to 450° F. Place roast on rack in an uncovered roasting pan; brush with marinade. Roast for 35 to 55 minutes, until meat thermometer registers 135° F (rare) to 145° F (medium-rare to medium). Carve as shown in illustration.
Serves 6 to 8.

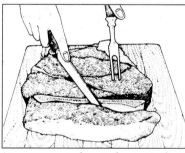

To carve, cut close to bones to divide chuck roast into several large pieces.

Then slice each section across the grain and serve, discarding bones.

Chuck Roast Marinated in Beer uses a combination of beer and lemon juice, seasoned with garlic and herbs, to make a tasty marinade that tenderizes an economical blade-cut chuck roast and also adds a lively flavor. Carve it as you would a big, tender steak.

Though not thought of as a roast, short ribs of beef can also be roasted in the oven. Cooked in a delicious barbecue sauce and served on a bed of poppy seed noodles, this dish makes a splendid meal.

BAKED SHORT RIBS WITH POPPY SEED NOODLES

Beef short ribs are not a roast in the usual sense, but like a roast they can be cooked in the oven, uncovered. These ribs are flavored with a tangy barbecue sauce and served with noodles.

>   3 to 4 pounds beef short ribs
>   1 package (12 oz) broad
>   egg noodles
>   1 tablespoon poppy seed
>   2 tablespoons butter or
>   margarine
>   ½ cup regular-strength
>   beef broth (homemade or
>   canned)
>   Chopped parsley, for garnish

Barbecue Sauce

>   1 medium onion, chopped
>   1 tablespoon butter or
>   margarine
>   1 clove garlic, minced or pressed
>   ½ teaspoon salt
>   ¼ teaspoon chili powder
>   1 tablespoon brown sugar
>   2 tablespoons cider vinegar
>   2 teaspoons Worcestershire sauce
>   ½ cup catsup
>   1 cup water

1. Preheat oven to 350° F. Cut short ribs in serving pieces. Arrange on a rack in an uncovered roasting pan. Bake until browned (30 to 45 minutes). Prepare Barbecue Sauce. Remove ribs and set aside. Remove rack. Pour off and discard fat.

2. Place ribs directly on bottom of roasting pan. Pour Barbecue Sauce over ribs. Continue baking, spooning sauce over meat occasionally, until ribs are tender (1 to 1½ hours).

3. About 20 minutes before ribs are done, cook noodles in boiling salted water, according to package directions; drain and rinse. Heat poppy seed in butter in a 2-quart saucepan until bubbly; stir in broth. Bring to a boil and cook for about 5 minutes to reduce slightly. Mix in well-drained noodles.

4. To serve, arrange ribs in center of a heated serving platter; keep warm. Spoon off fat in roasting pan. Add about ½ cup water to sauce in pan; heat and stir. Spoon sauce over meat. Surround with noodles. Sprinkle with chopped parsley.
Serves 6.

Barbecue Sauce In a 1½-quart saucepan, cook onion in butter or margarine until soft. Stir in garlic, salt, chili powder, brown sugar, cider vinegar, Worcestershire sauce, catsup, and water. Heat to boiling over medium heat, stirring occasionally.

SIRLOIN TIP ROAST WITH OVEN-BROWNED POTATOES AND STUFFED MUSHROOM CAPS

The sirloin tip is one of the most lean and tender of the less expensive beef oven roasts. For a really special dinner, serve this handsome roast with crusty potatoes baked in the meat drippings, and savory stuffed mushrooms. Accompany with asparagus spears and dinner rolls. For the salad course, toss mixed greens with blue cheese dressing and sprinkle with crisp bacon crumbles.

    1   clove garlic, thinly slivered
    1   boneless rolled sirloin
        tip roast (4½ to 5 lbs)
    ½   teaspoon dried tarragon
        Seasoned pepper
    6   medium baking potatoes
        (about 2¼ lbs)
    3   tablespoons salad oil
    1   teaspoon seasoned salt

Stuffed Mushroom Caps

    12 medium mushrooms
    3   tablespoons butter
    ¼   cup finely chopped
        smoked pork shoulder
        picnic or ham
    2   tablespoons finely
        chopped onion
    2   tablespoons chopped parsley
    ⅛   teaspoon dried tarragon
    ¼   cup each soft bread
        crumbs and shredded
        Monterey jack cheese

1. Preheat oven to 325° F. Cut thin slashes in fat covering roast, and into these insert garlic slivers. Place roast, fat side up, in center of a shallow roasting pan, about 10 by 15 inches. Sprinkle evenly with tarragon and seasoned pepper. Place in oven.

2. Peel and quarter potatoes. Mix with oil and seasoned salt. Arrange around roast in a single layer; drizzle with any remaining oil mixture. Replace in oven. Turn potatoes after 45 minutes.

3. Continue roasting until meat thermometer registers 135° F (rare) to 145° F (medium-rare to medium) and potatoes are tender, crusty, and golden (1½ to 2 hours). Slice meat thinly; serve with potatoes and mushrooms.

Serves 8 to 10.

Stuffed Mushroom Caps Remove stems from mushrooms and chop 6 stems finely. Sauté caps briefly in 2 tablespoons butter and remove from pan. Add remaining 1 tablespoon butter to pan, and in it cook mushroom stems, smoked pork, and chopped onions. Remove from heat and mix in parsley, tarragon, bread crumbs, and cheese. Mound stuffing mixture into mushroom caps. Arrange in a single layer in buttered baking dish; place in oven with roast during the last 15 minutes until heated through and lightly browned.

HARVEST VEAL OR TURKEY LOAF

Use either ground veal or ground turkey for this golden-flecked meat loaf that's made with shredded winter squash.

    2   cups shredded, peeled
        banana or Hubbard squash
    1½ pounds ground veal or turkey
    1   small onion, finely chopped
    1   can (2 oz) mushroom pieces
        and stems, drained
    1   cup soft bread crumbs
    1   teaspoon salt
    ⅛   teaspoon pepper
    ¼   teaspoon poultry seasoning
    1   cup sour cream

1. Preheat oven to 375° F. Lightly mix squash with ground meat, onion, mushrooms, bread crumbs, salt, pepper, poultry seasoning, and sour cream.

2. Pat meat mixture into 9- by 5-inch loaf pan. Bake uncovered until browned (1½ hours).

Serves 6.

ROAST BEEF HASH WITH FRIED EGGS

Leftover rare roast beef makes an extra-special hash, especially when served with dark bread, cucumber salad, and cold beer.

    ½   cup butter or margarine
    2   large onions, finely chopped
    ½   teaspoon sugar
    2   cups cubed cooked potatoes
    3   cups rare cooked roast
        beef, cut in ½-inch cubes
    ¼   cup regular-strength
        beef broth (homemade
        or canned)
    1   teaspoon Worcestershire sauce
    ½   teaspoon salt
    ⅛   teaspoon pepper
    4   to 6 eggs
        Chopped parsley, for garnish

1. In a large frying pan, heat about 3 tablespoons of the butter over moderate heat until foamy. Add onions and sugar; cook slowly, stirring occasionally until onions are soft and golden (about 20 minutes).

2. In another large frying pan, melt 3 tablespoons more butter over moderately high heat; add potatoes. Cook until browned on all sides.

3. Remove cooked onions from pan. Put another 1 tablespoon butter in pan and add beef, stirring until it is heated through and lightly browned.

4. To pan with potatoes, add cooked onions and beef; keep warm in a 250° F oven. To pan with beef, add broth, Worcestershire sauce, salt, and pepper; cook over high heat, stirring, until reduced by half. Lightly mix liquid into hash.

5. Fry eggs in remaining butter to desired doneness. Serve atop hash. Sprinkle with parsley.

Serves 4 to 6.

This lamb shoulder roast is seasoned with garlic and thyme, then roasted until the inside is a delicate pink color. The garlic-seasoned small white beans make a perfect side dish. Garnish the roast with bouquets of watercress.

LAMB AND VEAL

STUFFED LAMB SHOULDER PROVENÇALE

The tasty stuffing that accompanies this roast is made with pork and ripe olives.

- ½ teaspoon dried marjoram
- ¼ teaspoon each dried rosemary and thyme
- 1 egg
- 2 tablespoons milk
- 1 cup soft French bread crumbs
- 1 cup ground ham
- ½ pound ground lean pork
- 1 clove garlic, minced or pressed
- ¼ cup ripe olives, chopped
  Dash pepper
- 1 lamb shoulder roast (4¾ to 5 lbs), boned
  Olive oil

1. Preheat oven to 325° F. Combine marjoram, rosemary, and thyme. In a medium bowl beat egg lightly with milk. Mix in bread crumbs, then ham and pork, garlic, olives, pepper, and ½ teaspoon of the herb mixture.

2. Fill cavity of roast with stuffing mixture; sew edges closed with string or heavy thread. Rub surface of meat lightly with olive oil; sprinkle with remaining herb mixture. Place stuffed roast in an uncovered roasting pan; place the pan on an oven rack.

3. Roast until meat thermometer registers 170° F, about 2 hours. Remove string or thread; carve meat into ¾-inch slices. Use drippings to make gravy, if you wish (see page 28).

Serves 6.

ROLLED LAMB SHOULDER WITH WHITE BEANS

1 lamb shoulder roast (4 to 4½ lbs), boned
2 cloves garlic, slivered
¼ teaspoon dried thyme
   Black pepper, coarsely ground
   Watercress, for garnish

White Beans

7 cups water
1 pound dried small white beans (rinsed and drained)
2 teaspoons salt
1 onion, sliced
1 stalk celery, chopped
1 teaspoon dried marjoram
⅛ teaspoon white pepper
3 cloves garlic, minced or pressed
3 tablespoons butter
¼ cup chopped parsley

1. Preheat oven to 325° F. Roll and tie lamb shoulder roast. Cut small gashes in surface of lamb and insert garlic slivers. Sprinkle meat with thyme and pepper. Place on a rack in a shallow roasting pan. Roast, uncovered, until meat thermometer registers 140° F to 145° F, 1¼ to 1½ hours (interior color should be pink).
2. Carve lamb in ¼-inch-thick slices and accompany with white beans, spooning pan juices over all. Garnish with bouquets of watercress.
Serves 6.

White Beans In a large kettle bring water and white beans to a boil. Boil vigorously for 2 minutes. Cover, remove from heat, and let stand 1 hour. Add salt, onion, celery, marjoram, and pepper. Bring to a boil, reduce heat, and cover. Boil beans until most of the liquid is absorbed (1½ to 2 hours). In a large frying pan sauté garlic in butter until it begins to brown. Add beans and their liquid. Cook, uncovered, stirring occasionally, until contents are thickened but still moist. Add salt to taste. Stir in parsley.

Step-by-step

HOW TO BONE A LAMB SHOULDER ROAST

Before boning a lamb shoulder roast, examine the roast and its bone structure. Notice that the rib, back, and neck bones lie on the surface. Underneath the backbone and rib cage are two internal bones, the blade and arm bone. When removing these bones, take care to cut around the bones and not through the shoulder meat.

1. Holding the ends of the ribs, cut under the ribs toward the big middle chine bone. Lift the ribs away from the meat as you progress. After all of the ribs have been freed, cut closely along the underside of the chine bone to free the backbone and neckbone on the rib side.

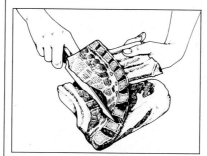

2. Turn the meat around. Pull the freed rib assembly up and toward you with one hand. Cut beneath the small feather bones, working from the backbone end down to the neck bone. Pull the entire section away from the meat and fold the rib assembly over upon the cutting board. Cut through any meat that remains attached along the feather bones and chine bone. Lift out the entire section.

3. Find the long narrow (internal) blade bone by bending the shoulder back and forth. Locate the point at which it joins the arm bone. Starting above the arm bone, cut through the meat above the blade. Fold back the meat so the blade is exposed. Then cut closely around the blade, taking care not to split the shoulder meat when cutting around the underside of the blade. Lift up the blade bone and cut through the joint at the arm bone. Pull the blade bone out.

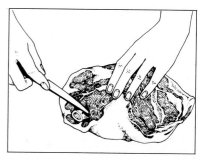

4. Cut through the meat to expose the arm bone. Cut carefully around and underneath until it can be removed. Turn the shoulder over and cut out the excess fat.

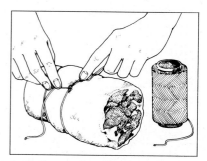

5. Roll meat lengthwise starting at the thin end. Roll it into a very tight cylinder. Put the seam side down. Starting in the middle, tie the roast at 1-inch intervals.

SPINACH-STUFFED BREAST OF VEAL

Breast of veal, a large and dramatic-looking dish, is actually cooked covered for part of the time to keep the meat moist.

This baked veal breast is frankly Italian, with its meaty stuffing of ground beef, spinach, and cheese. Accompanied by a salad or green vegetable, it will serve a large group economically and well.

> 1 *breast of veal (3 to 3½ lbs)*
> 2 *tablespoons olive oil or salad oil*
> 1 *cup each regular-strength chicken broth (canned or homemade) and dry white wine*

Ground Beef and Spinach Stuffing

> ½ *pound ground beef*
> 1 *medium onion, chopped*
> 1 *clove garlic, minced or pressed*
> 1 *can (2 oz) mushroom pieces, including stems*
> 1 *package (9 or 10 oz) frozen chopped spinach, thawed, and squeezed dry*
> ½ *cup soft bread crumbs*
> 1 *cup shredded Monterey jack cheese*
> 1 *egg, slightly beaten*
> ½ *teaspoon each salt and basil*
> ⅛ *teaspoon seasoned pepper*

1. When you buy the veal breast, have the meat dealer cut a pocket for the stuffing.

2. Preheat oven to 325° F. Fill the pocket with Ground Beef and Spinach Stuffing, then fasten the open end with small metal skewers. Place the meat in a large roasting pan. Brush with oil. Pour on ¾ cup *each* of broth and wine. Cover with foil and bake until meat is very tender (2 hours). Increase oven temperature to 350° F and continue baking, uncovered, for 25 to 30 minutes longer. Brush occasionally with pan drippings to brown meat. Remove meat to a heated platter and keep warm.

3. To loosen pan drippings, add remaining ¼ cup *each* broth and wine, stirring over high heat until liquid is reduced by about a third. Serve the sauce separately. To carve veal, cut between the rib bones.

Serves 6 to 8.

Ground Beef and Spinach Stuffing

Crumble ground beef into a large frying pan and brown it in its own drippings. Mix in onion, garlic, and mushroom pieces and stems. Cook, stirring occasionally, until onion is soft and begins to brown. Remove from heat and mix in spinach. Add bread crumbs, shredded Monterey jack cheese, egg, salt, basil, and pepper; mix lightly.

PORK

TANGY MARINATED ROAST PORK BUTT

Consider the versatile pork butt roast, a shoulder cut. It is juicy, flavorful, and often a very good buy. This roast is butterflied so that it will more fully absorb the striking flavors of the onion, pimiento, and garlic marinade.

> ½ *cup cider vinegar*
> ¼ *cup salad oil*
> 1½ *teaspoons salt*
> ½ *teaspoon dried oregano*
> ¼ *teaspoon freshly ground pepper*
> 2 *cloves garlic, minced or pressed*
> 1 *large onion, finely chopped*
> 1 *can (4 oz) pimientos, seeded and chopped*
> 1 *boneless pork butt roast (4½ to 5 lbs)*
> *Chopped parsley, for garnish*

1. In blender or a jar, combine vinegar, oil, salt, oregano, pepper, and garlic; whirl or shake until well blended. Add onion and pimientos.

2. Butterfly roast (see illustration below)—cut it horizontally through the center, almost to the opposite side, then open it flat. Place meat on a cutting board and score fat side diagonally with ½-inch-deep cuts, making about 3-inch squares. Place meat, scored side up, in a glass baking dish. Pour marinade over roast, spreading onions and pimientos evenly. Cover and refrigerate for 2 to 3 hours.

3. Preheat oven to 325° F. Remove pork from dish, reserving marinade with most of the onion and pimientos. Place meat, fat side up, on rack in a shallow roasting pan. Spoon on some of the marinade. Roast, uncovered, adding marinade occasionally, until meat thermometer registers 170° F, about 2 hours.

4. To serve, cut meat into squares along scored lines. Reheat remaining marinade for sauce; spoon warm sauce over meat. Sprinkle with chopped parsley.

Serves 8 to 10.

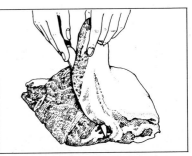

Use a clean sharp knife. Starting with fat side up, cut horizontally through center of boneless roast, almost to opposite side.

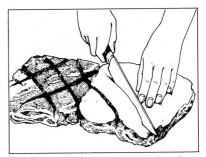

Spread meat flat, then score surface diagonally in big squares, in order to better absorb the flavors of the pimiento marinade.

ROAST COUNTRY-STYLE SPARERIBS WITH SAUERKRAUT

Moist and meaty, country-style spareribs are delicious baked with seasoned sauerkraut. Serve with new potatoes and crusty rye bread.

  1   can (27 oz) sauerkraut, rinsed and drained
½   teaspoon juniper berries or whole allspice
  1   bay leaf
  1   medium onion, thinly sliced
  4   to 5 pounds country-style spareribs
  1   tablespoon each kosher or coarse salt and caraway seed
½   teaspoon pepper
½   cup apple cider

1. Mix sauerkraut, juniper berries or allspice, bay leaf, and sliced onion. Spread evenly in an ungreased, shallow 2- to 3-quart casserole.

2. Preheat oven to 350° F. Rub spareribs on all sides with a mixture of salt, caraway seed, and pepper. Arrange in a single layer over the sauerkraut, bony side up. Cover and roast for 1 hour.

3. Turn spareribs, pour on cider, and return to oven. Continue baking, uncovered, until ribs are tender and well browned, 1¼ to 1½ hours. *Serves 6.*

CIDER-GLAZED SPARERIBS FLAMED IN BOURBON

Because pork spareribs, like short ribs of beef, are so easy to roast, they appear in the same chapter as the more substantial roasts. As the ribs finish baking, they are glazed with apple cider so that they become irresistibly sweet and succulent.

  4   pounds spareribs, cut in serving-sized pieces
        Garlic salt
        Pepper
½   cup apple cider
¼   cup bourbon whiskey

1. Preheat oven to 350° F. Sprinkle ribs on all sides with garlic salt and pepper. In a shallow roasting pan or broiler pan, arrange ribs in a single layer, bone side down. Bake 1 hour; pour off all the fat in the pan.

2. Pour cider over spareribs. Replace in oven and continue baking about 30 minutes, basting occasionally with pan drippings, until ribs are tender and well browned. Remove ribs to a warm serving platter.

3. Pour off fat in roasting pan. Add bourbon to warm roasting pan, stirring to dissolve drippings. Ignite, and spoon, flaming, over spareribs. Cut ribs apart, if desired. *Serves 4.*

Moist country-style spareribs are roasted with seasoned sauerkraut and sweet apple cider. Served with rye bread and new potatoes, these ribs make for a hearty meal on a chilly night.

GLAZED FRESH PICNIC SHOULDER ROAST

When this pork-shoulder roast is smoked, it is known as a *picnic*. A fresh (unsmoked) picnic is easy to bone and roll for this succulent, mahogany-glazed roast. Serve with a spicy fruit chutney.

- 1 bone-in fresh picnic shoulder roast (5½ to 6 lbs)
- ½ cup each *soy sauce, honey,* and *water*
- ¼ cup dry red wine
- 2 tablespoons sugar
- ½ teaspoon ground ginger
- 1 teaspoon each *salt* and *dry mustard*
- 2 cloves garlic, thinly slivered

1. Remove and discard picnic rind, if any. Bone and tie roast (see illustration). Place in a bowl or casserole slightly larger than the roast.

2. In a small saucepan heat remaining ingredients, stirring until honey and sugar are dissolved. Cool to room temperature, then pour over roast. Cover and refrigerate 8 hours or overnight, turning several times.

3. Preheat oven to 325° F. Remove meat, reserving marinade, and place, fat side up, on a rack in an open roasting pan. Roast, uncovered, until meat thermometer registers 170° F (2 to 2½ hours). During roasting time, brush occasionally with marinade. (Leftover marinade can be stored in the refrigerator and reused for chicken, steak, or hamburger.) Slice thinly to serve.

Serves 8 to 10.

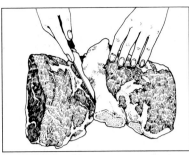

A picnic shoulder roast usually has only one major bone. (If the small hock end is present, cut it off at the joint and save it for soup). The big arm bone runs down the center. Cut in from one side to expose the bone. Remove bone and trim fat, then firmly roll the roast.

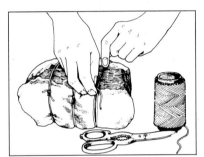

Tie the roast firmly at 1-inch intervals, using kitchen string.

ROAST PORK WITH MUSTARD POTATOES

- 2 teaspoons garlic salt
- ¼ teaspoon seasoned pepper
- ½ teaspoon dried summer savory
- 1 rolled boneless pork butt roast (4½ to 5 lbs)
- 6 medium-sized new potatoes (about 2½ lbs), thinly sliced
- 1 medium onion, finely chopped
- ½ cup each *chicken broth* (canned or homemade) and *half-and-half*
- 1 tablespoon Dijon mustard

1. Mix garlic salt, pepper, and savory. Rub most of mixture lightly over outside of roast, reserving a bit for the potatoes and onions. Coat these with the remaining seasoning mix. Mix broth, cream, and mustard until smooth; combine with potatoes.

Spread potato mixture in a large, shallow, greased baking dish. Place the seasoned roast, fat side up, in the center of the potatoes.

2. Preheat oven to 325° F. Bake until meat thermometer registers 170° F and potatoes are well browned, 2½ to 3 hours. Spoon off excess fat before slicing meat.

Serves 6 to 8.

POULTRY

HONEY-GLAZED BAKED CHICKEN QUARTERS

Here's another simple yet tasty oven dish: Baked chicken quarters with a sweet-and-sour glaze.

- ⅓ cup flour
- 1 teaspoon garlic salt
  Dash pepper
- 1 chicken (3 to 3½ lbs), quartered (see page 11)
- 6 tablespoons butter or margarine
- ¼ cup honey
- 3 tablespoons lemon juice
- 2 tablespoons soy sauce
  Dash ground ginger

1. Mix flour, garlic salt, and pepper, then coat chicken quarters thoroughly. As oven preheats to 350° F, melt 2 tablespoons of the butter in a shallow baking dish just large enough to hold the chicken in a single layer. Arrange chicken, skin side down, in butter. Bake, uncovered, 30 minutes.

2. Meanwhile, melt remaining 4 tablespoons butter with honey, lemon juice, soy sauce, and ginger. When chicken has baked 30 minutes, turn it skin side up. Evenly pour on butter mixture. Continue baking, brushing occasionally with sauce, until chicken is tender and richly browned (30 to 40 minutes more).

Serves 4.

Chicken quarters are first coated with a seasoned flour mixture and then baked with a glaze of honey, lemon juice, soy sauce, and ginger.

HOW TO MAKE PERFECT GRAVY

For many people, a beef roast or a turkey just isn't a meal without rich brown gravy. Here are some ideas for making your gravy smooth and flavorful.

1. *Think of gravy as a thickened sauce. First remove the meat from the roasting pan, then pour or spoon off the fat and measure it. For each cup of gravy, measure 1 to 2 tablespoons of fat into a saucepan. Discard the rest.*

2. *Loosen the drippings in the pan with liquid—beef or chicken broth, water, or red or white wine (or a combination of these). Heat and stir to loosen brown bits, and pour the liquid into a measuring cup; if there are large undissolved bits, pour liquid through a sieve. Don't add too much liquid, or the flavor will be weak.*

3. *For each cup of liquid, measure 1 to 2 tablespoons flour. Stir the flour into the fat in the saucepan and heat until bubbly. Remove from heat. Using a wire whisk, gradually stir in the liquid. Return to heat and cook, stirring constantly, until mixture is thickened. Boil 3–5 minutes more. Salt to taste.*

4. *If you prefer a creamy gravy for pork or chicken, use a liquid of about half milk, half broth or water.*

SAUSAGE-STUFFED ROAST CHICKEN

This roast chicken is made with a savory stuffing, which you can prepare ahead of time and refrigerate. But don't actually stuff the bird until you're ready to cook it.

> 1 *roasting chicken (5 lbs)*
> 3 *slices bacon*
> 1 *cup chicken broth (or ½ cup each chicken broth and dry white wine)*

Sausage Stuffing

> 1 *pound bulk pork sausage*
> 1 *onion, finely chopped Liver from the chicken, coarsely chopped*
> 1 *clove garlic, minced or pressed (optional)*
> 3 *cups cubed French bread*
> ½ *cup grated Parmesan cheese*
> ¼ *cup chopped parsley*
> ⅓ *cup chicken broth*

1. Preheat oven to 325° F. Rinse chicken with cool running water, inside and out, and pat dry with paper towels. Reserve liver for stuffing; save remaining giblets to make broth for later dish. Fill breast and body cavities with stuffing (see below); skewer closed. Place any extra stuffing in a buttered, covered casserole. Drape bacon slices over breast; insert meat thermometer in thickest part of breast. Place chicken on a rack in a shallow pan.

2. Roast chicken until thermometer registers 175° F or until a leg can be moved easily (1½ to 2 hours). Bake extra stuffing during last 30 minutes. Remove chicken to a carving platter and keep warm.

3. Skim off fat from roasting pan. To make gravy, add broth (or combined broth and wine) to pan and cook over direct heat, stirring constantly, to loosen brown drippings and reduce liquid by about a third. Serve gravy with slices of carved chicken.
Serves 6.

Sausage Stuffing Crumble sausage into a large frying pan and begin browning it over moderately high heat. Add onion, liver, and garlic. Continue cooking until sausage is browned and onion is soft. Remove from heat. Spoon off and discard fat. Add French bread, Parmesan cheese, and chopped parsley. Then lightly mix in chicken broth, just enough to moisten.
Makes 5 cups.

PIQUANT ROAST CHICKEN HALVES

Look for small chickens—two and a half pounds or less—to use in this recipe. Though low in calories, these roast chickens have a lot of flavor.

> 2 *small chickens (about 2½ lbs each), halved (see page 11)*
> 2 *tablespoons salad oil*
> 3 *tablespoons lemon juice*
> 2 *teaspoons salt*
> 1 *teaspoon each dried tarragon and paprika*
> ½ *teaspoon hot-pepper sauce*

1. Preheat oven to 375° F. Place chicken halves, skin side down, in a shallow nonstick baking pan. In a jar or small blender container, shake or whirl together oil, lemon juice, salt, tarragon, paprika, and hot-pepper sauce. Brush about half of the mixture generously over chicken.

2. Bake for about 1 hour. Turn chicken after the first 30 minutes. Brush several times during baking with remaining seasonings, until chicken is tender and nicely browned.
Serves 4.

FLAMING CORNISH HENS ON A SPIT

Here is a lavish way to cook frozen Rock Cornish game hens. If you find them on sale, take advantage of their price—they make a splendid dinner for two. Cooked on a rotisserie, the little birds are served flaming in your choice of brandy, whiskey, or orange liqueur.

> 2 Rock Cornish game hens (24 oz each)
> 2 tablespoons butter or margarine
> 1 teaspoon lemon juice
> ½ teaspoon grated orange rind
> ⅛ teaspoon whole white or black pepper, crushed
> Dash ground nutmeg
> ¼ cup brandy, bourbon, Scotch, or orange-flavored liqueur (such as Grand Marnier or Cointreau)

1. Arrange Cornish hens on a spit in oven or on a portable electric rotisserie. Heat together butter, lemon juice, orange rind, pepper, and nutmeg until bubbling.

2. Spit-roast hens, brushing occasionally with butter mixture, until skin is crisp and well browned, 1½ to 2 hours. Remove hens on spit to a warm, heat-proof (not wooden) platter; keep warm.

3. In a small long-handled pan, heat brandy, whiskey, or liqueur just until lukewarm (overheating will prevent it from flaming). Ignite and pour over hens. Keep spooning on the flaming liquid until flames are exhausted. Serve whole hen with juices spooned over, along with thick slices of warm French bread for mopping up juices. Eat with your fingers, if you like.

Serves 2.

ROAST TURKEY WITH CORNBREAD DRESSING

Festively stuffed with cornbread and sausage, turkey deserves its place of honor on holiday dinner tables. Try it for a special occasion outside the holiday season, too—it can be even more economical.

> 1 pound bulk pork sausage
> 2 onions, finely chopped
> 2 cups chopped celery
> 5 cups crumbled cornbread
> 3 cups cubed, day-old French bread
> ½ teaspoon salt
> ½ cup chopped parsley
> 1 turkey (12 to 15 lbs), thawed, rinsed, and patted dry
> 2 to 3 tablespoons soft butter or margarine

Crumbled Cornbread

> 1 cup sifted flour
> ¼ cup sugar
> 2 teaspoons baking powder
> ¾ teaspoon salt
> ½ teaspoon baking soda
> 1 cup yellow cornmeal
> 1 egg
> 1 cup buttermilk or sour milk
> 2 tablespoons salad oil

1. Preheat oven to 325° F. Crumble pork sausage into a large frying pan. Cook, stirring, until sausage is browned. Pour off all but about 3 tablespoons of the drippings. Add onions and celery and continue cooking, stirring occasionally, until vegetables are tender. In a large bowl combine cornbread and French bread. Lightly stir in sausage mixture, salt, and parsley. Gradually add broth, stirring just until stuffing is moistened.

2. Stuff the dressing lightly into the turkey breast and body cavities; skewer or sew closed. Tie legs together, if you wish. Place turkey on a rack in a shallow pan. Rub all over with butter. Insert thermometer in thick part of thigh.

3. Roast uncovered until thermometer registers 180° F to 185° F and drumstick moves easily, 2½ to 3½ hours. During roasting, baste several times with pan drippings. Place turkey on warmed platter, cover loosely with foil, and let stand for about 15 minutes before carving.

4. Meanwhile, make gravy from pan drippings, if you wish.

Serves 12 to 15.

Crumbled Cornbread Preheat oven to 425° F. Into a mixing bowl sift together flour, sugar, baking powder, salt, and baking soda. Mix in cornmeal. Make a well in center, and into it place egg, buttermilk or sour milk, and salad oil. Stir together quickly, just enough to moisten dry ingredients. Spread in a greased 8-inch-square pan. Bake for 15 to 20 minutes, until top is lightly browned and a wooden pick inserted near center comes out clean. Let cool, then crumble for the dressing.

Makes 5 cups.

Russian Marinated Lamb on Skewers (see page 33) acquires a piquant flavor from the pomegranate juice in the unusual marinade.

Thirty-Minute Meats

Enhance your evening meals
with these easy and elegant
thirty-minute meats.
Just because you're in a hurry
doesn't mean you have to buy the costliest
cuts. Many thrifty meats such as
top round, chuck roast,
liver, and chicken can be quickly
broiled, barbecued, sautéed,
or stir-fried in as little as half an hour
or less. Whether you're cooking
for family or for guests,
these dishes look and
taste as if they took hours
to prepare.

BROILING

Many of the most elegant meat dishes served in restaurants are broiled—and not all of them are fancy. With marinades, an attractive presentation, and judicious use of thrifty cuts of meat and poultry, you too can do what the restaurants do.

SWISS-STYLE SKEWERED LIVER AND BACON

The combination of liver and bacon is enjoyed in many parts of the world, including Zurich, where this dish is traditional. The Swiss usually serve it with *rosti* (the delicious potatoes that somewhat resemble hash browns). Fresh green beans add color and flavor to this dish.

    10 to 12 slices bacon, cut in
        half crosswise
     1 pound young beef liver, sliced
        White pepper
    ½ teaspoon ground sage
        Chopped parsley, for garnish

1. In a large sauté pan partially cook bacon until it is limp and beginning to brown; drain on paper towels.

2. Cut liver into strips 1 inch wide and about 2 inches long. Sprinkle lightly with pepper, then with sage. Wrap a partially cooked bacon strip around each liver strip. Thread on 8-inch bamboo skewers, about 3 to a skewer, to hold bacon in place.

3. Preheat broiler. Arrange skewers on rack in broiler pan. Broil, 3 to 4 inches from heat, until bacon is well browned on both sides, turning once (liver should be slightly pink in the center). Serve sprinkled with parsley.

Serves 3 to 4.

GIANT STUFFED HAMBURGER STEAKS WITH TANGY SAUCE

Filling plump hamburgers with a creamy, brandied blue-cheese butter gives them a special flavor; so does a tangy cold sauce spiked with horseradish. Accompany the hamburger steaks with crisp raw vegetables, warm French bread, and a red wine such as Beaujolais or a California Zinfandel.

     1 medium onion, chopped
     3 tablespoons butter or
        margarine
     2 cloves garlic, minced
        or pressed
     2 eggs
     2 pounds ground beef
     2 tablespoons chopped parsley
     1 teaspoon salt
    ⅛ teaspoon pepper
    ¼ cup crumbled blue cheese
     1 tablespoon brandy

Tangy Sauce

    ¼ cup each *chili sauce
        and mayonnaise*
    ½ cup catsup
    1½ teaspoons each *dry mustard
        and red wine vinegar*
     1 teaspoon Worcestershire sauce
        Dash hot-pepper sauce
    ¼ teaspoon ground ginger
     1 tablespoon each *pineapple
        juice and horseradish*

1. In a small frying pan cook onion in 1 tablespoon of the butter until it is soft but not browned. Mix in garlic; remove from heat. Beat eggs in a large bowl. Mix in onion mixture, ground beef, parsley, salt, and pepper. Shape into 8 flat oval patties.

2. In a small bowl mix blue cheese, remaining 2 tablespoons butter, and brandy until creamy and well combined. Place a quarter of the blue-cheese mixture in center of each of 4 of the patties. Top with remaining 4 patties; press edges together to seal.

3. Arrange stuffed hamburgers on rack in broiler pan. Broil about 4 inches from heat until well browned on both sides (a total of 12 to 15 minutes). To serve, spoon Tangy Sauce over each hamburger to taste.

Serves 4.

Tangy Sauce Mix together chili sauce, mayonnaise, catsup, dry mustard, red wine vinegar, Worcestershire sauce, hot-pepper sauce, ground ginger, pineapple juice, and horseradish.

Makes 1¼ cups.

Top four of the large oval ground beef patties with blue cheese filling.

Cover with remaining patties. Press edges together to seal before broiling.

RUSSIAN MARINATED LAMB ON SKEWERS

Many Russian recipes call for the piquant, magenta juice of autumn pomegranates for marinating lamb. Serve the skewered lamb with a rice pilaf and lightly sautéed zucchini. (See page 23 for step-by-step directions on how to bone a lamb shoulder roast for cubing.)

½ cup fresh pomegranate juice
2 tablespoons lemon juice
1 small onion, finely chopped
2 tablespoons salad oil
1 clove garlic, minced or pressed
½ teaspoon salt
  Dash pepper
2 pounds cubed boneless
  lean lamb shoulder or leg
2 green onions, thinly sliced
  (use part of tops), for garnish
  Lemon wedges and parsley
  sprigs, for garnish

1. In a shallow bowl mix pomegranate and lemon juices, chopped onion, oil, garlic, salt, and pepper. Stir in cubed lamb. Cover and refrigerate for 4 to 5 hours or overnight.

2. Preheat broiler. Drain meat and divide it among 6 skewers. Broil, about 4 inches from heat, turning once, until well browned on both sides, 8 to 10 minutes. Serve immediately, sprinkled with green onions and garnished with lemon and parsley.

Serves 6.

The piquant, magenta juice of pomegranates is an ingredient in many Russian recipes for marinating lamb. Squeeze this fresh fall fruit to make a tasty marinade for broiling boneless cubes of lamb on skewers. Take the precaution of wearing rubber gloves while handling the pomegranate to protect your hands from the vibrant purple stains.

Top round, a lean and versatile meat, is marinated in soy sauce, sherry, garlic, and onions. Strips of the steak are then threaded onto skewers, broiled with fresh pineapple, and topped with ground sesame seed. This tasty dish can be served with rice and a stir-fried vegetable such as snow peas.

BROILED STEAK SATAY WITH PINEAPPLE

Top round is a lean meat that, when marinated in soy sauce with sherry, garlic, and onions, becomes a tender and flavorful dish. Strips of steak are threaded onto skewers and broiled with wedges of pineapple, then sprinkled with ground sesame seed, Indonesian style. Rice and a stir-fried green vegetable—such as edible-pod peas—make a colorful and tasty accompaniment.

1½ to 2 pounds top round steak, ¾ inch thick
⅓ cup soy sauce
3 tablespoons dry sherry
2 tablespoons salad oil
1 small onion, finely chopped
3 cloves garlic, minced or pressed
¼ cup orange marmalade
⅛ teaspoon cayenne pepper
1 small pineapple (about 2 lbs)
2 tablespoons sesame seed, toasted and ground (see Note)
Plain, unflavored yogurt
Lime or lemon wedges

1. Cut steak into 6 long strips, each about ¾ inch wide. For marinade, mix in a bowl the soy sauce, sherry, oil, onion, and garlic. Place steak strips in bowl. Cover and refrigerate 1 to 2 hours.

2. Shortly before serving, preheat broiler. Whirl marmalade in blender with about 2 tablespoons of the marinade and all the cayenne. Peel pineapple, then quarter and remove core; cut in about 12 long wedges. Remove steak from marinade and thread strips on 6 metal or bamboo skewers, weaving skewer in and out of meat lengthwise to give a serpentine effect. Arrange skewers on rack of broiler pan. Broil 3 to 4 inches from heat until well browned on first side (4 to 5 minutes).

3. Turn skewers and arrange pineapple wedges around them; brush meat and fruit generously with marmalade mixture. Continue broiling—turning pineapple once and brushing again with marmalade mixture—until meat is browned to taste and pineapple is lightly browned.

4. Sprinkle meat with ground toasted sesame seed. Serve with hot broiled pineapple. Set out unflavored yogurt and lime or lemon wedges to add at the table.
Serves 6.

Note To toast and grind sesame seed, spread 2 tablespoons sesame seed in a shallow pan and bake in a 350° F oven until lightly browned (8 to 10 minutes); cool slightly. Whirl in small blender jar, or crush in a mortar, until powdery.

MARINATED LONDON BROIL

London broil traditionally is prepared with flank steak, yet the "London broil" you find in a supermarket meat case is usually top round cut from the most tender part next to the sirloin. This very high quality beef can be broiled or barbecued as is. However, you can use a more modest cut of top round and still produce a delicious London broil if you marinate it first to make it tender and flavorful.

    1½ to 2 pounds first-cut top
         round, about 1 inch thick
    ¼   cup each salad oil and
         dry red wine
    1   tablespoon Worcestershire
         sauce
    1   teaspoon Dijon mustard
    2   cloves garlic, minced
         or pressed
    ½   teaspoon salt
    ¼   teaspoon each sugar and
         dried rosemary
    1   bay leaf
         Seasoned pepper
         Chopped parsley, for garnish

1. Place meat in a shallow dish. In a covered jar or blender container, shake or whirl together oil, wine, Worcestershire sauce, mustard, garlic, salt, sugar, and rosemary until well combined. Pour over meat, turning to coat well. Place bay leaf in marinade. Cover and refrigerate, turning occasionally, for at least 8 to 10 hours.

2. Preheat broiler. Remove meat from marinade, reserving marinade. Place on rack in broiling pan. Sprinkle with pepper. Broil, about 6 inches from heat, until well browned on each side (allow about 10 minutes per side for rare), brushing occasionally with marinade.

3. Place on a wooden board and carve in thin diagonal slices. Sprinkle with chopped parsley.
Serves 6 to 8.

FRUITED CHICKEN EN BROCHETTE

Generous morsels of boneless chicken breast, first marinated in spices, wine, and yogurt, then skewered with onion and apricots, make a delicious and unusual entrée. A rice pilaf is a pleasant accompaniment.

    3   whole chicken breasts
         (6 halves, about 3 lbs),
         boned and skinned
         (see page 11)
    ½   cup plain, unflavored yogurt
    ¼   cup dry white wine
    ½   teaspoon ground cinnamon
    ¼   teaspoon curry powder
    ⅛   teaspoon ground cardamom
    ½   cup dried apricots
    ½   cup water
    2   tablespoons brown sugar
    1   tablespoon lemon juice
    ½   medium onion, separated
         into layers and cut in
         1-inch squares
         Sliced green onions (use
         part of tops), for garnish
         Lemon wedges

1. Cut boned chicken into bite-sized squares and place in a shallow glass bowl. In a small bowl blend yogurt, wine, cinnamon, curry powder, and cardamom until smooth. Pour over chicken, stirring to coat well. Cover and refrigerate 2 to 4 hours.

2. Meanwhile, place apricots in a small pan with water, brown sugar, and lemon juice. Bring to a gentle boil and simmer, uncovered, until apricots are just tender (about 10 minutes). Drain.

3. Preheat broiler. Remove chicken pieces from marinade and thread onto 6 metal skewers, alternating with onion squares and apricots. Place on rack in broiling pan, about 6 inches from heat; broil until chicken is cooked in the thickest part (test with a small sharp knife) and lightly browned (10 to 12 minutes per side). Sprinkle with green onions. Serve with lemon to squeeze over chicken.
Serves 6.

BARBECUING

What can compare with the flavor of meat cooked over charcoal? Just about any meat or poultry that can be broiled indoors can also be cooked outdoors, on a charcoal, gas, or electric grill. The following recipes are especially well suited to the barbecue.

BARBECUED PORK BUNS

For an easy family-barbecue meal, slice pork butt thinly and marinate it in a savory tomato sauce. Then grill the slices quickly and serve them in the marinade sauce, on toasted sesame rolls. These sandwiches are good with potato chips and salad or corn on the cob.

    1   pound boneless pork
         butt, trimmed of fat
         Tomato Barbecue Sauce
         (see page 41)
    4   hamburger buns with
         sesame seed
         Dill pickle slices

1. Freeze meat partially. Cut across the grain into large, thin slices. Place in a shallow bowl and lightly coat with sauce; cover and refrigerate for 2 to 3 hours or longer.

2. Remove meat from sauce. Place on grill above glowing coals. Cook, turning with tongs as the meat browns, just until nicely browned on both sides. As slices of meat cook, remove them to a covered dish; keep warm.

3. Reheat sauce. Split hamburger buns and toast on grill. Make sandwiches by filling toasted buns with cooked meat, spooning warm sauce over, and topping with pickles.
Serves 4.

menu

BARBECUED CHICKEN PICNIC

*Mustard-Barbecued
Chicken Legs*

Garden Potato Salad

Sliced Tomatoes

Garlic Bread

*Orange Chiffon Cake With
Strawberries and Cream*

White Table Wine

Milk

Coffee

*Set up a barbecue on
the patio, in the
park, or at the beach
for this festive picnic
featuring barbecued
chicken. When you
quarter a whole
chicken, save the
meaty leg and thigh
portions to barbecue
with this mustard-
and-herb marinade.*

GARDEN POTATO SALAD

    4   medium boiling potatoes
    1   clove garlic
    2   tablespoons salad oil
    ¼   cup tarragon wine vinegar
    1   teaspoon each *salt and sugar*
    ½   teaspoon dillweed
    3   hard-boiled eggs
    3   green onions, sliced
    3   large radishes, sliced
    1   small green pepper, quartered,
        seeded, and thinly sliced
    ¼   cup sliced ripe olives
    ⅓   cup mayonnaise
        Chopped parsley, for garnish

1. Cook unpeeled potatoes in boiling
salted water just until tender (about
35 minutes). While potatoes are
cooking, split garlic and place it in a
jar with oil; let stand for 10 minutes.
Remove and discard garlic. To
oil, add vinegar, salt, sugar, and
dillweed; shake well to blend. Drain
potatoes; peel while warm and cut
into ½-inch cubes (you should have
about 4 cups). Pour dressing over
warm potatoes. Cover and chill for
several hours or overnight.

2. To serve, slice 2 of the eggs. Add to
potatoes, along with green onions,
radishes, green pepper, ripe olives,
and mayonnaise. Mix lightly.
Slice remaining egg and use, with
parsley, as a garnish.
Serves 4.

MUSTARD-BARBECUED CHICKEN LEGS

    2   tablespoons Dijon mustard
    1   tablespoon dry white wine
    ¼   teaspoon each *dried
        basil, oregano, rosemary, and
        thyme*
    1   clove garlic, minced or pressed
    4   whole chicken legs
        (thighs attached)

1. In a small bowl mix mustard,
wine, herbs, and garlic until well
combined. Spread evenly over
all sides of chicken. Cover chicken
and refrigerate about 3 hours.

2. Arrange chicken on a barbecue
grill about 6 inches above glowing
coals. Grill chicken legs until
well browned on both sides, about 45
minutes in all (meat near the thigh
bones should no longer be pink or
run with pink juices when tested).
Serves 4.

ORANGE CHIFFON CAKE WITH STRAWBERRIES AND CREAM

    2¼   cups sifted cake flour
    1½   cups sugar
     3   teaspoons baking powder
     1   teaspoon salt
     2   oranges
     ½   cup salad oil
     5   egg yolks
     1   cup egg whites (use about
         8 eggs)
     ½   teaspoon cream of tartar
         Whipped cream
         Strawberries

1. Preheat oven to 325° F. Sift flour,
sugar, baking powder, and salt into a
medium-sized mixing bowl. Grate
the rind of the oranges and set aside.
Make a well in the center of the dry
ingredients and into it place, in
order: oil, egg yolks, and grated rind.
Squeeze and strain orange juice; measure and add water (if needed) to
make ¾ cup. Add to egg yolk mixture. Beat until smooth.

2. In a large bowl beat egg whites
and cream of tartar until very stiff
peaks form. Gradually pour
egg yolk mixture over egg whites,
folding gently until the two mixtures
are incorporated.

3. Pour batter into an *ungreased* 10-
inch tube pan. Bake until long
skewer inserted in thickest part comes
out clean (1 hour to 1 hour and 10
minutes). Invert pan and suspend on
a funnel or bottle to cool completely.
With a thin spatula, gently loosen
sides and bottom of cake; invert it
onto a serving plate.

4. To serve, top with whipped cream
and strawberries.
Serves 8 to 10.

The flavor of Mustard-Barbecued
Chicken Legs cooked over
charcoal in the park, at a tailgate
party, or on your own patio is
hard to beat.

Top round, marinated in a chile-garlic-tequila mixture then barbecued, is served with cheese-topped refried beans and a tomato rice casserole.

MEXICAN STEAK BARBECUE

Mexican Barbecued Top Round

Tomato-Rice Casserole

Refried Beans With Cheese

Corn Chips

Hot Sauce

Fresh Fruit

Sugar Cookies

Easy Sangria or Beer

An assertive chile-garlic-tequila marinade will help you turn a thick, first cut of top round (as in London broil) into a rare, juicy steak reminiscent of Mexico's carne asada. When served with sangria or beer, a baked tomato-rice casserole, and cheese-topped refried beans, this dish really invites a party.

REFRIED BEANS WITH CHEESE

  1 *large onion, chopped*
  3 *tablespoons lard, bacon drippings, or salad oil*
  1 *can (30 oz) refried beans*
  1 *clove garlic, minced or pressed*
  2 *teaspoons chili powder*
  1 *cup shredded Cheddar cheese*

1. In a heavy frying pan cook onion in heated lard, drippings, or oil, stirring until lightly browned. Mix in beans, garlic, and chili powder.

2. Cook over medium heat, stirring occasionally, until fat is absorbed and beans are heated through (about 5 minutes). Mix in ½ cup of the cheese until melted; top with remaining cheese and serve from frying pan. *Serves 6.*

TOMATO-RICE CASSEROLE

  3 *tablespoons salad oil*
1½ *cups long-grain rice*
  1 *large onion, finely chopped*
  1 *clove garlic, minced or pressed*
  1 *can (15 oz) tomato sauce*
1½ *cups regular-strength chicken broth (homemade or canned)*
  ¾ *teaspoon each salt and cumin*
  ⅛ *teaspoon cayenne pepper*
  ¾ *cup ripe olive wedges*
  2 *cups shredded Monterey jack cheese*

1. Preheat oven to 325° F. Heat oil in a large deep saucepan. Stir rice to coat it with hot oil, then stir in onion and garlic. Cook until onion browns lightly. Mix in tomato sauce, broth, salt, cumin, and cayenne. Bring to a boil, reduce heat, and cover tightly. Cook until rice is almost tender (about 20 minutes).

2. Mix in olive wedges and 1 cup of the cheese. Turn into a greased 1½- to 2-quart casserole. Sprinkle with remaining cheese. Bake, uncovered, until cheese is melted and lightly browned (about 15 minutes). *Serves 6 to 8.*

MEXICAN BARBECUED TOP ROUND

1½ *to 2 pounds first-cut top round, about 1 inch thick*
  ¼ *cup salad oil*
  3 *tablespoons tequila*
  1 *small, dried, hot chile pepper, crushed*
  1 *tablespoon chili powder*
  1 *teaspoon salt*
  ¼ *teaspoon dried oregano*
  2 *cloves garlic, minced or pressed*
  ¼ *cup each slivered red bell pepper, green bell pepper, and mild red onion*
     Radish roses, for garnish

1. Place meat in a shallow glass dish. In a covered jar or small blender container, shake or whirl together oil, tequila, dried chile, chili powder, salt, oregano, and garlic. Pour over meat. Cover and refrigerate, turning occasionally, for 8 to 10 hours.

2. Reserving marinade, remove meat. Place meat on grill about 6 inches above glowing coals. Barbecue, brushing occasionally with marinade (10 minutes per side for rare steak).

3. To serve, carve in thin, slightly diagonal slices. Top with mixture of red pepper, green pepper, and onion. Garnish with radishes. *Serves 6 to 8.*

EASY SANGRIA

  1 *can (12 oz) frozen limeade concentrate, thawed*
  1 *quart dry red wine*
     Orange, lemon, lime, and strawberry slices
  1 *quart chilled club soda*

1. In a 10- to 12-cup pitcher, stir together limeade concentrate and wine. Mix in fruit slices to taste. Cover and chill for 3 to 4 hours.

2. To serve, mix in club soda, then add ice. Garnish with additional sliced fruit, if you wish. *Serves 6 to 8.*

Thick slices of zucchini lie next to colorful brochettes of pork, peppers, and onions. Both are marinated in wine, lemon, and herbs and grilled over charcoal to a golden brown.

SKEWERED PORK AND RED PEPPER

This marinade of wine, lemon, and herbs is meant for pork—but it also makes a flavorful baste for big, thick, diagonal slices of zucchini. Grill the zucchini over the charcoal fire along with these colorful brochettes of pork, peppers, and onions.

- 1½ to 2 pounds lean boneless pork butt, cut in 1-inch cubes
- ½ cup dry white wine
  Juice of 1 lemon
- 2 tablespoons olive oil or salad oil
- 1 teaspoon each *salt and paprika*
- ¼ teaspoon each *black pepper and dried rosemary*
- 1 large onion
- 1 large red bell pepper, halved and seeded

1. Place pork cubes in a shallow bowl. In blender, shake or whirl together wine, lemon juice, oil, salt, paprika, pepper, and rosemary. Cut onion in half; reserve one half, and chop the other half finely and add to pork. Pour marinade over pork. Cover and refrigerate 8 to 10 hours or overnight.

2. Remove pork from bowl, reserving marinade. Cut remaining half-onion in wedges; then separate into layers and cut into squares. Cut red pepper into 1-inch squares. Using 4 to 6 skewers, alternate pork cubes with onion and red pepper squares.

3. Grill skewered pork about 6 inches above glowing coals, brushing occasionally with reserved marinade, until nicely browned on each side (8 to 10 minutes per side).

Serves 4 to 6.

THREE VERSATILE MARINADES FOR BARBECUED MEATS

Marinating meat and poultry before barbecuing them can make a big difference in terms of flavor and tenderness. Here are three different styles of marinades.

For marinating, use a container that holds the meat snugly in a single layer. A glass or stainless steel bowl or casserole is a good choice, as it won't be affected by acid ingredients. Cover the marinating meat with plastic wrap or the casserole cover, and refrigerate it for several hours. (For maximum flavor, marinate it overnight.)

Store any leftover marinade in a covered jar in the refrigerator. It will keep for up to a month. (Teriyaki marinade keeps for several months.)

MUSTARD AND HERB MARINADE

⅓ cup salad oil
¼ cup dry white wine
1 tablespoon each *red wine vinegar and lemon juice*
1 large clove garlic, minced or pressed
1½ tablespoons Dijon mustard
¼ teaspoon each *salt and sugar*
⅛ teaspoon each *dried thyme, oregano, summer savory, and tarragon*
Dash white pepper

1. Combine oil, wine, vinegar, lemon juice, garlic, mustard, salt, sugar, herbs, and pepper in blender container; whirl until smooth.

2. Use as a marinade for lamb or chicken.
Makes just under 1 cup.

TERIYAKI MARINADE

½ cup soy sauce
3 tablespoons sugar
2 teaspoons grated fresh ginger, or ½ teaspoon ground ginger
1 clove garlic, minced or pressed
2 tablespoons dry sherry

1. In a bowl or tightly covered jar, mix or shake soy sauce, sugar, ginger, garlic, and sherry well, until sugar is dissolved.

2. Use as a marinade for beef steaks or for chicken pieces, quarters, or halves. Brush meat with marinade while cooking.
Makes about ¾ cup.

TOMATO BARBECUE SAUCE

1 tablespoon salad oil
1 medium onion, finely chopped
1 large clove garlic, minced or pressed
½ teaspoon each *salt and chili powder*
¼ teaspoon dry mustard
2 tablespoons brown sugar
3 tablespoons cider vinegar
1 tablespoon Worcestershire sauce
¾ cup each *catsup and dry red wine*

1. In a 1½- to 2-quart saucepan, heat oil and sauté onion until soft but not browned. Stir in garlic, salt, chili powder, dry mustard, brown sugar, vinegar, Worcestershire sauce, catsup, and wine. Stir until sugar dissolves and mixture begins to boil; simmer for 3 to 5 minutes, then remove from heat.

2. Cool, then use as a marinade for uncooked meat and poultry such as pork, beef, or chicken. Or brush, warm, over hamburgers or frankfurters as they cook on grill.

Warm sauce can also be used for reheating sliced cooked beef, pork, or chicken. (This recipe is used in Barbecued Pork Buns, page 35.)
Makes 2 cups.

LEMON-BARBECUED LAMB SHOULDER CHOPS

This spicy Mediterranean marinade—lemon, garlic, and oregano—enhances the flavor of economical lamb shoulder chops.

4 round-bone lamb shoulder chops, about ¾ inch thick (about 2 lbs)
3 tablespoons each *olive oil or salad oil and lemon juice*
½ teaspoon each *salt, paprika, and dried oregano*
2 cloves garlic, minced or pressed
¼ teaspoon each *sugar and whole black pepper, coarsely crushed*
1 teaspoon grated lemon rind
1 bay leaf

1. Trim any excess fat from lamb chops. Arrange in a single layer in a shallow baking dish.

2. In a jar or small blender container, shake or whirl together oil, lemon juice, salt, paprika, oregano, garlic, and sugar until well combined. Mix in pepper, lemon rind, and bay leaf; pour over lamb chops. Cover and refrigerate 2 to 4 hours, turning at least once.

3. Remove chops, reserving marinade. Grill about 6 inches above glowing coals, brushing occasionally with marinade, until well browned (about 5 minutes per side).
Serves 4.

TOP-OF-THE-RANGE COOKING

There are several ways to cook meat quickly—on your range top, in an electric frying pan, or even over a hot plate! *Pan broiling* is done in a frying pan over moderately high heat, using little if any cooking fat. *Pan-frying* or *sautéeing*, another means of quick skillet cooking, uses more fat than pan broiling. And *stir-frying* is familiar to all devotees of Chinese cooking (see page 56).

When preparing a meat dish using any of these quick-cooking techniques, it's a good idea to have all your ingredients peeled, chopped, measured, and ready to use. Success depends on putting the various elements together swiftly and smoothly.

STEAK AND ONIONS FOR TWO

Many people love this German-origin combination: sweetly pungent onions heaped abundantly over quickly cooked steaks. It goes deliciously with chunky butter-browned potatoes, a green vegetable, and a light red wine.

> 2 medium onions, thinly sliced
> 2 tablespoons butter or margarine
> 1 tablespoon salad oil
> 1 clove garlic, minced or pressed
> 2 boneless steaks from blade-cut chuck roast (see page 9)
>   Salt and white pepper
> ¼ cup dry white wine
>   Chopped parsley, for garnish

1. Separate onions into rings. In a 9- to 10-inch frying pan, heat 1 tablespoon of the butter with all the oil. Add onions and garlic. Cook slowly over low heat, stirring occasionally, until onions are limp and golden (20 to 25 minutes). Increase heat to brown onions slightly; remove onions from pan and keep them warm in a 250° F oven.

2. Sprinkle steaks with salt and pepper. Add remaining butter to same pan. Over moderately high heat, brown steaks quickly on both sides (3 to 4 minutes per side); remove to warm serving plates. Add wine to pan and cook quickly to reduce by about half, stirring in browned juices from pan. Reduce heat to moderate and mix in onions. Spoon onion mixture over steaks. Sprinkle with parsley.

Serves 2.

BEEF STROGANOFF

A typical 5-pound blade chuck roast, when boned and trimmed of fat, should yield about one-half pound meat from the top section (or flatiron muscle). This recipe uses that section from two roasts.

> 1 pound beef chuck from atop blade bone, trimmed of fat (see page 9)
> 2 tablespoons butter or margarine
> 1 tablespoon salad oil
> ¼ pound mushrooms, sliced
> 1 small onion, finely chopped
> ¾ teaspoon salt
> 1 teaspoon Worcestershire sauce
>   Dash each paprika and white pepper
> ½ cup sour cream
>   Chopped parsley, for garnish
>   Noodles

1. Slice meat across the grain about ¼ inch thick; cut into bite-sized strips.

2. In a large frying pan over moderately high heat, heat 1 tablespoon of the butter with salad oil until foamy. Add mushrooms and onion and cook quickly, stirring often, until browned. Remove mushroom mixture from pan with a slotted spoon, and reserve.

3. If needed, add 1 tablespoon more butter to the pan. Add strips of meat and cook over high heat, turning meat and shaking pan, just until meat browns. Remove pan from heat; stir in mushroom mixture, salt, Worcestershire, paprika, pepper, and sour cream.

4. Return pan to low heat, stirring constantly. Cook just until sauce is heated through (do not allow to boil). Sprinkle with parsley; serve with noodles.

Serves 3 to 4.

JOE'S SPECIAL

This meal-in-one-skillet dish is a San Francisco favorite. The mushrooms are a nice addition, but you can omit them to keep the cost down. For a quick supper, it's nearly complete—simply add a crusty loaf of French bread and a hearty red wine.

> 1 pound ground beef, crumbled
> 1½ tablespoons olive oil or salad oil
> 1 large onion, finely chopped
> 1 clove garlic, minced or pressed
> ¼ pound mushrooms, sliced (optional)
> 1 teaspoon salt
> ⅛ teaspoon each pepper and dried oregano
>   Dash ground nutmeg
> 2 cups chopped fresh spinach
> 3 eggs
>   Freshly grated Parmesan cheese

1. In a large heavy frying pan over high heat, heat oil and brown ground beef well. Add onion, garlic, and mushrooms (if used); reduce heat and continue cooking, stirring occasionally, until onion is soft. Stir in seasonings and spinach; cook about 5 minutes longer, stirring several times.

2. Add eggs to meat mixture; stir quickly over low heat just until eggs begin to set. Serve immediately. Sprinkle cheese over each serving to taste.

Serves 3 to 4.

GYPSY-STYLE STEAK

Mushrooms, onions, and sweet red-pepper strips in a sour cream sauce cover this rare steak. (After adding the sour cream, heat the sauce to *just below* the boiling point, since more heat may cause it to separate.) Fluffy white rice is a natural accompaniment.

> 2 tablespoons butter or
>   margarine
> 1 tablespoon salad oil
> 1 medium onion, finely chopped
> 1 sweet red pepper, seeded
>   and cut in strips
> ¼ pound mushrooms, sliced
> 1 clove garlic, minced or pressed
> 4 boneless steaks from 2
>   blade-cut chuck roasts (see
>   page 9)
>   Salt and paprika
> ⅓ cup dry white wine
> ½ cup sour cream
>   Chopped parsley, for garnish

1. In a large frying pan heat 1 tablespoon of the butter and salad oil. Cook onion, red pepper, mushrooms, and garlic, stirring frequently, until tender; remove vegetable mixture from the pan.

2. Sprinkle steaks with salt and paprika. Add remaining butter to pan in which vegetables were cooked. Brown steaks quickly on both sides over high heat (about 4 minutes per side). Remove to a warm serving platter.

3. Add wine to pan and cook quickly to reduce slightly, stirring to loosen browned juices from pan. Reduce heat to moderate, mix in vegetables, and cook until heated through. Over low heat, smoothly mix in sour cream (do not boil). Spoon sauce over steaks. Sprinkle with parsley.

Serves 4.

Gypsy-Style Steak, accompanied by fluffy white rice and lightly cooked fresh zucchini slices, is a quick and easy dinner that will add a colorful boost to the end of a hectic day.

Sauté boneless chuck steaks and serve them topped with a flavorful herb butter for a novel version of this favorite meat. Accompanied by baked potatoes, this elegant dish will provide a relaxing candlelight dinner for two.

STEAK WITH TANGY HERB BUTTER

Steaks made from the bottom third of a chuck roast provide some of the best-tasting beef you can find. Why not give them an all-out elegant treatment—a delicious parsley-watercress butter. Use any remaining butter on baked potatoes.

> *Lower section blade-cut chuck roast, bone removed (see page 9)*
> ½ *tablespoon each butter or margarine and salad oil*
> *Salt*
> *Watercress, for garnish*

Herb Butter

> ¼ *cup soft butter or margarine*
> 1 *tablespoon lemon juice*
> 2 *tablespoons each finely chopped parsley and watercress*
> ½ *teaspoon Worcestershire sauce*
> *Dash white pepper*

1. Trim and discard fat from meat; cut the piece of meat in half, crosswise, into two equal slices, each ¾ to 1 inch thick. If necessary, roll slightly and fasten with wooden picks to make more compact steaks.

2. In a heavy frying pan over medium-high heat, heat butter and oil together until foamy; cook steaks quickly until well browned on each side (4 to 5 minutes per side). Remove to warm serving plates. Sprinkle with salt.

3. Serve topped with a chunk of Herb Butter, accompanied by a bouquet of watercress.

Serves 2.

Herb Butter Beat butter or margarine until fluffy; gradually beat in lemon juice until well combined, then mix in parsley, watercress, Worcestershire sauce, and pepper. Shape into a roll or a cube, wrap in plastic film, and chill several hours to blend flavors.

ELEGANT EYE OF ROUND STEAKS

One good way to make this compact cut of meat tender is to slice it thinly, pound it, then brown the steaks very quickly. The result is meat that is rare and juicy. Serve with slender french fries, tender-crisp green beans, and a red wine, such as Zinfandel.

> 2 eyes of round from full-cut round steaks (see page 10), about 12 ounces total, trimmed of fat
> Coarsely ground pepper
> Flour
> 1 tablespoon each butter or margarine and salad oil
> Salt
> ¼ pound small mushrooms, quartered
> 2 shallots, finely chopped, or 2 tablespoons very finely chopped mild onion
> ¼ cup dry red wine
> Chopped parsley, for garnish

1. Freeze eye of round steaks partially, just until ice crystals begin to form. Slice each steak horizontally into 2 thin slices. Using the flat side of a meat mallet, place steaks between pieces of waxed paper and pound them until they are about ¼ inch thick. Sprinkle with pepper and dust lightly with flour, shaking off excess.

2. In a large frying pan, heat butter and oil over high heat. Brown steaks very quickly on both sides; remove to a heated platter, sprinkle with salt, and keep warm. Add mushrooms to pan and brown them quickly; stir in shallots and wine. Cook, stirring, until most of the liquid is gone. Salt to taste, then spoon mushroom mixture over steaks. Sprinkle with parsley. Serve immediately with vegetables.
Serves 2.

QUICK LIVER AND MUSHROOMS

One thing liver doesn't need is overcooking. When browned quickly, the center stays pink and moist, and the texture and flavor are at their best. Here the liver is further enhanced by a light sauce made with onions, mushrooms, and wine.

> 1 pound sliced young beef liver, cut in serving pieces
> Salt, pepper, and flour
> 3 tablespoons butter or margarine
> 1 small onion, finely chopped
> 1 can (4 oz) mushroom pieces and stems, drained
> 2 tablespoons lemon juice
> ¼ cup dry white wine
> Chopped parsley, for garnish

1. Sprinkle liver with salt and pepper; coat lightly with flour. Heat 2 tablespoons of the butter in a large frying pan, and brown liver quickly on both sides. Remove to a heated serving platter, and keep warm in a 250° F oven.

2. Add remaining 1 tablespoon butter to pan, and in it brown onion and mushrooms; stir in lemon juice and wine. Bring to a boil and cook, stirring to mix in brown bits, until slightly reduced. Spoon mushroom sauce over liver; sprinkle with parsley.
Serves 3 to 4.

MUSTARD AND PEPPER STEAK

Here is that marvelously flavorful and tender steak from the chuck again (see page 9), in a version for two that's elegant enough to make a French chef proud. Serve it with baked potatoes or noodles with butter and parsley, and broiled tomato halves covered with melted cheese.

> 2 boneless steaks from blade-cut chuck roast (see page 9)
> 1 teaspoon whole white or black peppercorns, coarsely crushed
> ¼ teaspoon dried rosemary
> 1 tablespoon each butter or margarine and salad oil
> Salt
> 1 tablespoon Dijon mustard
> ¼ cup each dry vermouth or white wine and whipping cream

1. Trim and discard fat from meat; if necessary, roll slightly and fasten with wooden toothpicks to make more compact steaks. Mix pepper and rosemary; press mixture into steaks on both sides.

2. In a heavy frying pan, over medium-high heat heat butter and oil together until foamy; cook steaks quickly until well browned on each side (about 4 minutes per side). Remove to warm serving plates; sprinkle with salt. Pour off fat.

3. Add to cooking pan mustard, vermouth, and cream, stirring to blend well and loosen browned juices from pan. Boil, stirring, until reduced and slightly thickened. Pour sauce over steaks.
Serves 2.

ALPINE LIVER STRIPS IN WINE CREAM SAUCE

This Swiss favorite features quickly cooked, bite-sized strips of calf or young beef liver in a wine-flavored cream sauce. Accompany it with fresh noodles or hash brown potatoes and buttered broccoli.

  1½ *pounds sliced young beef or calf liver, cut into 2- by ½-inch strips*
      Salt, white pepper, and nutmeg
      Flour
  ¼   *cup butter or margarine*
  2   *tablespoons vegetable oil*
  2   *shallots, chopped, or 2 tablespoons very finely chopped onion*
  ½   *cup dry white wine*
  ¾   *cup whipping cream*
      Chopped parsley, for garnish

1. Sprinkle liver with salt, pepper, and nutmeg; coat lightly with flour, shaking off excess. In a large heavy frying pan heat 2 tablespoons of the butter with the oil over moderately high heat until the mixture is foamy. Brown half the liver, cooking just until well browned on both sides. Remove liver and keep it warm. Add 1 tablespoon more butter to pan; heat, then cook remaining liver. Add it to previously cooked liver.

2. Add remaining 1 tablespoon butter to pan. In it cook shallots until they are lightly browned. Add wine and cream; cook, stirring briskly, until sauce boils and is reduced by about half. Salt to taste.

3. Return liver and its juices to sauce, stirring over medium heat until heated through. Sprinkle with chopped parsley to serve.

Serves 4 to 6.

HAMBURGERS AU POIVRE

These elegant hamburgers are coated with coarsely crushed pepper and flamed with brandy for a dramatic finishing touch. Serve them with tiny green peas and thin, crisp French fried potatoes. They are perfect dinner fare to serve before or after a sporting event or other informal gathering.

  1½ *pounds ground lean beef*
  ½   *teaspoon garlic powder*
  1   *teaspoon each salt, Worcestershire sauce, and Dijon mustard*
  1   *teaspoon whole black peppercorns, coarsely crushed*
  1   *tablespoon each butter or margarine and salad oil*
  ⅓   *cup regular-strength beef broth (homemade or canned)*
  2   *tablespoons very finely chopped onion*
  3   *tablespoons brandy*
      Watercress, for garnish

1. In a large bowl lightly mix ground beef, garlic powder, salt, Worcestershire sauce, and mustard. Shape into 4 large patties. Rub and press crushed pepper into both sides of patties. Cover with waxed paper and let stand at least 30 minutes.

2. In a large heavy frying pan, heat combined butter and oil over moderately high heat until foamy. Cook meat patties in the heated mixture until well browned (2½ to 4 minutes on each side). Remove to a heated platter and keep warm.

3. Pour off the cooking fat. Stir broth and onions into pan, stirring in browned bits. Boil, stirring until most of the liquid is gone. Remove from heat, add brandy, and swirl to mix and heat it slightly. Ignite and spoon, flaming, over burgers. Garnish with bouquets of watercress. Serve immediately.

Serves 4.

MEDITERRANEAN PARSLIED MEATBALLS

Meatballs are always a favorite family meal, but with a little imagination they can be elegant enough for company, too. These light-textured meatballs have a definite Greek influence—oregano, lots of chopped parsley, and tart lemon butter. Serve with rice and sautéed zucchini.

  1   *medium onion, chopped*
  ¼   *cup water*
  1   *egg*
  ¼   *cup milk*
  ⅓   *cup fine dry bread crumbs*
  1   *clove garlic, minced or pressed*
  1   *teaspoon salt*
  ¼   *teaspoon dried oregano*
  ⅛   *teaspoon pepper*
  1   *pound ground lean beef*
  ½   *cup chopped parsley*
  2   *tablespoons butter or margarine*
  2   *tablespoons lemon juice*

1. Place onion and water in a small pan. Cook covered, until onion is transparent; drain. In a large bowl, beat egg with milk. Mix in bread crumbs, garlic, salt, oregano, and pepper; let stand for a few minutes. Then lightly mix in drained onion, ground beef, and parsley. Shape into meatballs about 1½ inches in diameter.

2. In a large frying pan, melt butter and slowly brown meatballs on all sides. Remove to a warm serving dish. Add lemon juice to pan drippings; stir to loosen browned bits. Pour drippings over meatballs. Sprinkle with a little additional chopped parsley.

Serves 3 to 4.

SCANDINAVIAN MEATBALLS

These beef-and-pork meatballs are gently spiced and served in a creamy sauce that is good with either noodles or rice. Dark rye bread and a dilled cucumber salad complete the meal.

    1   egg
    1½ cups milk
    ½   cup fine dry bread crumbs
    1   teaspoon each *salt and sugar*
    ¼   teaspoon each *ground ginger,
        nutmeg, and allspice*
    1   pound *ground lean beef*
    ½   pound *ground pork*
    1   small onion, finely chopped
    ¼   cup butter or margarine
    1   tablespoon flour
        Chopped parsley, for garnish

1. In a large bowl beat egg with ½ cup of the milk. Blend in bread crumbs, salt, sugar, and spices. Thoroughly mix in ground meats and onion. Shape into meatballs about the size of walnuts.

2. In a large, heavy frying pan, brown meatballs well in heated butter or margarine. As they brown, remove them to a heated dish in a 250° F oven to keep warm.

3. Pour off all but about 1 tablespoon of the fat. Cook flour in same pan, stirring, until bubbly and lightly browned. Gradually mix in the remaining 1 cup milk, cooking until thickened and smooth. Salt to taste. Return meatballs to pan, cover, and simmer 15 minutes. Sprinkle with parsley.

Serves 4 to 6.

For a warm meal with friends or family on a cold winter night, serve creamy Scandinavian Meatballs. These hearty meatballs are good with egg noodles or rice and a cucumber salad with dill.

Your dinner guests will enjoy a bubbly Beef Fondue cooked right at the table. Complement the tenderized, cooked top round with a dip of spicy garlic mayonnaise for a rich taste. Serve with a fresh green salad and warm French bread.

BEEF FONDUE

Tenderized boneless top round can make an elegant yet economical beef fondue to cook at the table. Serve with warm French bread and a green salad.

> 1½ to 2 pounds boneless
>   top round
>   *Unseasoned powdered meat tenderizer*
> 2 cups salad oil
>   *Salt and pepper*

Spicy Garlic Mayonnaise

> 1 *egg*
> 2 *teaspoons Dijon mustard*
> 1 *teaspoon paprika*
> 1 *clove garlic, minced or pressed*

> ½ *teaspoon salt*
> 2 *tablespoons white wine vinegar*
> ¼ *cup olive oil*
> ¾ *cup salad oil*
> 1 *tablespoon each chili sauce and drained capers*
> 1 *teaspoon Worcestershire sauce*
> 2 *tablespoons snipped fresh chives or thinly sliced green onions*
> 2 *tablespoons chopped sour pickle*

1. Trim fat from meat. Cut meat into ¾-inch cubes. Sprinkle with meat tenderizer and let stand at room temperature about 30 minutes, according to tenderizer directions.

2. Heat oil on top of range or in an electric fondue pot to about 360° F. If using range top, transfer to fondue pot over alcohol or canned heat burner.

3. At the table, each person cooks steak cubes, one at a time, on fondue forks or bamboo skewers. Allow 20 to 30 seconds (depending on heat of oil) for meat to brown lightly on outside, yet remain juicy and rare in center. Transfer cooked meat to plate, sprinkle with salt and pepper, spear with another fork (metal fondue forks get too hot from cooking to be used for eating), and dip into Garlic Mayonnaise or other favorite fondue sauces.
Serves 4 to 6.

Spicy Garlic Mayonnaise In blender container combine egg, mustard, paprika, garlic, salt, vinegar, and olive oil. Cover and whirl at low speed. Immediately uncover and pour in salad oil in a slow, steady stream. Whirl until thick and smooth. Pour into a mixing bowl and add chili sauce, capers, Worcestershire sauce, chives or green onions, and pickle. Cover and chill.
Makes about 1½ cups.

VEAL KIDNEYS IN SHERRY AND MUSTARD SAUCE

Kidneys are another variety meat that benefits from fast cooking. If overcooked, they can become strong-tasting and tough, but when sautéed quickly they are delicious and tender. Try them over rice or buttered English muffins, topped with a robustly flavored sauce that suits their distinctive taste.

> 6 *veal kidneys (about 1 lb)*
> *Salt and white pepper*
> 3 *tablespoons butter or*
> *margarine*
> ¼ *pound mushrooms, sliced*
> ¼ *cup finely chopped onion*
> ¼ *cup dry sherry*
> 2 *teaspoons Dijon mustard*
> ½ *cup sour cream*
> *Chopped parsley, for garnish*

1. To prepare kidneys, cut away fatty membrane, then cut in slices ½ inch thick. Sprinkle with salt and pepper.

2. In a large frying pan heat 2 tablespoons of the butter over moderately high heat. Add mushrooms and cook until browned; remove and reserve. Add a little more butter, and in it cook onion lightly. Add kidneys and remaining butter and cook quickly, stirring, just until firm and lightly browned. Add kidneys to mushrooms.

3. Add sherry and mustard to pan, cooking and stirring until smooth and slightly reduced. Return kidney mixture to cooking pan. Over low heat, stir sour cream into kidneys, cooking just until heated through (do not boil). Salt to taste. Sprinkle with parsley.
Serves 4.

CREAMY PORK AND APPLE SAUTÉ

Lean pork can substitute for veal in many dishes. It is a delicate and tender dish, especially when cooked with apple wedges, wine, and cream and served with hot rice or noodles.

> 1½ *to 2 pounds lean,*
> *boneless pork butt*
> ⅓ *cup flour*
> 1½ *teaspoons salt*
> ½ *teaspoon each paprika*
> *and ground nutmeg*
> ⅛ *teaspoon white pepper*
> 2 *to 3 tablespoons butter*
> *or margarine*
> 1 *tablespoon salad oil*
> 1 *small onion, finely chopped*
> 2 *medium-sized tart cooking*
> *apples, peeled and cut*
> *in ½-inch wedges*
> ¾ *cup dry white wine*
> ½ *cup whipping cream*
> *Chopped parsley, for garnish*

1. Cut pork into thin strips about 2 inches long and ½ to ¾ inch wide. Mix flour, salt, paprika, nutmeg, and pepper. Lightly coat pork strips with the flour mixture, shaking off excess. In a large frying pan heat 2 tablespoons of the butter with the oil. Brown pork strips on all sides, about a third at a time. Remove them when they are well browned.

2. Add more butter, if needed. Cook onion, stirring occasionally, until lightly browned. Return pork and any juices to the frying pan. Add apple wedges. Pour on wine and cream. Bring to a boil, reduce heat, cover, and simmer until pork is tender (about 20 minutes). With a slotted spoon, remove pork and apples to a warm serving dish.

3. Bring pan juices to a boil and stir briskly over high heat until sauce is smooth; add salt to taste. Pour over pork and apples. Sprinkle with parsley.
Serves 4.

ITALIAN VEAL SAUTÉ

Although most cuts of veal are usually fairly expensive, occasionally you can find a good value in a boneless roast. Cut it up yourself—in slices for scaloppine, or in strips or cubes for a quick sauté such as this—and you are bound to come out ahead.

> 2 *pounds boneless veal, cut*
> *in small cubes*
> *Salt, white pepper, ground*
> *nutmeg, and flour*
> 3 *tablespoons butter or*
> *margarine*
> 2 *tablespoons olive oil or*
> *salad oil*
> 1 *medium onion, finely chopped*
> ½ *teaspoon Italian herb*
> *seasoning blend*
> 2 *cloves garlic, minced*
> *or pressed*
> ½ *cup dry white wine or*
> *regular-strength chicken broth*
> *(homemade or canned)*
> ¼ *cup chopped parsley*
> ¼ *cup dry Marsala or sherry*
> *Lemon wedges*

1. Sprinkle veal with salt, pepper, and nutmeg; coat cubes lightly with flour, shaking off excess. In a large frying pan heat 2 tablespoons of the butter with all the oil over medium heat. Brown veal, about half at a time, on all sides, removing cubes as they brown.

2. When all the veal is well browned, add remaining 1 tablespoon butter and brown onion lightly. Return veal to pan. Sprinkle with herb mixture and garlic, and add wine or broth. Cover and simmer 15 minutes. Uncover; stir in parsley and Marsala or sherry. Salt to taste. Accompany with lemon wedges.
Serves 6.

menu

PITA BREAD SANDWICH PARTY

Ground Lamb in Pita Bread

Golden Rice Salad

Orange-Lemon Pound Cake

Nuts and Fruits: Almonds and Walnuts in Shells, Tangelos, Bananas, Dates, Dried Papaya Strips, Apples, Grapes

Chilled Dry Rosé Wine or Beer

Stuffed with a saucy ground lamb mixture and topped with cool yogurt and crisp, fresh vegetables, the hot sandwiches featured in this informal party menu are light and refreshing Middle Eastern fare.

GOLDEN RICE SALAD

2½ cups water
1 teaspoon each *olive oil or salad oil, turmeric, and salt*
1¼ cups long-grain rice
1 cup thawed frozen peas
1 jar (4 oz) sliced pimiento, drained
¼ cup each *finely chopped parsley and sliced green onions (use part of tops)*
2 teaspoons drained capers
Romaine or leaf lettuce

Lemon Mayonnaise

1 egg yolk
1 teaspoon each *grated lemon rind and Dijon mustard*
½ teaspoon garlic salt
2 teaspoons lemon juice
1 tablespoon white vinegar
Dash cayenne pepper
3 tablespoons olive oil
⅔ cup salad oil

1. In a 2-quart saucepan combine water, oil, turmeric, and salt; bring to a boil. Gradually pour in rice. Cover, reduce heat, and simmer until rice is just tender (22 to 25 minutes). Chill thoroughly.

2. Fluff chilled rice with a fork. Lightly mix in peas, pimiento, parsley, green onions, capers, and Lemon Mayonnaise. Cover and chill for several hours to blend flavors.

3. Serve in a bowl lined with romaine or leaf lettuce. Sprinkle with additional sliced green onions.
Serves 6 to 8.

Lemon Mayonnaise In blender combine egg yolk, lemon rind, mustard, garlic salt, lemon juice, white vinegar, cayenne, and olive oil. Cover and turn motor on low speed. Immediately uncover and pour in salad oil in a slow, steady stream. Whirl until thick and smooth.

Makes just under 1 cup.

GROUND LAMB IN PITA BREAD

These sandwiches make great party fare and good family fare, too. The basic recipe makes four servings. For a party, double it, using a large can (15 oz) of tomato sauce. The recipe can also be tripled, using one 8-ounce and one 15-ounce can of tomato sauce.

1 pound ground lamb, crumbled
1 medium onion, chopped
1 clove garlic, minced or pressed
1 can (8 oz) tomato sauce
¾ teaspoon salt
½ teaspoon ground cumin
¼ teaspoon each *dried oregano and ground allspice*
4 pita breads
Unflavored yogurt, chopped cucumber, slivered green pepper, and thinly sliced green onions (use part of tops)

1. Preheat oven to 350° F. In a large, heavy frying pan, brown lamb in its own drippings. Spoon off excess fat. Mix in onion and cook, stirring, until lightly browned. Stir in garlic, tomato sauce, salt, cumin, oregano, and allspice. Bring to a boil, cover frying pan, reduce heat, and simmer gently 15 minutes.

2. Meanwhile, wrap pita breads in foil and heat in oven 10 to 15 minutes. Cut in halves. Spoon in ground lamb mixture. At the table, add yogurt, cucumber, green pepper, and green onions to taste.
Serves 4.

ORANGE-LEMON POUND CAKE

2¼ cups sifted flour
¼ teaspoon baking soda
2¼ cups granulated sugar
1½ cups soft butter or margarine
2 tablespoons lemon juice
1 tablespoon each *vanilla extract and orange flower water*
1 teaspoon each *grated orange and lemon rind*
7 eggs, separated (at room temperature)
½ teaspoon cream of tartar
Confectioners' sugar

1. Preheat oven to 325° F. In a medium bowl mix flour with soda and 1¼ cups of the granulated sugar. Place butter in large bowl of electric mixer and, with mixer at low speed, add flour mixture, mixing just until combined. Blend in lemon juice, vanilla, orange flower water, and orange and lemon rind. Add egg yolks, one at a time, blending after each addition.

2. In a separate bowl, beat egg whites with cream of tartar until frothy. Gradually add remaining 1 cup granulated sugar, beating constantly until soft peaks form. Gently but thoroughly fold egg whites into batter. Spread in a floured and greased 10-cup fluted tube pan, about 10 inches in diameter.

3. Bake until cake begins to pull away from sides of pan and tests done when a long skewer is inserted in thickest part (about 1 hour and 10 minutes). Turn off heat and leave cake in oven for 15 minutes longer.

4. Remove to a wire rack and let cake stand in pan at room temperature for about 15 minutes. Then carefully invert cake onto rack to complete cooling. While still warm, sprinkle with confectioners' sugar. When cool, wrap in foil and let stand for up to 24 hours before serving.

5. Sprinkle with additional confectioners' sugar before serving.

Serves 10 to 12.

An informal pita bread sandwich party is a perfect excuse for a gathering of old friends on a Sunday afternoon. These pocket breads can be stuffed with spicy ground lamb, served with a golden rice salad, and complemented with a chilled rosé wine.

A refreshing Shish Kebab Sauté uses boneless top round strips that have been marinated in a red wine marinade and sautéed with fresh vegetables for a tasty meal.

SHISH KEBAB SAUTÉ

    1½ to 2 pounds boneless
         top round
     1   medium onion, quartered
         and thinly sliced
     5   tablespoons butter or
         margarine
     1   green pepper, quartered,
         seeded, and cut into crosswise
         strips
    ½   pound mushrooms, quartered
     1   medium tomato, cut in
         8 wedges
         Salt

Red Wine Marinade

    ½   cup dry red wine
     2   tablespoons salad oil
     1   tablespoon Worcestershire
         sauce
     1   clove garlic, minced
         or pressed
     1   teaspoon onion salt
    ¼   teaspoon dried rosemary
    ⅛   teaspoon dried thyme
         Dash pepper

1. Trim fat and cut steak across the grain into bite-sized strips. Place in marinade in a shallow bowl; cover and chill for 2 to 3 hours or longer. Drain meat well on paper towels, reserving marinade for use later.

2. In a large frying pan over medium heat, cook onion in 2 tablespoons of butter or margarine until lightly browned. Add green pepper; cook, stirring, until limp and bright green. Remove and reserve vegetables. Brown mushrooms in 2 tablespoons more butter in the same pan; add to green pepper mixture. In remaining butter cook steak strips quickly, in three batches, turning with tongs until browned on both sides.

3. Return all the steak and vegetables to the pan; add tomato wedges and 2 tablespoons of the reserved marinade. Cook, stirring lightly, just until mixture is heated through. Salt to taste.

Serves 6.

Red Wine Marinade Thoroughly mix in small bowl all ingredients.

CHICKEN BREASTS WITH MUSHROOMS, SWISS CHEESE, AND WHITE WINE

Cooked with its own luscious sauce of mushrooms, cheese, and wine, this entrée is delicious accompanied by green beans and butter-browned new potatoes.

- 3 *whole chicken breasts (6 halves, about 3 lbs in all), halved, boned, and skinned (see page 11)*
  Salt, white pepper, and ground nutmeg
- 2 *tablespoons butter or margarine*
- 1 *tablespoon salad oil*
- ¼ *pound mushrooms, sliced*
- 2 *shallots, chopped, or 2 tablespoons very finely chopped mild onion*
- ½ *cup dry white wine*
- ½ *cup shredded aged natural Swiss cheese*
- ½ *cup whipping cream*
  Dash paprika
  Cherry tomatoes and thinly sliced green onions, for garnish

1. Sprinkle chicken breasts on all sides with salt, white pepper, and nutmeg. In a large frying pan heat together butter and oil over medium heat. Add chicken breasts and brown lightly; turn, add mushrooms and shallots around chicken, and continue cooking until chicken breasts are lightly browned on both sides.

2. Pour wine over chicken; cover and simmer just until chicken is cooked through (15 to 20 minutes). Using a slotted spoon, remove chicken to a heated serving dish; keep warm. Bring liquid to a boil, stirring until reduced by about half. Mix in cheese, cream, and paprika. Cook over moderate heat, stirring, until cheese melts and sauce is slightly thickened. Salt sauce to taste. Spoon over chicken. Garnish with cherry tomatoes and a sprinkling of green onions.

Serves 4 to 6.

HUNGARIAN CHICKEN BREASTS

Red- and green-pepper strips give paprika-seasoned chicken breasts a colorful embellishment. Serve with twisted noodles or rice.

- 3 *whole chicken breasts (6 halves, about 3 lbs in all), halved, boned, and skinned (see page 11)*
  Salt, white pepper, and flour
- 1 *tablespoon each butter or margarine and salad oil*
- 1 *small onion, finely chopped*
- 1 *each red and green bell pepper, quartered, seeded, and cut into thin crosswise strips*
- 1 *can (2 oz) mushroom pieces and stems, drained*
- 1 *teaspoon paprika*
- ⅓ *cup dry white wine*
- ⅔ *cup sour cream*

1. Sprinkle chicken breasts lightly with salt and pepper. Coat with flour, shaking off excess. In a large frying pan heat butter and oil over medium heat. Add chicken breasts and brown well on both sides. Top with onion, red- and green-pepper strips, and mushrooms; sprinkle with paprika. Pour on wine. Bring to a boil, reduce heat, cover, and simmer until chicken is cooked through (test with a small, sharp knife in thickest part—about 20 minutes). Using a slotted spoon, remove chicken and vegetables to a heated serving dish; keep warm.

2. Bring cooking liquid to a boil, loosening browned juices from pan; cook until reduced by about half. Remove from heat; stir in sour cream. Return to low heat just to heat through (do not boil). Salt to taste. Pour sauce over chicken breasts and vegetables.

Serves 4 to 6.

SWEET-AND-SOUR CHICKEN WINGS

When you cut up whole frying chickens, save the wings for your soup kettle—or use them in this tart and colorful main dish. Serve with steamed rice or Chinese noodles.

- 2 *pounds chicken wings*
- 2 *tablespoons salad oil*
- 1 *onion, thinly sliced and separated into rings*
- 1 *carrot, thinly sliced*
- 1 *clove garlic, minced or pressed*
- ⅓ *cup vinegar*
- ⅓ *cup firmly packed brown sugar*
- ¼ *cup each catsup and unsweetened pineapple juice*
- 1 *tablespoon soy sauce*
- 1 *green pepper, halved, seeded, and cut into 1-inch squares*
- 2 *teaspoons cornstarch, smoothly mixed with 1 tablespoon water*

1. Separate each chicken wing (at joints) into 3 pieces; discard (or reserve for soup) wing tips. In a large frying pan heat oil and brown wings well, about a third at a time. Pour off fat. Return all browned chicken wings to pan.

2. Add onion, carrot, and garlic. Mix vinegar, brown sugar, catsup, pineapple juice, and soy sauce together until smooth; pour over chicken and vegetables. Cover and cook for 15 minutes; add green pepper and cook until chicken is cooked through and carrots are tender-crisp (about 5 minutes longer). Remove chicken and vegetables to a warm serving dish.

3. Remove sauce from heat; blend in cornstarch mixture. Return to heat and cook, stirring, until thickened and clear. Salt to taste. Pour sauce over chicken and serve.

Serves 3 to 4.

One of the most elegant ways to serve boneless chicken breasts is in a wine-cream sauce with seedless grapes. Accompany the dish with rice, a simple green vegetable, and a fruity white wine.

CHICKEN BREASTS WITH GRAPES

Once you have mastered the technique of boning chicken breasts, you can save money at the meat counter again and again. There is an almost limitless variety of quick, elegant ways to cook boneless chicken breasts. Follow the step-by-step directions on page 11, and after a few tries you will be able to prepare classic dishes like this one in no time at all. Accompany these chicken breasts with fluffy rice and a fruity white wine such as Chenin Blanc.

3 whole chicken breasts (6 halves, about 3 lbs in all), halved, boned, and skinned
Salt and ground nutmeg
2 tablespoons butter or margarine
1 tablespoon orange marmalade
¼ teaspoon dried tarragon
1 green onion, thinly sliced (use part of top)
⅓ cup dry white wine
1 cup seedless grapes
¼ cup whipping cream

1. Sprinkle chicken breasts with salt and nutmeg. In a large frying pan heat butter over medium-high heat and brown chicken lightly. Add marmalade, tarragon, green onion, and wine. Cover, reduce heat, and simmer 10 minutes; add grapes, cover again, and continue cooking until chicken is cooked through (test with a small, sharp knife in thickest part)—about 10 minutes longer.

2. Using a slotted spoon, remove chicken and grapes to a heated serving dish; keep warm. Add cream to liquid in pan. Bring to a boil, stirring; cook until sauce is reduced and slightly thickened. Salt to taste. Pour sauce over chicken.

Serves 4 to 6.

GOLDEN TURKEY BREAST PARMIGIANA

Turkey parts are often reasonably priced. Bone, skin, and slice turkey breast to use as you would veal scaloppine. (Save the bones for the soup on page 71.) It is delicious marinated, then lightly coated with flour and Parmesan cheese and sautéed.

> 2 *pounds turkey breast*
> 3 *tablespoons lemon juice*
> ⅓ *cup olive oil or salad oil*
> ¼ *teaspoon each* salt and white pepper
> ½ *cup each* flour and grated Parmesan cheese
> 6 *tablespoons butter or margarine (approximately)*
> *Lemon wedges*

1. Bone and skin turkey breast. Place on a cutting board, smooth side up. Cut meat across the grain into large slices about ½ inch thick. Place turkey pieces, one at a time, between two sheets of waxed paper; pound each with flat side of a meat mallet to about ¼-inch thickness.

2. Beat or shake together lemon juice, oil, salt, and pepper until well combined. Pour over pounded turkey in a shallow dish; cover and refrigerate for about 1 hour. Drain turkey.

3. Coat turkey pieces generously with mixture of flour and cheese. In a large frying pan heat 4 tablespoons of the butter. Quickly sauté turkey slices, 4 or 5 at a time, until lightly browned on each side, 3 to 5 minutes for each side, adding more butter as needed. Keep cooked turkey warm in a 250° F oven while cooking remainder. When cooked, serve at once with lemon.

Serves 4 to 6.

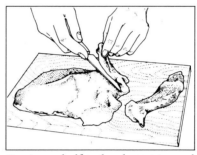

Boning a half turkey breast is much like boning chicken. Cut away rib bones, if any, then cut out wishbone.

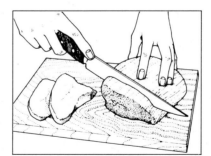

Slice across grain, about ½ inch thick.

SPAGHETTI WITH CHICKEN LIVERS

Here is an impromptu spaghetti sauce that is nice for a late-evening supper. Serve with bread sticks, butter or leaf lettuce salad with an herb dressing, and a robust red wine.

> 2 *slices bacon, diced*
> 1 *pound chicken livers, cut in halves*
> 1 *onion, finely chopped*
> 1 *can (4 oz) mushroom pieces and stems, drained*
> 1 *clove garlic, minced or pressed*
> 1 *can (6 oz) tomato paste*
> 1 *can (13¾ oz) regular-strength chicken broth, or* 1¾ *cups homemade chicken broth*
> 1 *teaspoon Italian herb seasoning blend*
> ½ *teaspoon each* salt and sugar *Dash pepper*
> ¼ *cup chopped parsley*
> 1 *pound spaghetti, cooked and drained*
> 2 *tablespoons soft butter or margarine Freshly grated Parmesan cheese*

1. In a large frying pan cook bacon until crisp and browned; remove with a slotted spoon and drain on paper towels. In bacon drippings, cook chicken livers, about half at a time, until nicely browned on all sides; remove from pan and reserve.

2. Add onion and mushrooms to pan; cook until tender and beginning to brown. Mix in garlic, tomato paste, chicken broth, Italian seasoning, salt, sugar, and pepper. Bring to a boil, reduce heat, and simmer, uncovered, for 15 to 20 minutes, stirring occasionally.

3. Return chicken livers and bacon to sauce; cook 5 minutes longer. Stir in parsley. Lightly mix hot cooked spaghetti with butter; top with chicken liver sauce. Add grated Parmesan cheese to taste.

Serves 4 to 6.

STIR-FRYING

Stir-frying, a quick-cooking technique similar to sautéing, is used to prepare many Chinese dishes. In stir-frying, the ingredients are cut into bite-sized pieces and cooked over high heat. The pieces cook quickly and in an equal amount of time. As the name suggests, foods are stirred or lifted frequently as they cook. Even if you are not skilled at Chinese cooking, you can easily borrow the stir-fry idea for quick-cooking main dishes. You don't need any special equipment; a wok is traditional for this style of cooking, but many simple dishes—such as the four that follow—can be cooked in a standard frying pan or electric skillet. The important thing is to have all the ingredients ready.

PORK WITH TOFU

Tofu, or soy bean curd, is creamy and mild flavored. High in protein, yet relatively inexpensive, it can be used to stretch higher-priced meats. Like pasta, tofu has a way of setting off the fuller-flavored foods that are cooked with it. Serve the mixture in shallow soup bowls atop rice.

- 1 pound lean boneless pork butt
- 1 tablespoon salad oil
- ½ cup soy sauce
- 2 tablespoons sugar
- ¼ cup water
- 1 medium onion, thinly sliced and separated into rings
- 1 clove garlic, minced or pressed
- 2 teaspoons peeled, grated fresh ginger or ½ teaspoon ground ginger
- 2 slices tofu or soy bean cake (about 12 oz), cut in 1-inch cubes
- 1 bunch (6 to 8) green onions, cut in 1-inch pieces (use part of tops)

1. Thinly slice pork, then cut it into 1- by 2-inch strips; heat oil in a large frying pan or wok over high heat, add pork strips, and brown.

2. Add soy sauce, sugar, water, onion, garlic, and ginger. Bring to a boil, reduce heat, and simmer, uncovered, 5 minutes.

3. Mix in tofu and cook just until heated through. Stir in green onions; serve immediately.

Serves 4 to 6.

LAMB WITH FIVE-SPICE AND GREEN ONIONS

The dominant flavor in Chinese five-spice powder is anise (the mixture also includes fennel, cloves, cinnamon, and pepper). It is especially complementary to this lean, tender lamb. Use lamb shoulder you have boned yourself (see page 23). Freeze the rest for stew or curry.

- 1 pound lean boneless lamb shoulder, thinly sliced and cut in bite-sized strips
- ¾ teaspoon Chinese five-spice powder
- 1 clove garlic, minced or pressed
- 2 tablespoons soy sauce
- ⅓ cup dry sherry
- 2 tablespoons salad oil
- 1 teaspoon cornstarch, smoothly mixed with 1 tablespoon water
- 1 bunch (6 to 8) green onions, cut in diagonal slices about ½-inch thick

1. Mix lamb with five-spice powder, garlic, soy sauce, and sherry; cover and refrigerate 1 to 4 hours. Drain meat, reserving marinade.

2. Heat oil in a large heavy frying pan or wok. In it cook lamb, about half at a time, turning and stirring until it is just browned. Remove pan from heat; return all the cooked lamb to the pan. Blend cornstarch mixture into reserved marinade; add to meat.

3. Return to heat and cook, stirring, until sauce is thickened. Stir in green onions. Serve immediately.

Serves 3 to 4.

GINGERED FLANK STEAK WITH SNOW PEAS

Flank steak, frequently thought of as a less costly cut of beef, is not as expensive as some loin cuts. But it is by no means a rock-bottom bargain, either—the cost per pound is likely to be double that of any other meat suggested in this book! However, flank steak is lean and boneless, and delicious in a stir-fry dish such as this. (If you prefer to use a less expensive cut, substitute an equal weight of boneless chuck, using the flatiron muscle atop the blade bone: see page 9.) Serve with rice.

- 1 pound flank steak, partially frozen
- ⅓ cup water
- 2½ teaspoons cornstarch
- 2 tablespoons dry sherry
- ¼ cup soy sauce
- 2 teaspoons peeled, grated fresh ginger or ½ teaspoon ground ginger
- 1 clove garlic, minced or pressed
- 3 tablespoons salad oil
- ½ pound mushrooms, sliced
- ½ pound snow peas, stems and strings removed

1. Slice flank steak diagonally into thin strips about 1 inch wide and 2 inches long. In a small bowl mix water, cornstarch, sherry, soy sauce, ginger, and garlic until cornstarch dissolves.

2. In a large frying pan or wok, heat 2 tablespoons of the oil over high heat; in it brown beef strips quickly on both sides, about half at a time, removing them as soon as they brown.

3. When all the beef is browned and removed from pan, add remaining 1 tablespoon oil. In it brown mushrooms lightly, stirring; mix in peas, stirring until bright green. Add seasoned cornstarch liquid and cook, stirring, until thickened and clear. Return beef strips to pan and cook just until heated through. Serve immediately.

Serves 4.

SZECHWAN CHICKEN AND PEANUTS

People who enjoy bold seasonings know that Szechwan-style Chinese food can be quite as satisfyingly mouth-searing as the most flamboyant Mexican cooking. While this chicken dish won't make you breathe fire, it does have the perceptible heat that only dried chile peppers can generate. Accompany it with steamed rice.

   2 *whole chicken breasts*
     (4 halves, about 2 lbs in all),
     halved, boned, and skinned
     (see page 11)
   2 *teaspoons cornstarch*
   ¼ *teaspoon ground ginger*
   2 *tablespoons each water*
     and dry sherry
   ¼ *cup soy sauce*
   1 *tablespoon each sugar*
     and white vinegar
   2 *cloves garlic, minced*
     or pressed
   5 *small, dried, hot red*
     chile peppers
   3 *tablespoons salad oil*
   ½ *cup dry roast peanuts*
   1 *large green pepper,*
     quartered, seeded, and cut
     in ¾-inch squares

1. Cut chicken into bite-sized ½-inch-wide strips. Mix cornstarch, ginger, water, sherry, soy sauce, sugar, vinegar, and garlic until smooth. Slit red peppers; remove and discard seeds.

2. In a large, heavy frying pan or wok, heat oil. Add chile peppers and peanuts. Cook, stirring, over medium-high heat until peanuts are browned; remove peanuts and peppers with a slotted spoon, discarding peppers. Drain peanuts on paper towels.

3. Add chicken strips to pan and cook, stirring, until chicken is white and opaque-looking throughout. Add green peppers and cook, stirring, about 2 minutes longer. Stir soy sauce mixture and add it to chicken. Cook, stirring, until sauce is thickened and clear. Return peanuts to pan and continue cooking until peppers are tender-crisp.

Serves 3 to 4.

Stir-fried Szechwan Chicken and Peanuts is a hot and exuberant meal for those who enjoy this traditional Chinese manner of cooking. Along with garlic, this recipe incorporates dried hot red chile peppers, ground ginger, sherry, and soy sauce for a bold, fiery flavor.

This savory Chicken and Escarole Soup, with its generous amounts of chicken and rich broth, is a classic Italian dish that makes a hearty meal.

Elegant Whole-Meal Soups

W hen people reminisce
about family meals
of long ago, often what they
really miss is mother's or grandmother's
homemade soups—how delicious
they tasted and how aromatic
they smelled as they simmered for hours
on the back burner.
Cooking soup from scratch
was not only an economical move;
it was also downright
satisfying to create something
marvelous from next
to nothing—"In those days,
butchers *gave* soup
bones away."

HEARTY SOUPS

Creating complete meals from the soup kettle offers many advantages: economy, make-ahead convenience, and wonderful flavor. These days, unfortunately, hardly anyone gives anything away; but the bony cuts of meat that make the best-flavored and sturdiest soups are still relatively economical.

Main-dish soups make fine family meals, of course, but they also can be great party fare. Although it generally requires several hours of cooking, once it's at the simmering stage, a soup needs virtually no attention. Made with meat or poultry, vegetables and potatoes, rice or noodles all in one bowl, a soup requires only a few accompaniments to become a full meal. Just add bread or crackers, a salad or crisp raw vegetable relishes, and a simple dessert, if you wish.

BEEF AND SAUERKRAUT SOUP

Crowded with vegetables and meat, this sauerkraut soup has a pleasantly tart flavor, enhanced by sour cream added at the table.

> 1 tablespoon each *butter or margarine and salad oil*
> 4 *beef shanks (about 3 lbs), trimmed of fat*
> 2 *medium onions, finely chopped*
> 1 *carrot, shredded*
> 1 *large clove garlic, minced or pressed*
> 1 *can (1 lb) sauerkraut*
> 4 *cups water*
> 1 *can (1 lb) tomatoes, coarsely chopped, liquid reserved*
> ⅛ *teaspoon pepper*
> 1 *bay leaf*
> *Salt*
> *Sour cream*

1. In a 5½- to 6-quart Dutch oven, heat butter and oil and brown beef shanks on all sides. Add onions and carrot and cook, stirring, until onion is limp. Add garlic, sauerkraut, water, tomatoes and their liquid, pepper, and bay leaf. Bring to a boil, reduce heat, cover, and simmer until meat is very tender, about 3 hours.

2. Remove beef shanks with a slotted spoon. Discard bones and any fat. Return meat to soup in chunks. (At this point, soup may be covered and chilled until ready to serve; skim fat before reheating, if necessary.)

3. Reheat soup to serving temperature. Taste and add salt, if needed.

Serves 4 to 6.

BEEFY FRENCH ONION SOUP

The traditional onion soup of the legendary Paris market, Les Halles, is a rich beef broth, dense with onions, crowned with cheese-laden toast, and so filling it is *almost* a main dish. Here, to take it one rich step further, the broth is made with meaty beef shanks. All this soup needs to become a meal is a leafy salad with an oil and vinegar dressing, and a robust red wine. The broth can be prepared a day or more in advance.

> 6 *tablespoons butter or margarine*
> 1 *tablespoon salad oil*
> 3½ *to 4 pounds beef shanks*
> 1 *large onion, finely chopped*
> 2 *large carrots, thinly sliced*
> 1 *tablespoon salt*
> ½ *teaspoon whole black peppercorns*
> 5 *sprigs parsley*
> 1 *bay leaf*
> 8 *cups water*
> 8 *medium onions, thinly sliced and separated into rings*
> 1 *clove garlic, minced or pressed*
> 2 *tablespoons flour*
> 1 *cup dry white wine*
> 6 *thick slices French bread*
> 1 *cup each shredded Swiss and Parmesan cheese*

1. In a large soup kettle (at least 6-quart size), heat 1 tablespoon of the butter and all of the oil. Add beef shanks and brown well on all sides. Add chopped onion, carrots, salt, pepper, parsley, bay leaf, and water. Bring to a boil, reduce heat, cover, and simmer for about 3 hours, until broth is richly flavored.

2. Strain broth into a large bowl. When meat is cool enough to handle, cut into chunks and return it, with marrow from bones, to broth; discard vegetables and bones. Chill soup; skim off fat. (This much can be done 1 to 2 days ahead.)

3. In the same large soup kettle, heat remaining 5 tablespoons butter. Add sliced onions, cover, and cook until limp, about 10 minutes. Uncover and cook over low heat, stirring frequently, until onions brown lightly, about 30 minutes longer. (Reduce heat if onions become too brown.) Stir in garlic and flour. Cook and stir until bubbly. Remove from heat and stir in about 4 cups of the broth. Return to heat; mix in remaining broth with beef; add wine. Bring to a gentle boil, cover, reduce heat, and simmer until ready to serve. Salt to taste.

4. Meanwhile, place bread in a single layer on a baking sheet in a 250° F oven. Toast until bread is very dry and barely browned (about 30 minutes). Sprinkle about ⅓ cup of the mixed cheeses over each toast slice.

5. To serve, ladle soup into heatproof bowls. Top each with a cheese-and-toast slice. Place under broiler, about 5 inches from heat, until cheese is melted and lightly browned, 3 to 5 minutes. Serve immediately.

Serves 6.

A golden slice of bread with melted cheese floats on top of Beefy French Onion Soup. Serve with a fresh green salad and a California Zinfandel.

QUICK ITALIAN SAUSAGE AND BEAN SOUP

Aromatic with anise and other herbs, Italian sausage gives body to this easy, chili-like soup. This is a perfect hearty soup to serve with crusty French bread and butter on a cold winter day.

- 1 pound mild Italian-style pork sausages
- 1 large onion, finely chopped
- 1 clove garlic, minced or pressed
- 1 green pepper, seeded and chopped
- 1 teaspoon mixed Italian herb seasoning
- 1 can (1 lb) tomatoes, coarsely chopped, liquid reserved
- 1 can (8 oz) tomato sauce
- 1 can (13¾ oz) regular-strength beef broth, or 1¾ cups homemade beef broth
- 1 can (1 lb) red kidney beans
- ½ cup dry red wine
  Salt (optional)
  Grated Parmesan cheese

1. Remove casings and crumble Italian sausage into a 3- to 4-quart saucepan. Cook, stirring, until sausage browns lightly. Add onion and cook until it begins to brown. Spoon off most of the sausage drippings.

2. Add garlic, green pepper, herb seasoning, tomatoes and their liquid, tomato sauce, broth, and kidney beans and their liquid. Bring to a boil, cover, reduce heat, and simmer 30 minutes.

3. Stir in wine and cook, uncovered, about 3 minutes. Salt to taste. Serve with Parmesan cheese. *Serves 4.*

MEATBALL AND RAVIOLI SOUP

This soup is so substantial that it can almost be eaten with a fork. It needs only green salad and red jug wine to make a complete meal.

- 1 tablespoon olive oil or salad oil
- 1 large onion, finely chopped
- 1 clove garlic, minced or pressed
- 1 can (28 oz) tomatoes, coarsely chopped, liquid reserved
- ¼ cup tomato paste
- 1 can (13¾ oz) regular-strength beef broth or 1¾ cups homemade beef broth
- ½ cup dry red wine
- 1 cup water
- ½ teaspoon each sugar and dried basil
- ¼ teaspoon each dried thyme and oregano
- 1 package (12 oz) frozen ravioli (plain, without sauce), thawed
- ¼ cup chopped parsley
  Grated Parmesan cheese

Meatballs

- 1 egg
- ¼ cup each soft bread crumbs and grated Parmesan cheese
- ¾ teaspoon onion salt
- 1 clove garlic, minced or pressed
- 1 pound ground lean beef

1. In a 4- to 6-quart Dutch oven, brown meatballs carefully in heated oil. Mix in onion and garlic and cook about 5 minutes, taking care not to break up meatballs. Add tomatoes and their liquid, tomato paste, broth, wine, water, sugar, basil, thyme, and oregano. Bring to a boil, reduce heat, cover, and simmer 30 minutes.

2. Add ravioli and cook, covered, at a gentle boil for as long as specified on package (10 to 15 minutes), until they are just tender and no longer taste starchy. Salt to taste. Stir in parsley. Serve with cheese to sprinkle over the thick soup. *Serves 4 to 6.*

Meatballs In a medium bowl lightly beat egg; mix in soft bread crumbs, Parmesan cheese, onion salt, garlic, and beef. Shape into 1-inch balls.

MILANESE VEGETABLE-BEEF SOUP

A sort of *minestrone* (translation: big soup), this boasts a grand assortment of vegetables. The most fragile are added at the end, to retain their fresh texture and brilliant green color.

- 1 blade-cut chuck roast (3½ to 4 lbs)
- 2 tablespoons olive oil or salad oil
- 2 large sweet red onions, sliced and separated into rings
- 2 carrots, thinly sliced
- 2 stalks celery, thinly sliced
- 2 cloves garlic, minced or pressed
- ½ cup chopped parsley
- 1 tablespoon salt
- 1 teaspoon dried basil
- 10 cups water
- 1 can (1 lb) tomatoes, coarsely chopped, liquid reserved
- 1 medium boiling potato, thinly sliced
- 1 package (9 oz) frozen Italian green beans, thawed
- 2 medium zucchini, thinly sliced
- 2 cups chopped fresh spinach
  Grated Parmesan cheese
- 1 cup dry red wine

1. Cut roast into large chunks, trimming and discarding as much fat as possible. In a large kettle (at least 6-quart size), heat oil and brown meat and bones well. Mix in onions and cook until limp. Add carrots, celery, garlic, parsley, salt, basil, and water. Bring to a boil, cover, reduce heat, and simmer for about 3 hours, until meat is very tender and broth is flavorful.

2. Remove meat and bones with a slotted spoon. Discard bones and fat; return meat in chunks to soup. (At this point, soup may be covered and chilled until ready to serve; skim fat from surface before reheating.)

3. To soup add tomatoes and their liquid, and potato. Bring to a gentle boil and cook, uncovered, until potato is tender (about 30 minutes). Add beans and zucchini and cook for about 10 minutes longer, just until tender. Stir in spinach and cook about 3 minutes. Salt to taste. At the table, sprinkle with Parmesan cheese and pour in wine, to taste.

Serves 6.

Milanese Vegetable-Beef Soup incorporates an incredible variety of vegetables, such as carrots, celery, tomatoes, potatoes, green beans, zucchini, and fresh spinach. It can be flavored at the table with freshly grated Parmesan cheese and red wine for a special meal.

Corned Beef and Cabbage Soup reunites two familiar ingredients for a refreshingly simple and elegant dish. Serve with a dollop of sour cream and a sprig of dill.

CORNED BEEF AND CABBAGE SOUP

The richly flavored liquid in which corned beef has been cooked is the basis for an appealing soup that is simplicity itself. Shredded cabbage, added a few minutes before serving, stays colorfully green, fresh tasting, and slightly crisp.

> 1 *corned beef brisket (3½ to 4lbs)*
> 16 *cups water*
> 1 *bay leaf*
> 1 *cinnamon stick, broken into 2 or 3 pieces*
> 1 *tablespoon mixed pickling spices, tied in a square of cheesecloth*
> 2 *medium onions, thinly sliced and separated into rings*
> 1 *stalk celery, thinly sliced*
> 1 *small head (about 1½ lbs) cabbage*
> *Sour cream*
> *Snipped fresh dill or dried dillweed (optional)*

1. Rinse corned beef well under cold running water, then place in a 5- to 6-quart kettle or Dutch oven. Cover with 8 cups of the water and bring to a boil; drain. Add bay leaf, cinnamon stick, pickling spices, onions, and celery. Cover with 8 cups hot water. Bring to a boil, cover, reduce heat, and simmer for about 4 hours or until meat is very tender.

2. Remove corned beef; discard pickling spices and bay leaf. Cut corned beef into thick slices and return to soup. Quarter cabbage, cut in thin shreds, and return to soup. Bring to a boil and cook, uncovered, for 2 to 3 minutes, just until cabbage is limp but still bright green. Serve immediately in broad soup bowls; top each serving with a dollop of sour cream and a sprinkling of fresh or dried dill, if you wish.

Serves 6 to 8.

RUTH'S BARLEY AND WHITE BEAN SOUP

This is somewhat lighter than many bean soups, with chewy, nutlike kernels of plump barley in a full-flavored vegetable broth.

- ½ cup small white beans, rinsed and drained
- 8 cups water
- 2 tablespoons butter or margarine
- 1 small onion, finely chopped
- 2 leeks, well rinsed and thinly sliced
- ⅓ cup pearl barley
- 1 clove garlic, minced or pressed
- 1 stalk celery, finely chopped
- 1 medium carrot, shredded
- 2 smoked ham hocks (1½ to 2 lbs) or 1 meaty ham bone
- 1 bay leaf
- ⅛ teaspoon white pepper
- 1 cup milk
  Salt (optional)
  Chopped parsley or snipped chives, for garnish

1. In a medium saucepan bring beans and 2 cups of the water to a boil; boil for 2 minutes. Remove from heat, cover, and let stand for 1 hour.

2. In a 5½- to 6-quart kettle or Dutch oven, melt butter. In it cook onion, leeks, and barley until onion is transparent. Stir in garlic, celery, and carrot and cook 2 to 3 minutes. Add ham hocks or bone, remaining 6 cups water, beans and their liquid, bay leaf, and pepper.

3. Bring to a boil, cover, reduce heat, and simmer until meat separates easily from bone (2½ to 3 hours). Remove ham hocks or ham bone; when they are cool enough to handle, remove and discard bones and skin. Discard bay leaf. Return meat in chunks to the soup.

4. Gradually stir in milk and reheat to serving temperature (do not boil). Salt to taste. Sprinkle each portion with parsley or chives, and serve. *Serves 6.*

CHILI BEAN SOUP

If your family likes chili, this pork-studded red bean soup is sure to please. Accompany it with a green salad and tortilla chips for a hearty, Mexican-accented meal. For a hotter, more authentic Mexican soup, replace the chili powder with 3 fresh or dried chopped *ancho* chiles.

- 1 pound dried red beans, rinsed and drained
- 7 cups water
- 1 tablespoon salad oil
- 2 pounds country-style spareribs
- 1 green pepper, seeded and chopped
- 2 medium onions, sliced
- 2 cloves garlic, minced or pressed
- 2 teaspoons salt
- 2 tablespoons chili powder
- ½ teaspoon ground cumin
- 1 can (8 oz) tomato sauce
  Shredded Monterey jack cheese

1. Place beans in a large bowl; add 4 cups of the water and let stand overnight. (Or bring beans and 4 cups water to a boil in a 4-quart kettle, boil briskly for 2 minutes, then remove from heat and let stand, covered, for 1 hour.)

2. In a 5- to 6-quart Dutch oven or deep kettle, heat oil. In it brown spareribs well on all sides. Add green pepper, onions, and garlic; brown lightly. Add remaining 3 cups water, bring to a boil, reduce heat, cover, and simmer for 1½ to 2 hours, until meat is tender.

3. Remove spareribs from pan. Slice meat from bones and return to the cooking liquid in chunks; discard bones and fat. (At this point, you may refrigerate the stock overnight, then skim off fat and reheat.)

4. Add soaked beans and their liquid, salt, chili powder, and cumin; bring to a boil. Cover, reduce heat, and simmer for 1½ hours, until beans are almost tender. Mix in tomato sauce. Cook for about 1 hour longer, until beans are very tender. Serve sprinkled with cheese. *Serves 6 to 8.*

FRESH CORN AND POLISH SAUSAGE CHOWDER

Creamy and colorful, this quick soup features the crisp freshness of corn, green pepper, and cabbage.

- 1½ pounds Polish sausage (kielbasa), sliced about ¼ inch thick
- 2 medium boiling potatoes, cut in ½-inch cubes
- 1 bay leaf
- 1 green pepper, seeded and chopped
- 1 jar (2 oz) sliced pimientos
- 1 medium onion, thinly sliced and separated into rings
- 1 can (13¾ oz) regular-strength chicken broth, or 1¾ cups homemade chicken broth
  Corn cut from 2 ears (1½ to 2 cups)
- 2 cups shredded cabbage
- 2 cups milk
  Salt, white pepper, and paprika

1. Place sausage slices in a 4- to 6-quart kettle or Dutch oven; cook over medium heat, stirring, to brown sausage lightly in its own drippings. Spoon off fat. Add potatoes, bay leaf, green pepper, pimientos, onion, and broth. Bring to a boil, reduce heat, cover, and simmer for 20 to 25 minutes, until potatoes are tender.

2. Stir in corn and cabbage and boil gently, uncovered, about 3 minutes. Add milk. Heat slowly just until soup is steaming hot (do not boil). Season to taste with salt and white pepper. Sprinkle with paprika. *Serves 4 to 6.*

SWEDISH YELLOW SPLIT PEA SOUP

If ever a soup could be called beautiful, this is the one—golden yellow, flecked with the orange of carrots and the deep rose of simmered ham.

  1 tablespoon butter or margarine
  1 medium onion, finely chopped
  2 medium carrots, thinly sliced
  1 stalk celery, thinly sliced
  2 smoked ham hocks (1½ to 2 lbs) or 1 meaty ham bone
  1 pound yellow split peas, rinsed and drained
  1 can (12 oz) beer
  6 cups water
  1 whole cardamom pod, crushed
  ¼ teaspoon dried marjoram
    Dash cayenne pepper
  1 tablespoon cider vinegar
    Salt (optional)

1. In a 5½- to 6-quart kettle or Dutch oven, melt butter. In it cook onion, carrots, and celery, stirring occasionally, until onion is soft but not browned. Add ham hocks or bone, peas, beer, water, cardamom, marjoram, and cayenne. Bring to a boil, cover, reduce heat, and simmer until ham and peas are tender (2½ to 3 hours).

2. Remove ham hocks or bone; when they are cool enough to handle, remove and discard bones and skin. Return meat to soup in chunks. Stir in vinegar. Salt to taste and reheat to serving temperature.
Serves 6.

DILLED LAMB AND BARLEY SOUP

Here is a very substantial lamb soup that tastes good with red-cabbage cole slaw, dark rye bread, and a lemon dessert.

  ⅔ cup pearl barley
  2 tablespoons butter or margarine
  4 lamb shanks (about 3 lbs)
  2 onions, finely chopped
  2 cloves garlic, minced or pressed
  2 stalks celery, thinly sliced
  2 carrots, sliced about ⅛ inch thick
  6 cups water
  ¼ cup chopped parsley
  2 teaspoons salt
  1 bay leaf
  ⅛ teaspoon white pepper
  1 teaspoon dillweed
    Sour cream

1. Soak barley in water to cover. Meanwhile, heat butter in a 5- to 6-quart Dutch oven or deep kettle. In it brown lamb shanks well on all sides. Mix in onions, garlic, celery, and carrots. Then add the water, parsley, salt, bay leaf, pepper, and dillweed. Bring to a boil, cover, and simmer slowly until lamb is very tender (2½ to 3 hours).

2. Remove lamb shanks from soup. Take meat off bones; discard bones, fat, and skin. Return meat in chunks to soup. Discard bay leaf. (At this point, you may chill soup and let barley stand overnight, then skim off fat.)

3. Drain soaked barley and add it to the soup. Bring soup to a boil again; cook, covered, until barley is tender, 45 minutes to 1 hour. Salt to taste. Spoon sour cream on each serving.
Serves 6.

GREEN SPLIT PEA SOUP WITH HAM HOCKS

Here is a soup for a cold, rainy day— you can count on its robust flavor and nourishing substance to warm your very bones. Accompany it with corn muffins and, for dessert, spicy baked apples.

  3 to 4 small smoked ham hocks (2 to 2½ lbs)
  12 cups water
  2 medium onions, chopped
  2 stalks celery, chopped (including leaves)
  1 teaspoon dried tarragon
  ½ cup chopped parsley
  ⅛ teaspoon each ground nutmeg and white pepper
  1 pound green split peas, rinsed and drained
  1 tablespoon lemon juice
    Salt

1. Place ham hocks in a 6- to 8-quart kettle with the water, onions, celery, and tarragon. Bring to a boil, reduce heat, cover, and simmer until meat is very tender (3 to 4 hours). Remove ham hocks; when they are cool enough to handle, discard bones and skin. Return meat to broth in large chunks.

2. Add parsley, nutmeg, pepper, and split peas. Simmer, uncovered, 1½ to 2 hours longer, stirring occasionally. If possible, refrigerate the soup several hours or overnight. Skim off fat and reheat the soup over medium heat to serving temperature, stirring occasionally. Stir in lemon juice. Add salt to taste.
Serves 6 to 8.

SHORT RIBS AND CELERY ROOT SOUP

The gnarled, knobby, unsung celery root is one of the least glamorous-looking of vegetables. But its rich, earthy flavor makes it a mainstay of German soups and boiled dinners. Try it in this beefy soup—the broth is clear and golden, and the fresh tomatoes and parsley stirred in just before serving time make it glisten and gleam. Serve the soup with hot, buttery garlic bread. If you like, add a spoonful of tart yogurt or a squeeze of lemon.

> 1 tablespoon each *butter or margarine and salad oil*
> 3 pounds *beef short ribs*
> 1 *celery root (about 1½ lbs), peeled and cut in julienne strips*
> 2 *carrots, thinly sliced*
> 1 *red bell pepper, seeded and cut in 2-inch-long strips*
> 2 *medium onions, thinly sliced and separated into rings*
> 1 *large clove garlic, minced or pressed*
> 8 *cups water*
> 1 *tablespoon salt*
> ¼ *teaspoon white pepper*
> 1 *bay leaf*
> ½ *teaspoon dried thyme*
> 1 *tomato, peeled and finely chopped*
> ½ *cup chopped parsley Plain, unflavored yogurt or lemon wedges (optional)*

1. In a 5- to 6-quart kettle or Dutch oven, heat butter and oil and brown short ribs well on all sides. Spoon off drippings. Add celery root, carrots, red pepper, onions, garlic, water, salt, pepper, bay leaf, and thyme. Bring to a boil, cover, and simmer for 3 to 4 hours, until meat is very tender and broth is richly flavored.

2. Remove short ribs with a slotted spoon. When meat is cool enough to handle, remove it from bones and return it to soup in chunks. Discard bones and fat. (If possible, cover and chill soup for several hours or overnight.)

3. Skim and reheat soup to serving temperature. Salt to taste. Stir in tomato and parsley. Serve with yogurt or lemon wedges to add at the table.

Serves 4 to 6.

This tray of vegetables and short ribs includes celery root—a knobby, crunchy vegetable whose rich flavor enhances many German dishes. Simmer the celery root with the other vegetables and the short ribs for a hearty, beefy soup.

OXTAIL SOUP SUPPER

Beet and Herring Salad

Sherried Oxtail Soup

Buttermilk Rye Bread

Butter

Fresh Fruit Bowl:
Tangerines, Apples, Nuts
in Shells

Suggested beverage: Beer

Thick, rich oxtail soup suggests a German menu. Start the meal with a tangy first course of herring and beets in a creamy dressing, arranged on lettuce leaves. Accompany the soup with a wonderful homemade rye bread, sliced thickly and served slightly warm. After such a sturdy repast, a light, help-yourself dessert is in order—a bowl of fresh seasonal citrus fruits, crisp apples, and nuts.

BEET AND HERRING SALAD

    1 jar (12 oz) herring
      fillets in wine sauce
    1 can (16 oz) julienne-style
      beets, well drained
    ½ cup thinly sliced celery
    ⅓ cup each mayonnaise and
      sour cream
      Butter or leaf lettuce
      Snipped chives
    2 hard-boiled eggs, sliced

1. Drain liquid from herring jar, and discard bay leaf and whole peppers. Cut herring into bite-sized pieces. In a medium bowl lightly combine herring, beets, and celery with mixture of mayonnaise and sour cream. Cover and chill for several hours to blend flavors.

2. Serve herring mixture on lettuce leaves. Sprinkle the salad with chives and garnish with slices of hard-boiled eggs.
Serves 6.

SHERRIED OXTAIL SOUP

    3 pounds oxtails, cut
      into segments
      Salt, white pepper, ground
      allspice, and flour
    2 tablespoons butter or
      margarine
    3 onions, chopped
    3 carrots, shredded
    1 small rutabaga (about ½ lb),
      peeled and sliced
    1 small celery root (about
      12 oz), peeled and cubed
    5 cups water
    1 teaspoon each salt and
      paprika
    ⅛ teaspoon each white pepper,
      cayenne pepper, and dried
      thyme
    1 bay leaf
    ½ cup dry sherry

1. Sprinkle oxtails lightly with salt, white pepper, and allspice, then coat lightly with flour. Heat butter in a 5- to 6-quart kettle or Dutch oven;

brown oxtails well on all sides in heated butter, removing them as they brown. When all are browned, pour off most of the drippings. Add onions and carrots; cook, stirring occasionally, until onion is limp and lightly browned. Return oxtails to pan with rutabaga, celery root, water, salt, paprika, white pepper, cayenne, thyme, and bay leaf. Bring to a boil; reduce heat, cover, and simmer until meat is very tender (about 4 hours).

2. Skim off fat, then strain the soup to separate out the meat and vegetables. Return the liquid to the kettle. Discard bay leaf. Remove meat from bones and add meat to broth. Place strained vegetables in blender with a little of the broth; whirl until smooth. Mix puréed vegetables into broth.

3. Boil soup gently, uncovered, to reduce liquid slightly (about 20 minutes). Stir in the sherry. Add salt to taste.

Serves 4 to 6.

BUTTERMILK RYE BREAD

    1 package active dry yeast
    1 tablespoon honey
    1 cup warm water
    3½ cups unsifted all-purpose
      flour (approximately)
    2 cups buttermilk
    1 tablespoon salt
    1 cup graham flour or
      whole wheat flour
    2½ cups rye flour
    1 egg white, slightly beaten
      with 1 teaspoon water
    1 tablespoon poppy seed

1. In large bowl of an electric mixer, stir together yeast, honey, and water. Stir in 1 cup of the all-purpose flour. Let stand in a warm place until bubbly (20 to 25 minutes).

2. Mix buttermilk and salt into the risen mixture. Add 2 cups more all-purpose flour, mix to blend, then beat with mixer at medium speed for 5 minutes. Stir in graham and rye flours, about 1 cup at a time, to make a stiff dough. Turn out on a floured board or pastry cloth and knead until dough is smooth and springy, kneading in up to ½ cup more all-purpose flour, if necessary. Place dough in a greased bowl, cover lightly, and let rise until doubled (about 1¼ hours).

3. Preheat oven to 350° F. Punch dough down, let rest 5 minutes, then divide in half. Shape each half into a loaf and place in a greased 9- by 5-inch loaf pan. Let rise again until doubled, about 45 minutes. Brush lightly with egg white mixture; sprinkle with poppy seeds. Bake for 40 to 45 minutes, until loaves are well browned and sound hollow when tapped lightly.

Makes 2 loaves.

EASY EGGPLANT SOUP

For short-notice meals, it's a good idea to have a few quick-cooking soups in your culinary repertoire. One that is notable is this tomatoey vegetable soup; it is ready to serve in less than an hour.

> 1 tablespoon each *butter or margarine and olive oil or salad oil*
> 1 *pound ground beef, crumbled*
> 1 *large onion, chopped*
> 1 *large clove garlic, minced or pressed*
> 1 *medium eggplant (about 1½ lbs), cut in ¾-inch cubes (unpeeled)*
> 2 *medium carrots, shredded*
> 1 *green pepper, seeded and cut in 2-inch-long strips*
> 1 *can (28 oz) tomatoes, coarsely chopped, liquid reserved*
> 1 *teaspoon each salt, sugar, and dried basil*
> ½ *teaspoon ground nutmeg*
> ¼ *teaspoon pepper*
> 2 *cans (13¾ oz each) regular-strength beef broth, or 3½ cups homemade beef broth*
> ½ *cup chopped parsley Grated Parmesan cheese*

1. In a 5- to 6-quart Dutch oven, heat butter and oil and brown beef and onion. Add garlic, eggplant, carrots, and green pepper. Cook, stirring occasionally, until eggplant browns lightly.

2. Stir in tomatoes and their liquid, salt, sugar, basil, nutmeg, pepper, and broth. Bring to a boil, reduce heat, cover, and simmer for 45 to 50 minutes, until the eggplant is very tender.

3. Stir in parsley. Salt to taste. Serve with cheese at the table.

Serves 4 to 6.

Easy Eggplant Soup, a quick and simple dish, can be prepared when unexpected guests arrive for dinner. Fresh eggplant and Italian vegetables are cooked with ground beef and seasonings to produce a full-bodied soup. Serve topped with freshly grated Parmesan cheese.

Lamb meatballs, zucchini, and lemon are combined in a glistening Greek soup. The distinct taste of ground seasoned lamb, with the underlying hint of lemon and tender, cooked zucchini, produce a savory meal for four.

GREEK MEATBALL AND ZUCCHINI SOUP

Exceptionally simple and quick to assemble, this soup gets its character from ground lamb meatballs, accented with fresh lemon. It is especially tasty when made with homemade chicken stock (see page 13). Serve with a loaf of braided egg bread.

> *1½ tablespoons olive oil or salad oil*
> *1 large onion, finely chopped*
> *½ teaspoon dried oregano*
> *2 cans (13¾ oz each) or 3½ to 4 cups homemade regular-strength chicken broth*
> *2 tablespoons long-grain rice*
> *2 medium zucchini (about ¾ lb), thinly sliced*
> *Salt (optional)*
> *Lemon wedges*

Lamb Meatballs

> *1 egg*
> *1 teaspoon salt*
> *1 clove garlic, minced or pressed Dash pepper*
> *¼ cup soft bread crumbs*
> *1 pound ground lamb*

1. In a 4- to 6-quart Dutch oven, heat oil and brown meatballs on all sides. Add onion, oregano, broth, and rice. Bring to a boil, cover, reduce heat, and simmer until rice is tender (about 25 minutes).

2. Add zucchini and cook, uncovered, until just tender (4 to 6 minutes). Salt to taste, and serve with lemon wedges.
Serves 4.

Lamb Meatballs In a medium bowl, beat egg. Mix in salt, garlic, pepper, and bread crumbs. Lightly mix in lamb. Shape into ¾-inch meatballs.

SPANISH GARBANZO AND SPINACH SOUP

1 pound dried garbanzo beans, rinsed and drained
8 cups water
2 tablespoons olive oil or salad oil
1 large onion, finely chopped
1 stalk celery, thinly sliced
2 cloves garlic, minced or pressed
2 cups ½-inch-wide strips smoked pork shoulder picnic or ham
1 bay leaf
1 small dried red chile pepper, crushed
½ teaspoon dried thyme
1 can (1 lb) tomatoes, coarsely chopped, liquid reserved
1 bunch (8 to 10 oz) fresh spinach
Salt
1 hard-boiled egg, pressed through a sieve

1. Place beans in a large bowl, add the water, and let stand overnight. (Or, if you prefer, bring beans and water to a boil in a 4-quart kettle, boil briskly for 2 minutes, then remove from heat and let stand, covered, for 1 hour.)

2. Heat oil in a 5½- to 6-quart kettle or Dutch oven. In it cook onion, celery, garlic, and pork or ham strips until vegetables are soft. Add beans and their liquid, bay leaf, red pepper, and thyme. Bring to a boil, cover, reduce heat and simmer for 1 hour. Add tomatoes and their liquid. Continue cooking until beans are tender, about 2 hours longer.

3. Meanwhile, rinse and drain spinach well, remove and discard stems, and chop leaves coarsely. Stir spinach into soup and continue cooking, uncovered, about 5 minutes. Salt to taste. Serve in broad, shallow bowls, sprinkled with sieved hard-boiled egg.

Serves 6.

GOODBYE-TO-THE-THANKSGIVING-TURKEY SOUP

As good tasting as it is economical, this soup is made with the very last of a festive turkey. Enhance the flavor, if need be, by adding canned or homemade chicken broth toward the end of the cooking process.

Meaty turkey carcass and large bones
2 carrots, thinly sliced
1 stalk celery, sliced
1 onion, cut in eighths
1 bay leaf
2 sprigs parsley
⅛ teaspoon each ground nutmeg and dried thyme
1 teaspoon salt
½ teaspoon whole white or black peppercorns
9 cups water
½ cup thinly sliced celery
2 to 4 cups chicken broth (if needed)
½ cup tiny shell macaroni
¼ cup frozen peas, thawed

1. Break up turkey carcass and place bones in a 5- to 6-quart Dutch oven or deep kettle. Add 1 of the carrots, the stalk of celery, onion, bay leaf, parsley, nutmeg, thyme, salt, pepper, and water. Bring to a boil, reduce heat, and simmer, covered, 3 hours. Uncover and simmer 1 hour longer to reduce liquid.

2. Strain into large bowl. Discard bones and vegetables, returning any meat to the broth. (At this point, soup may be refrigerated, then skimmed.)

3. Return soup to the cooking pot. Add the second carrot, sliced celery, and additional broth, if needed to enhance flavor. Bring to a boil again, reduce heat, and simmer, covered, until carrots and celery are tender (about 1 hour).

4. Add macaroni and cook at a gentle boil until nearly tender—about 10 minutes. Stir in peas and continue cooking about 3 minutes. Salt to taste.

Serves 4 to 6.

TIPS FOR FREEZING SOUPS

Few kinds of cooked dishes freeze as well as soups. Serious cooks use their freezers during several stages of the soup-making process.

☐ *Freeze bones until you are ready to make broth or soup.*

☐ *Freeze beef or chicken broth or beef concentrate (see page 13) to have available for other dishes.*

☐ *You can freeze soups in plastic or coated cardboard freezer containers, in coffee or shortening cans, or in large glass jars. Be sure to leave at least an inch at the top: The liquid will expand as it freezes.*

☐ *Frozen soups should be used within four months, so it is a good idea to label soups with a date.*

☐ *You can heat most frozen soups over direct low heat; stir frequently. Reheat soups containing milk in a double boiler.*

☐ *Soups thickened with eggs, will taste best if you first let the frozen soup thaw, reheat it, and then add the egg mixture.*

☐ *If a recipe tells you to add some of the fresh vegetables at the very end of the cooking time to enhance their color and texture, omit them from the soup you plan to make ahead and freeze. Later, when you take the soup from the freezer and reheat it, add the vegetables as directed in the original recipe.*

CHICKEN AND ESCAROLE SOUP

This is a main-dish version of an Italian soup that generally is served as a first course. By adding a generous quantity of chicken and serving with bread sticks and vegetable relishes, presto!—it becomes a hearty meal.

1 frying chicken (3½ to 4 lbs), cut up
1 large onion, finely chopped
1 small carrot, thinly sliced
1 sprig parsley
1 bay leaf
1 stalk celery, chopped (including leaves)
2 teaspoons salt
⅛ teaspoon each ground nutmeg and white pepper
¼ teaspoon dried thyme
4 cups water
¼ cup tiny shell macaroni
2 cups escarole, inner leaves only, thinly sliced
2 tablespoons butter or margarine
Grated Parmesan cheese

1. In a 4- to 6-quart kettle or Dutch oven, combine chicken pieces, onion, carrot, parsley, bay leaf, celery, salt, nutmeg, pepper, thyme, and water. Bring to a boil, reduce heat, cover, and simmer for about 2 hours, until chicken is very tender. Strain broth; remove and discard skin and bones from chicken. Cut chicken into large pieces. Discard vegetables and whole seasonings. Return chicken to broth. (This much can be prepared ahead, if you wish, and reheated later.)

2. Reheat soup to gentle boil. Add macaroni and cook, uncovered, until just tender. (See package directions for cooking time.)

3. Meanwhile, in a medium frying pan, cook escarole in heated butter, stirring until it is wilted and bright green—about 3 minutes. Stir escarole mixture into soup. Salt to taste. Serve in broad soup bowls with Parmesan cheese.

Serves 4.

VELVETY CHICKEN AND MUSHROOM SOUP

This creamy, rich chicken soup has elegance and finesse both in its flavor and appearance. It makes a lovely light supper served with a salad of fresh greens, warm French bread, and a nice white wine such as Chardonnay. If you wish, you can prepare it ahead through step 2 and then freeze for later use. Wait to add the cream, chicken, and the lemon-egg mixture until just before serving.

½ pound mushrooms, sliced
2 tablespoons butter or margarine
1 small onion, finely chopped
1½ tablespoons flour
⅛ teaspoon dried thyme Dash white pepper
1 teaspoon catsup
1 cup half-and-half
1 egg, slightly beaten
1 tablespoon lemon juice Salt

Chicken Breasts and Broth

3 half chicken breasts (about 1½ lbs)
1 stalk celery, thinly sliced
1 medium onion, chopped
1 teaspoon salt
2 whole allspice
2½ cups water

1. Prepare chicken breasts and broth according to directions; set meat and broth aside separately.

2. In a 3-quart saucepan, cook sliced mushrooms in heated butter until lightly browned; set aside about ¼ cup of the mushrooms for garnish.

Add onion to remaining mushrooms in pan; cook and stir until limp but not browned. Mix in flour until bubbly. Add thyme, pepper, and catsup. Remove from heat and gradually mix in broth. Cook, stirring, until soup boils gently. Cover and simmer 15 minutes. Whirl until smooth in blender; return soup to cooking pan.

3. Stir in half-and-half and chicken; cook until soup is steaming hot. Beat egg with lemon juice. Stir in a little of the hot soup. Pour egg mixture into hot soup. Cook, stirring, until very hot but not boiling. Salt to taste. Stir in reserved mushrooms. Serve the soup steaming hot.

Serves 3 to 4.

Chicken Breasts and Broth In a 2½- to 3-quart saucepan, combine chicken breasts, celery, onion, salt, allspice, and water. Bring to a boil, cover, reduce heat, and simmer 45 minutes. Pour through a colander, reserving broth. Discard seasonings, bones, and skin. Break or cut the chicken into generous bite-sized pieces.

FLEMISH CHICKEN SOUP

A plump stewing chicken gives this Belgian soup a rich flavor, which is accented by egg yolks, cream, and lemon juice. As an accompaniment, you might serve an endive salad with a mustard dressing, a coarse-textured whole wheat bread, and sweet butter.

3 tablespoons butter or margarine
2 stalks celery, thinly sliced
2 leeks, well rinsed and thinly sliced (white and pale green parts only)
2 medium onions, thinly sliced and separated into rings
1 stewing hen (4 to 5 lbs), cut up
6 cups water
1 cup dry white wine
2 teaspoons salt
2 sprigs parsley
½ bay leaf
½ teaspoon dried thyme
⅛ teaspoon each ground nutmeg and white pepper
Juice of 1 lemon
3 egg yolks
½ cup whipping cream
Lemon slices, for garnish

1. Melt butter in a deep 6- to 8-quart kettle or Dutch oven. Add celery, leeks, and onions. Cook, stirring, until soft but not browned. Add chicken pieces, water, wine, salt, parsley, bay leaf, thyme, nutmeg, and pepper. Bring to a boil, reduce heat, cover, and simmer until chicken is very tender (about 2 hours).

2. With a slotted spoon, remove chicken pieces. Discard bones and skin. Place chicken, in good-sized chunks, in a warm soup tureen. Ladle on a little of the cooking liquid; cover and keep warm in a 250° F oven until ready to serve.

3. Remove and discard bay leaf and parsley from the broth. Mix lemon juice into broth. In a bowl, beat egg yolks with cream until well blended. Gradually pour in about 1 cup of the hot broth, stirring constantly. Stir egg yolk mixture into broth. Cook over low heat, stirring constantly with a wire whisk, until steaming hot (do not boil). Salt to taste. Pour broth over chicken in tureen. Garnish with lemon slices.

Serves 6.

A diverse selection of fresh ingredients goes into this Flemish Chicken Soup. This rich and elegant soup can be enhanced with a chilled light white wine, such as Chenin Blanc. Round out the meal with an endive salad and whole wheat bread.

Hungarian Goulash Soup, topped with a spoonful of sour cream and served with a butter lettuce salad and dark rye bread, makes a delicious dinner.

HUNGARIAN GOULASH SOUP SUPPER

Butter Lettuce Salad

Tart Dressing

Hungarian Goulash Soup

Dark Rye Bread

Sweet Butter

Fresh Lemon Bars

Suggested wine: California Zinfandel

Goulash, or gulyás, takes many forms in Hungary. One of them is a hefty soup made with red bell peppers and seasoned with caraway seed, paprika, and garlic. Accompany it with dark rye bread and a red wine such as California Zinfandel.

HUNGARIAN GOULASH SOUP

2 tablespoons each *salad oil and butter or margarine*

3 pounds boneless English-cut short ribs, *cut in about 1½-inch chunks*

2 large onions, *chopped*

1 clove garlic, *mashed*

1 tablespoon paprika

5 cups water

1 large red bell pepper, *seeded and cut in thin strips*

2 teaspoons salt

⅛ teaspoon white pepper

1 teaspoon caraway seed

2 tomatoes, *peeled and coarsely chopped*

1 small, dried, hot red chile pepper, *crushed*

2 medium potatoes, *cut lengthwise in eighths*
Sour cream

1. In a 4½- to 5-quart Dutch oven, heat oil and brown meat, about a fourth at a time. When all the meat is browned, pour off pan drippings and discard them. Melt butter in the same pan. Add onions and garlic, and cook over medium heat until onions are soft and golden; blend in paprika.

2. Stir in browned meat and its juices, water, red pepper, salt, white pepper, caraway seed, tomatoes, and chile pepper. Bring to a boil, reduce heat, cover, and simmer about 2½ hours, until meat is tender. Cover and refrigerate several hours or overnight.

3. Skim off and discard fat. Bring soup to a simmer. Add potatoes and cook until tender, about 30 minutes longer. Taste; add salt if needed. Serve with sour cream to spoon on at the table.
Serves 6 to 8.

FRESH LEMON BARS

These zesty lemon bars are an irresistible treat, perfect to serve any time of day, whether it be for dessert or an afternoon tea. Made in two layers—a shortbread crust with a lemon custard topping—they are a perfect summertime sweet.

1 cup butter or margarine, *softened*

½ cup confectioners' sugar

1 teaspoon vanilla extract

2 cups flour

4 eggs

2 cups granulated sugar
Grated rind of 1 lemon

6 tablespoons lemon juice
Confectioners' sugar

1. Preheat oven to 350° F. In large bowl of electric mixer, cream butter, the ½ cup confectioners' sugar, and vanilla until fluffy; mix in flour until well blended. Spread evenly in a well-buttered 13- by 9-inch baking pan. Bake for 20 minutes.

2. Meanwhile, in a medium bowl stir (do not beat) eggs, granulated sugar, lemon rind, and lemon juice until combined. Pour egg mixture over baked layer. Continue baking for 18 to 22 minutes longer, until topping is set and lightly browned.

3. While cookies are still warm, sift additional confectioners' sugar to cover top generously. Cut into bars. Cool before serving.
Makes 3 dozen bars.

menu

TURKEY AND BARLEY SOUP SUPPER

Turkey and Barley Soup

Spicy Pumpkin Muffins

Butter

Molded Citrus Salad

Date and Walnut Brownies

Vanilla Ice Cream

Suggested wine: White Table Wine

Nowadays you can buy turkey already cut into parts, and drumsticks are one of the most economical parts of all. You can make this rich, delicious soup from only two or three large drumsticks.

SPICY PUMPKIN MUFFINS

Muffins are one of the fastest quick breads, and with only a little planning, you can stir up a batch almost anytime. They consist of a dry and a liquid mixture. To prepare for speedy assembly, mix the dry ingredients in one bowl, the liquid in another. (Refrigerate liquid mixture if done more than an hour ahead.)

Have muffin pans greased and ready to use. Then quickly combine the two mixtures, and spoon the batter into the pans. In less than half an hour the muffins will be ready to eat, and temptingly hot.

1½ cups unsifted flour
½ cup sugar
2 teaspoons baking powder
¾ teaspoon salt
1 teaspoon ground cinnamon
½ teaspoon ground ginger
¼ teaspoon ground cloves
½ cup raisins
1 egg
½ cup each *milk and canned pumpkin*
¼ cup salad oil
2½ teaspoons sugar, mixed with ½ teaspoon ground cinnamon

1. Preheat oven to 400° F. In a large bowl stir together flour, sugar, baking powder, salt, cinnamon, ginger, and cloves until well combined; mix in raisins, coating them well with flour mixture. In a smaller bowl, beat egg with milk, pumpkin, and oil.

2. Stir egg mixture, all at once, into flour mixture, mixing only until combined. Fill greased or nonstick muffin pans two-thirds full of batter; sprinkle with sugar and cinnamon mixture. Bake until nicely browned (20 to 25 minutes). Serve warm. *Makes 12 muffins.*

DATE AND WALNUT BROWNIES

⅔ cup unsifted flour
½ teaspoon baking powder
⅓ cup butter or margarine
2 squares (2 oz) unsweetened chocolate
1 cup sugar
2 eggs
1 teaspoon vanilla extract
⅓ cup each *chopped walnuts and snipped dates*

1. Preheat oven to 350° F. Sift flour with baking powder. In a small, heavy saucepan over low heat, slowly melt butter with chocolate; cool slightly. In a large bowl beat eggs. Add sugar gradually; beat until smooth and well combined. Blend in chocolate mixture and vanilla. Add flour mixture; mix well. Stir in walnuts and dates.

2. Spread batter evenly in a greased or nonstick, 8-inch square baking pan. Bake until edges begin to pull away from pan sides and a wooden toothpick comes out clean when inserted near the center (about 25 minutes).

3. Place pan on a wire rack; cool for 20 to 30 minutes. Cut into 2-inch squares. Brownies are at their best served slightly warm, topped with vanilla ice cream or whipped cream. *Makes 16 brownies.*

TURKEY AND BARLEY SOUP

If you like turkey drumsticks, you'll love this soup. Rich and flavorful, it's also easy to make.

  2 to 3 turkey drumsticks
     (2½ to 3 lbs)
  2 tablespoons butter or
     margarine
  1 large onion, finely chopped
  3 stalks celery, thinly sliced
  2 large carrots, sliced
  1 clove garlic, minced or pressed
  ¼ teaspoon poultry seasoning
  1½ teaspoons seasoned salt
  6 cups water
  1 cup dry white wine
  ¼ cup pearl barley
     Salt (optional)
  ¼ cup finely chopped parsley

1. In a broad 5½- to 6-quart kettle or Dutch oven, melt butter and brown turkey drumsticks well on all sides.

2. Add onion, celery, carrots, garlic, poultry seasoning, seasoned salt, water, wine, and barley. Bring to a boil; cover, reduce heat, and simmer until turkey is very tender (2½ to 3 hours).

3. Remove turkey from soup. When it is cool enough to handle, discard bones, tendons, and skin. Return turkey in chunks to soup. Salt to taste. Reheat to serving temperature and stir in parsley. Serve very hot.

Serves 4 to 6.

Savory Turkey and Barley Soup is accompanied by warm pumpkin muffins and a molded salad. The soup is made from rich and flavorful turkey drumsticks, so you don't have to buy an entire turkey to make the soup. Look for specials on these at your meat dealer.

LAMB BORSCH SUPPER

Eggplant Caviar

Rye Melba Toast

Lamb-Bone Borsch

Cherry Streusel Pie

Suggested wine: Beaujolais

Colorful borsch is the focus of this soup supper. Precede it with a tangy eggplant spread, a poor-man's caviar. A light, fruity Beaujolais is a pleasing complement to the soup. A crumbly almond-topped cherry pie makes a fine dessert; serve with milk or full-bodied after-dinner coffee.

EGGPLANT CAVIAR

    2 small eggplants (about
       1 pound each), unpeeled
    1 large onion, finely chopped
    6 tablespoons olive oil
    3 cloves garlic, minced or
       pressed
    ⅓ cup catsup
    ½ cup chopped parsley
    2 tablespoons drained capers
   1½ teaspoons salt
    ½ teaspoon pepper
    ¼ teaspoon ground cinnamon
    1 tablespoon each *dried
       mint, grated lemon rind, and
       lemon juice*
    2 tablespoons red wine vinegar
       Melba toast

1. Preheat oven to 350° F. Cut eggplants in half lengthwise; place cut side down in an oiled baking pan. Bake, uncovered, until eggplant is very tender (50 to 60 minutes).

2. Meanwhile, in a 1½-quart saucepan, heat oil and sauté onion, stirring occasionally, until lightly browned. Stir in garlic and catsup. Simmer, uncovered, for 15 minutes.

3. When eggplant is tender, scoop out the meat and discard peel. Mash coarsely in a bowl. Stir in onion mixture, parsley, capers, salt, pepper, cinnamon, mint, lemon rind, lemon juice, and vinegar. Cover and chill to blend flavors for several hours or overnight. Spread on Melba toast to serve.

Makes about 3½ cups.

CHERRY STREUSEL PIE

    1 package (20 oz) frozen,
       unsweetened red sour pitted
       cherries, thawed
    2 tablespoons quick-cooking
       tapioca
    1 cup sugar
    ⅛ teaspoon salt
    ¼ teaspoon ground nutmeg
    1 9-inch unbaked pastry shell

Almond Streusel

    ¾ cup unsifted flour
    ½ cup firmly packed brown
       sugar
    ½ cup butter or margarine
    ½ cup slivered blanched
       almonds

1. Preheat oven to 375° F. Mix cherries and their juice, tapioca, sugar, salt, and nutmeg. Let stand for 15 minutes. Spread in pie shell. Spoon Almond Streusel mixture evenly over cherries.

2. Bake until filling is bubbly all over and topping is well browned (45 to 50 minutes). Cool.

Serves 6 to 8.

Almond Streusel In a medium bowl mix flour and brown sugar; cut in butter or margarine until mixture is crumbly. Lightly mix in almonds.

LAMB-BONE BORSCH

This traditional Russian soup is delightfully different from most soups because of its refreshing flavor and bright color. It can be made from bones saved from lamb shoulder roasts, or with savory inexpensive lamb neck bones.

> 5 pounds (approximately) meaty lamb bones
> 9 cups water
> 1 tablespoon salt
> ¼ teaspoon pepper
> 1 bay leaf
> 2 medium onions, sliced
> 2 stalks celery, thinly sliced (including leaves, chopped)
> 6 to 8 medium-sized beets
> 2 large carrots, coarsely shredded
> 1 large boiling potato, diced in ½-inch cubes
> 1 can (1 lb) tomatoes, coarsely chopped, liquid reserved
> 1 small head (about 1 lb) cabbage
> 1 tablespoon sugar
> 2 tablespoons red wine vinegar
> Sour cream
> Snipped fresh dill or dried dillweed

1. In a large soup kettle (at least 8-quart size), combine lamb bones, water, salt, pepper, bay leaf, onions, and celery. Bring to a boil, cover, reduce heat, and simmer for 1 hour.

2. Meanwhile, cut tops from beets (cook greens separately, as a vegetable) and scrub them. Add whole, unpeeled beets to kettle and continue cooking, covered, 1 hour longer. Remove bones with a slotted spoon and reserve them until they are cool enough to handle. Remove beets; peel and dice them in ½-inch cubes.

3. To soup add cut beets, carrots, potato, and tomatoes and their liquid. Remove meat from bones and add it to the soup, discarding bones. Bring soup to a boil; boil gently, uncovered, about 1 hour.

4. Chill soup overnight, or at least for several hours. Skim off fat. Reheat until soup boils gently. Cut cabbage into long thin wedges; remove core and discard it. Add cabbage to soup. Continue cooking, uncovered, until cabbage is just tender (about 10 minutes). Stir in sugar and vinegar. Salt to taste. Serve in large bowls, topped with dollops of sour cream sprinkled with dill.

Serves 8.

This unusual supper features lamb borsch—the traditional Russian soup made from beets—and an eggplant spread for crisp rye toast. For dessert serve Cherry Streusel Pie with milk or coffee.

Tender veal stew with carrots and fresh peas is a perfect dish for spring. Accompany the main dish with butter-browned new potatoes.

Stews for Special Meals

Here's a secret known by good cooks around the world: Slow cooking in liquid brings out a wealth of flavor and tenderness in the humblest meats and poultry. In fact, some of the most famous dishes around the world are stews, and they all make delightful special meals for family or friends. Here you will find recipes for everything from Burgundy Beef Stew to Italian Veal Shanks in Tomato Sauce.

STEWS FOR SPECIAL MEALS

Some of the best-known main dishes around the world are basically stews: *sauerbraten* from Germany, *pot au feu* from France, and the traditional New England boiled dinner. All these diverse dishes are made with less tender—and therefore less expensive—meats.

Thrifty cooks have long known that certain cuts of meat respond best to such slow, moist-heat cooking methods as stewing, braising, and fricasseeing. The terms *braising* and *stewing* can be used somewhat interchangeably (stewing, it is generally agreed, involves more cooking liquid than braising). Unlike braised and stewed meats, meat or poultry that is *fricasseed* usually is not browned first.

Cooking meat slowly in liquid is a good way to tenderize it. Because meat protein tends to toughen at high temperatures, meat will be more meltingly tender if the cooking liquid stays below the boiling point. This gentle motion, says one good cook, is "a tremble, with only an occasional bubble."

Cooking in liquid brings out the meat's full flavor as well as its tenderness. It is also a good medium for adding other tastes—wine, fruit, or vegetable juices, herbs and spices, and hearty root vegetables.

Of the world's famous stews, few are regarded as grand or formal dishes. Why not? One theory is that most were created by practical women who had more pressing demands on their time than fussing for hours in the kitchen—so they found main dishes that could be put on to cook unattended while they spent the day doing other chores.

For today's cooks, stews have a similar appeal, whether for family meals or for entertaining.

When you think of meats to use for stew, you probably think of those tidily cut and wrapped packages of perfect cubes found in the supermarket. But is your supermarket meat manager's idea of "stew meat" necessarily the best, or even most appropriate, choice? Probably not. It takes practically no work at all to cut up a boneless roast, yet usually the roast is priced somewhat less per pound than comparable cubed-and-packaged stew meat. For example, if a boneless veal shoulder roast costs less per pound than veal stew meat, it can be well worth the few minutes it takes to cube it for a stew. A boneless beef chuck or rump roast, also, is often a very economical choice for stew. So it pays to take a good look at the meat counter specials before you pick up that handy package labeled "stew."

There is more than one way to cook a stew. The most obvious is in a big deep pot on top of the range, but you can also use an electric frying pan, your oven, or a special cooking utensil such as a fanciful ceramic baker or an electric slow cooker.

TOP-OF-THE-RANGE STEWS

You can use a variety of utensils to cook the meats you simmer atop the range. To hold the cooking heat well, select a tightly covered frying pan or Dutch oven made from a heavy material.

SAVORY BRAISED BEEF SHANKS

A beef shank, according to many good cooks, is a single-portion pot roast. Indeed, the two are cooked much the same way. Bones with marrow offer a special bonus: delicate flavor. This dish is splendid with mashed potatoes or buttered egg noodles and a salad of fresh greens.

> 4 *meaty beef shanks (3 to 3½ lbs), about 1 inch thick*
> *Salt, pepper, and flour*
> 1 *tablespoon each butter or margarine and salad oil*
> 1 *medium onion, finely chopped*
> 2 *cloves garlic, minced or pressed*
> 1 *tablespoon Dijon mustard*
> 1 *can (13¾ oz) regular-strength beef broth or 1¾ cups homemade beef broth (see page 13)*
> 1 *cup dry red wine*
> *Chopped parsley, for garnish*

1. Lightly sprinkle beef shanks on both sides with salt and pepper; coat with flour, shaking off excess. In a large frying pan, over medium high heat, melt butter and brown beef well on all sides.

2. Mix in onion, garlic, mustard, beef broth, and wine. Bring to a boil, cover, reduce heat, and simmer until meat is very tender (2 to 2½ hours).

3. With a slotted spoon, remove meat to a warm serving dish. Bring cooking liquid to a boil and cook, stirring, until reduced and thickened. Taste and add salt, if needed. Pour sauce over beef shanks. Sprinkle with parsley and serve.
Serves 4.

BURGUNDY BEEF STEW

This flavorful stew is made from the center portion of the chuck roast. Serve it with tiny new potatoes cooked in their jackets, French bread, and a forthright red jug wine.

1½ pounds center section beef chuck, from under blade bone (see page 9), trimmed of fat, cubed

2 tablespoons butter or margarine

½ cup ½-inch-wide strips smoked pork shoulder picnic or ham

2 medium onions, thinly sliced

1 clove garlic, minced or pressed

1 medium carrot, cut in ½-inch slices

¼ cup chopped parsley

1 bay leaf

½ teaspoon salt

⅛ teaspoon pepper

¼ teaspoon dried thyme

1 tablespoon tomato paste

1 cup dry red wine

1 can (4 oz) mushroom pieces and stems

1. In a large frying pan, brown beef well (about half at a time) in heated butter. When beef is browned, add ham strips and brown them.

2. Add onions, garlic, carrot, parsley, bay leaf, salt, pepper, thyme, and tomato paste. Stir in wine. Mix in mushrooms and their liquid. Bring to a boil, reduce heat, cover, and simmer until meat is very tender (about 2 hours). With a slotted spoon, remove meat and vegetables to a serving dish; keep warm.

3. Bring cooking liquid to a boil, and cook, stirring frequently, until reduced and slightly thickened. Salt to taste. Pour over meat and serve.

Serves 4 to 6.

A traditional French dish, Burgundy Beef Stew uses the center portion of the chuck roast simmered with a hearty red wine for a rich and tangy taste. This substantial stew, served with small potatoes and French wine, is a toasty comfort for a cold winter night.

CARAWAY BEEF PAPRIKA

Caraway seeds give this thick stew a middle European flavor. The dish uses the center section of a chuck roast (separate it from the two more tender parts—you can use them in other dishes). Complement Caraway Beef Paprika with broad noodles, rye bread, and dark beer.

  2 to 2½ pounds *center-section beef chuck (from under blade bone—see page 9), trimmed of fat*
  2 tablespoons *butter or margarine*
  1 tablespoon *salad oil*
  ½ pound *mushrooms, sliced*
  3 medium *onions, finely chopped*
  1 clove *garlic, minced or pressed*
  1 can (6 oz) *tomato paste*
  1 cup *dry white wine*
  1 tablespoon *paprika*
  1 *bay leaf*
  1 teaspoon *salt*
  ½ teaspoon *caraway seed*
  ⅛ teaspoon *pepper*
  ½ cup *sour cream*

1. Cut beef into bite-sized cubes. In a large frying pan or Dutch oven, heat butter and oil. Add beef and brown, about half at a time, removing meat as it browns. When all the meat is browned, brown mushrooms lightly; remove from pan. Cook onions in the same pan, stirring occasionally, until they brown lightly.

2. Return beef, mushrooms, and their juices to pan. Mix in garlic, tomato paste, wine, paprika, bay leaf, salt, caraway seed, and pepper. Bring to a boil, cover, and reduce heat. Simmer until tender (about 2½ hours).

3. Just before serving, mix in sour cream, stirring over low heat until hot but not boiling. Salt to taste.
Serves 6.

SAUERBRATEN-STYLE STEAK STRIPS

Simmer strips of bottom round slowly, with spices, in a sweet-sour sauce. This German-inspired main dish goes well with noodles and, unlike most beef dishes, a chilled white wine such as Rhine or Mosel.

  1 pound *bottom round, trimmed of fat*
    Salt, pepper, and flour
  1 tablespoon each *salad oil and butter or margarine*
  ¼ cup *red wine vinegar*
  1 cup *dry white wine*
  1 medium *onion, thinly sliced and separated into rings*
  ½ *bay leaf*
  ¼ teaspoon *ground cinnamon Dash each ground allspice and cloves*
  2 tablespoons *raisins*
  1 *gingersnap, finely crushed*

1. Cut meat across the grain into ¼-inch-thick strips, about 2 inches long and 1 inch wide. Sprinkle lightly with salt and pepper, then dust with flour, shaking off excess. In a large, deep frying pan, melt butter with oil and brown beef, about half at a time.

2. Return all the browned meat to the pan. Mix in vinegar, wine, onion, bay leaf, cinnamon, allspice, cloves, and raisins. Bring to a boil, cover tightly, and reduce heat. Simmer until meat is very tender (about 2 hours). Remove bay leaf. Salt to taste. Stir in gingersnap crumbs.
Serves 4.

KENTUCKY BURGOO

This Southern stew was once a hunter's creation, rich with such small game as squirrel and rabbit. Now it is more likely to be made with a plump chicken and bony cuts of beef, pork, veal, and lamb. It is so hearty that few side dishes are needed—perhaps just a leafy salad. It is traditionally served at Louisville parties during the week before the Kentucky Derby.

Burgoo takes a long time to cook—a total of 7 to 9 hours. If you wish, you can begin it one day and complete it the next. Cook the meats and chicken for several hours, remove the bones, return the meat to the broth, then refrigerate it overnight. The following day, skim the fat from the broth, reheat, it and add the vegetables to cook 4 or 5 hours.

  2 pounds each *pork, veal, beef, and lamb shanks*
  1 large *chicken (about 4 lbs), preferably a stewing hen*
  5 quarts *water*
  6 each *onions, medium potatoes, and carrots*
  1 can (28 oz) *tomato purée*
  2 *green peppers, seeded and cut in strips*
  2 cups *cabbage, shredded*
  1 package (10 oz) *frozen baby lima beans, thawed*
  1 cup *chopped celery*
  2 small *dried red chile peppers, crushed*
  2 tablespoons *salt*
  2 ears *corn*
    Worcestershire sauce
  ½ cup *chopped parsley*

1. Place meats and chicken in a very large pot (about 15 quarts). Add water and bring to a boil. Reduce heat, cover, and simmer until meats are so tender they fall from the bones (3 to 4 hours).

2. Remove meat and chicken from the broth; cool slightly. Separate meat from the bones, discarding bones and chicken skin. Return meat in large chunks to the cooking liquid.

3. Chop onion; cut potatoes in ½-inch cubes; slice carrots thinly. Add prepared vegetables, along with tomato purée, green peppers, cabbage, lima beans, celery, dried red peppers, and salt to the meat and broth. Simmer, uncovered, until thickened (about 4 to 5 hours longer). Stir frequently as the mixture becomes thick.

4. About 15 minutes before serving, cut kernels of corn from the cobs and add to the burgoo. Season to taste with salt and Worcestershire sauce. Stir in parsley.

Serves 12 to 15.

BEEF AND EGGPLANT SAUTÉ

A good buffet dish, this stew can be made ahead and reheated. Serve with noodles, green salad, and red wine.

> 1 *small eggplant (1 to 1½ lbs)*
>   *Salt*
> ½ *cup olive oil or salad oil (approximately)*
> 2 *to 3 pounds boneless top round, trimmed of fat and cubed*
> 1 *large onion, finely chopped*
> 2 *cloves garlic, minced, or pressed*
> 2 *large tomatoes, peeled and chopped*
> 1 *tablespoon tomato paste*
> ½ *teaspoon each salt, dried basil, and dried rosemary*
> ⅛ *teaspoon each ground nutmeg and white pepper*
> ¼ *cup dry red wine*
>   *Chopped parsley, for garnish*

1. Remove stem of unpeeled eggplant and cut into ¾-inch cubes. Spread cubes out on several thicknesses of paper towels; sprinkle with salt. Let stand for 20 minutes. Blot surface moisture with paper towels.

2. In a large frying pan heat ¼ cup of the oil. Brown eggplant cubes in heated oil, removing and reserving browned eggplant and adding more oil, 1 tablespoon at a time, as needed.

3. When all the eggplant is browned, brown beef cubes well on all sides in the same frying pan. Mix in onion and garlic; cook until onion is soft.

4. Add tomatoes, tomato paste, salt, basil, rosemary, nutmeg, pepper, and wine. Bring to a boil, cover, and reduce heat. Simmer until meat is very tender (2 to 2½ hours).

5. Gently stir in browned eggplant. Cover again, and continue cooking for 10 to 15 minutes longer, until eggplant is tender. Salt to taste. Sprinkle with chopped parsley.

Serves 6 to 8.

Enjoy top round sautéed with fresh eggplant, plump tomatoes, and a bouquet of herbs and seasonings. To round out this savory meal, accompany it with noodles and a crisp green salad.

POT AU FEU

Just about every Western culture boasts a boiled dinner (which, for best results, should be gently simmered, never actually boiled). The meat most commonly used is a brisket of beef. Most briskets today end up as corned beef, so you may have to locate a traditional meat dealer to find this cut at all. But the effort is worth it!

Serve the delicious cooking broth from this classic dish first, as a clear soup, with warm French bread. Then bring on the sliced beef, surrounded by the vegetables that shared the pot (keep them warm in a low-temperature oven while you enjoy the first course). Traditional accompaniments to this homey main dish are mustard, coarse salt, and the tiny sour pickles called cornichons.

1 fresh beef brisket (3½ to 4 lbs)
3 or 4 leeks, well rinsed, with green tops trimmed to about 5 inches
2 turnips, quartered
3 large carrots, quartered lengthwise, or 15 baby carrots
3 stalks celery, cut in 3-inch lengths (including leaves, chopped)
5 sprigs parsley
1 tablespoon salt
1 bay leaf
¼ teaspoon each whole cloves, whole allspice, and dried thyme
1 clove garlic, slivered
4 cups water
1 cup pearl onions
¼ pound small whole mushrooms
1 pound green beans
Dijon mustard, coarse salt, and cornichons (sour pickles)

1. Place meat in a large kettle (at least 8-quart size) with leeks, turnips, carrots, celery, parsley, salt, bay leaf, cloves, allspice, thyme, garlic, and water. Bring slowly to a boil, cover, and reduce heat. Simmer about 3 hours.

2. Add onions and mushrooms and continue to simmer, covered, about 40 minutes longer, until meat is very tender. Add green beans and simmer, uncovered, about 10 minutes. Remove brisket and vegetables to a heatproof platter, and spoon on a little broth to keep them moist. Cover with foil and keep warm in a 250° F oven.

3. Strain broth to remove seasonings. Salt to taste. Serve as a first course. Then carve brisket in ¼-inch slices and serve surrounded by vegetables. Pass mustard, salt, and cornichons.

Serves 6 to 8.

BRAISED EYE OF ROUND STEAKS

The eye of round responds well to long, slow cooking, becoming tender and flavorful. Serve with curly egg noodles.

When you buy an economical full-cut round steak (see page 10) and separate the top and bottom round for other uses, freeze the compact eyes of round until you have accumulated six. Then use them in this savory dish.

6 eye of round steaks (about 2½ lbs total)
Salt, seasoned pepper, and flour
1 tablespoon each butter or margarine and salad oil
3 medium onions, thinly sliced
1 clove garlic, minced or pressed
¾ teaspoon dry mustard
1 teaspoon Italian herb seasoning or herbes de Provence
1 can (12 oz) vegetable juice cocktail

1. Sprinkle steaks with salt and seasoned pepper; coat lightly with flour. Heat butter and oil in a large heavy frying pan over medium high heat; brown pieces of floured meat well on both sides.

2. Top with onions. Sprinkle with garlic, dry mustard, and herb mixture. Pour on vegetable juice. Bring to a boil, cover, reduce heat, and simmer until meat is very tender (about 2½ hours). Salt to taste. Spoon sauce over meat and serve.

Serves 6.

MEXICAN PORK WITH GREEN CHILES

Here is a wonderful filling for burritos: Scoop the steaming meat into warm flour tortillas; add toasted pine nuts or almonds, cilantro (also known as Chinese parsley), and steamed rice; then roll up into burritos.

To warm flour tortillas, first wet your fingertips with water, then rub the tortillas so that they become moist. Heat individually on a seasoned griddle for several minutes, turning occasionally. Stack them as they are heated, cover, and keep warm in oven.

3 pounds lean boneless pork butt, cut in 1-inch cubes
2 tablespoons lard or shortening
2 large onions, chopped
2 cloves garlic, minced or pressed
1 large tomato, peeled and coarsely chopped
1 can (7 oz) diced green chiles
2 teaspoons salt
1 teaspoon ground cumin
¾ teaspoon dried oregano
¼ cup chopped cilantro
1 cup water
2 teaspoons lime or lemon juice
½ to 1 cup pine nuts or slivered almonds
Chopped cilantro or parsley, for garnish
Warm flour tortillas
Rice

1. In a 5- to 6-quart Dutch oven, heat lard and brown meat, about a third at a time. When all the meat is browned, pour off excess fat, if necessary.

2. Return meat and its juices to pan; add onions, garlic, tomato, green chiles, salt, cumin, oregano, cilantro, and water. Bring to a boil, cover, reduce heat and simmer until meat is very tender (about 2 hours). Meanwhile, toast nuts by spreading them in a shallow pan and baking in a 350° F oven until lightly browned (8 to 10 minutes).

3. Uncover meat and continue cooking at a gentle boil for about 20 minutes, stirring occasionally, until slightly thickened. Stir in lime or lemon juice. Salt to taste.

4. To serve, sprinkle with pine nuts or almonds and chopped cilantro. Serve spooned into warm flour tortillas with a little rice. (Or, if you wish, spoon over rice in shallow bowls, and accompany with hot, buttered flour tortillas.)

Serves 6 to 8.

Beef brisket and fresh vegetables adorn this platter for an elegant and appealing meal. The ingredients for the traditional dish Pot au Feu are gently simmered in the same pot, then served garnished with mustard, coarse salt, and cornichons.

BEEF ROLLS PROVENÇALE

A ground ham filling gives these tender beef rolls a smoky flavor. The generous red sauce is delicious over fluffy rice.

- 2 pounds boneless top round, about ½ inch thick, trimmed of fat
  Flour
- 2 tablespoons olive oil or salad oil
- 1 medium onion, finely chopped
- 2 cloves garlic, minced or pressed
- ¼ pound mushrooms, quartered
- ½ cup each tomato juice and dry red wine
  Salt (optional)
  Chopped parsley, for garnish

Ham Filling

- Smoked pork shoulder picnic, enough for 1 cup ground pork
- 1 small onion, finely chopped
- 1 tablespoon olive oil or salad oil
- 1 clove garlic, minced or pressed
- ½ teaspoon dried Italian herb seasoning or herbes de Provence

1. Cut meat into 6 to 8 pieces of equal size. Place each piece between sheets of waxed paper and pound with the flat side of a mallet, until meat is less than ¼ inch thick. Spread each piece with Ham Filling, then tuck in sides and roll up firmly. Fasten ends with small metal skewers, or tie firmly at each end with clean white string.

2. Coat meat rolls lightly with flour, shaking off excess. In a large frying pan heat oil and brown meat rolls well on all sides. Add onion, garlic, and mushrooms, stirring to brown lightly. Pour on tomato juice and wine, bring to a boil, reduce heat, cover, and simmer until meat is very tender when tested with a fork (about 2½ hours).

3. Remove beef rolls to a warm serving dish. Skim fat from pan liquid, then bring liquid to a boil. Cook, stirring to loosen browned bits from pan, until sauce is reduced and slightly thickened. Taste and add salt, if needed. Pour sauce over beef rolls. Sprinkle with parsley and serve.

Serves 6 to 8.

Ham Filling Trim fat from smoked pork shoulder picnic. Grind ham with fine blade of food chopper, to make 1 cup. Sauté onion in olive oil or salad oil until it starts to brown; remove from heat and stir in garlic, ground ham, and Italian herb seasoning.

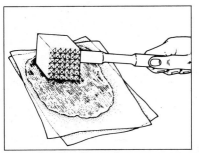

Use side of mallet to flatten meat.

Spread each piece of pounded meat with Ham Filling.

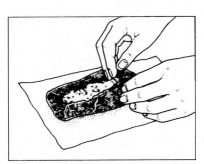

Fold in sides, then roll up rectangles to enclose filling snugly; fasten with skewers or string.

CHICKEN ARLÉSIENNE

Just a pinch of saffron imparts a very special flavor to this chicken dish from the south of France. Accompany with rice, zucchini cooked just until tender-crisp, and bread sticks.

- 1 frying chicken (3 to 3½ lbs), quartered
  Salt and white pepper
- 2 tablespoons butter or margarine
- 1 small onion, finely chopped
- 1 clove garlic, minced or pressed
- ¼ teaspoon each dried thyme and rosemary
  Pinch saffron threads or powdered saffron
- 1 teaspoon Dijon mustard
- 1 jar (2 oz) sliced pimiento, liquid reserved
- 1 can (8 oz) tomato sauce
- ⅓ cup dry white wine
- ½ cup frozen peas, thawed

1. Sprinkle chicken pieces with salt and white pepper. In a large, deep frying pan, melt butter and brown chicken lightly on both sides. Sprinkle with onion, garlic, thyme, rosemary, and saffron. Mix mustard, pimiento and its juice, tomato sauce, and wine; pour sauce mixture over chicken.

2. Bring to a boil, cover, reduce heat, and simmer until chicken is tender (about 50 minutes). Remove chicken pieces to a heated serving dish and keep warm.

3. Skim and discard fat from cooking liquid, then bring to a boil. Cook, stirring, until slightly reduced and thickened. Mix in peas and cook, uncovered, until they are heated through, about 3 minutes longer. Taste and add salt, if needed. Pour sauce over chicken and serve.

Serves 4.

MEXICAN SHORT RIBS

Flavored with oranges and green olives and spiced with cumin, this meaty dish is good with rice and hot buttered corn tortillas.

> 4 pounds beef short ribs, cut in serving pieces
> Salt, pepper, and flour
> 2 tablespoons olive oil or salad oil
> 1 large onion, thinly sliced and separated into rings
> 1 clove garlic, minced or pressed
> 1 can (1 lb) tomatoes, coarsely chopped, liquid reserved
> 1 cup dry red wine
> 1 teaspoon grated orange rind
> Juice of 1 orange
> ½ cup sliced pimiento-stuffed green olives
> ⅛ teaspoon cayenne pepper
> 1 teaspoon ground cumin
> Chopped cilantro (Chinese parsley) or parsley, for garnish

1. Sprinkle short ribs with salt and pepper, then coat lightly with flour, shaking off excess. In a large frying pan or Dutch oven heat oil and brown ribs, about half at a time. Remove them from pan as they brown. When all the ribs have been browned, pour off most of the drippings. In fat remaining in pan, cook onion rings and garlic until onion is tender and lightly browned.

2. Return browned short ribs to pan with tomatoes and their liquid, wine, orange rind, orange juice, olives, cayenne, and cumin. Bring to a boil, reduce heat, cover, and simmer until meat is very tender (2½ to 3 hours).

3. Remove short ribs to a warm serving dish and keep warm. Bring sauce to a boil, stirring occasionally; boil, uncovered, until reduced and slightly thickened. Taste and add salt, if needed. Spoon sauce over meat. Sprinkle short ribs with chopped cilantro or parsley.

Serves 6.

For an original addition to a potluck dinner, try short ribs cooked with the Mexican seasonings cilantro and cumin. Simmered with oranges, wine, olives, and tomatoes, the moist short ribs soon absorb an exciting and distinctive flavor that invites a second helping.

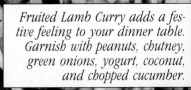

Fruited Lamb Curry adds a festive feeling to your dinner table. Garnish with peanuts, chutney, green onions, yogurt, coconut, and chopped cucumber.

FRUITED LAMB CURRY

1 *lamb shoulder roast (4 to
    5 lbs)*
2 *tablespoons butter or
    margarine*
4 *medium onions, thinly sliced
    and separated into rings*
3 *large tart green apples, peeled,
    cored, and sliced*
2 *cloves garlic, minced
    or pressed*
2 *tablespoons each flour
    and curry powder*
¼ *cup golden raisins*
1½ *teaspoon ground ginger*
1 *stick cinnamon, broken in
    2 pieces*
1 *teaspoon salt*
1 *cup each regular-strength
    beef broth (homemade or
    canned) and dry red wine*
1 *teaspoon lemon juice*
    Cooked rice
    *Condiments: chopped dry-
    roasted peanuts, toasted
    unsweetened coconut,
    chutney, sliced green onions,
    diced unpeeled cucumber,
    plain yogurt*

1. Bone roast (see page 23), trim fat, and cut into bite-sized cubes (at least 4 cups cubed meat).

2. In a large frying pan or Dutch oven, melt butter and brown cubed lamb, about half at a time. Remove meat as it browns. When all the meat is browned, pour off all but 2 tablespoons of the drippings. In fat remaining in pan, sauté onions until golden. Add apples; cook, stirring lightly, about 3 minutes longer. Mix in garlic, flour, and curry powder.

3. Return meat and its juices to pan with raisins, ginger, cinnamon stick, salt, broth, wine, and lemon juice. Bring to a boil, cover, reduce heat, and simmer until meat is very tender and flavors are well blended (1½ to 2 hours).

4. Serve with rice; pass condiments in small bowls.
Serves 6 to 8.

CHICKEN, HUNTER'S STYLE

A savory mixture of herbs, mushrooms, red wine, and a touch of tomato gives chicken legs a clear brown sauce similar to that used for game. Accompany with baked new potatoes in their jackets.

6 *chicken legs with thighs
    attached*
    Salt, pepper, and paprika
2 *tablespoons butter or
    margarine*
1 *tablespoon salad oil*
3 *shallots, finely chopped,
    or 3 tablespoons shallots*
1 *small tomato, peeled
    and chopped*
¼ *pound mushrooms, quartered*
2 *cloves garlic, minced
    or pressed*
½ *teaspoon dry mustard*
¼ *teaspoon each dried thyme
    and rosemary*
2 *tablespoons Beef Concentrate
    (see page 13) or 1 tablespoon
    powdered beef stock base*
¾ *cup dry red wine*

1. Sprinkle chicken legs with salt, pepper, and paprika. In a large heavy frying pan, heat butter and oil until foamy. Add chicken legs and brown slowly on all sides. Spoon off excess fat.

2. Sprinkle chicken with shallots, tomato, mushrooms, garlic, mustard, thyme, and rosemary. Add Beef Concentrate and wine. Bring to a boil. Reduce heat, cover, and simmer until chicken is tender (about 1 hour).

3. Using a slotted spoon, remove chicken and mushrooms to a warm serving dish. Bring cooking liquid to a boil; cook, stirring, until reduced and thickened. Taste and add salt, if needed; pour the thickened sauce over chicken.
Serves 6.

JOYCE'S NEW ORLEANS RED BEANS AND RICE

From a city noted for its culinary excellence and diversity, here is a beloved family dish. It is said to have been a favorite meal on washdays: One could start the beans cooking, then go about the numerous and exhausting tasks of heating water, feeding clothes through a hand-operated wringer, and hanging them out to dry. By the time the laundry dried, the beans were ready for dinner. Even now, when automatic equipment does the wash, the dish still tastes delicious.

1 *pound dried red beans,
    rinsed and drained*
8 *cups water*
2 *large onions, chopped*
1 *bay leaf*
¼ *teaspoon pepper*
1 *meaty ham bone or 2 smoked
    ham hocks (1½ to 2 lbs)*
1 *green pepper, finely chopped*
1 *tablespoon white vinegar*
½ *teaspoon hot-pepper sauce*
    Salt (optional)
    Cooked rice

1. In a 4- to 6-quart kettle or Dutch oven, bring beans and water to a boil. Boil briskly for 2 minutes, then remove from heat. Cover; let beans stand for 1 hour.

2. Add onions, bay leaf, pepper, and ham bone or ham hocks. Bring to a boil, cover, reduce heat, and simmer for 3 hours. Remove ham bone or ham hocks. When they are cool enough to handle, remove and discard bones, fat, and skin. Return meat to beans in chunks.

3. Mix in green pepper, vinegar, and hot-pepper sauce. Continue simmering, uncovered, stirring occasionally, until beans are thick and very tender (2 to 2½ hours). Salt to taste. Serve over rice.
Serves 6.

SAUTÉED LAMB WITH SPRING VEGETABLES

Peas and asparagus added just at the end give this elegant stew a spring-time freshness. Accompany with small, buttered new potatoes cooked in their jackets. Serve a leafy green salad *after* the main dish.

1 lamb shoulder roast
  (3¾ to 4½ lbs)
  Salt and white pepper
2 tablespoons butter or
  margarine
1 medium onion, finely chopped
1 small clove garlic, minced
  or pressed
¼ teaspoon each dried tarragon
  and rosemary
⅛ teaspoon each ground nutmeg
  and cloves
3 medium carrots, cut lengthwise in quarters
2 small turnips, quartered
1 cup dry white wine
½ cup fresh or thawed
  frozen peas
1 cup cut fresh asparagus
  (about 1-inch pieces)
1 teaspoon lemon juice
  Chopped parsley, for garnish

1. Bone roast (see page 23), trim fat, and cut meat into bite-sized cubes (about 4 cups).

2. Sprinkle meat with salt and white pepper. In a large, deep frying pan or Dutch oven, melt butter and brown meat, about half at a time. When all the lamb is browned, pour off fat and return lamb and its juices to pan.

3. Add onion, garlic, tarragon, rosemary, nutmeg, cloves, carrots, turnips, and wine. Bring to a boil, cover, reduce heat, and simmer until meat is fork-tender (1½ to 2 hours).

4. Uncover and mix in peas and asparagus. Continue cooking, uncovered, until green vegetables are tender-crisp (5 to 8 minutes longer).

Serves 6.

With a slotted spoon, remove the lamb and vegetables to a heated serving dish; keep warm.

5. Bring cooking liquid to a boil. Cook, stirring, until liquid is reduced and slightly thickened. Mix in lemon juice. Taste and add salt, if needed. Pour sauce over the lamb and vegetables. Sprinkle with parsley and serve.

Serves 6.

VEAL BREAST BRAISED WITH TARRAGON

For this creamy stew, ask your meat dealer to cut through the veal breast-bone in several places so you can separate the meat into single-rib sections. Serve with noodles or rice and wax beans.

1 breast of veal (3 to
  3½ lbs), cut in serving pieces
  Salt, white pepper, and
  ground nutmeg
2 tablespoons butter
1 tablespoon salad oil
1½ teaspoons dried tarragon
1 small onion, finely chopped
¼ cup shredded carrot
½ cup each dry white wine
  and whipping cream
¼ cup chopped parsley

1. Sprinkle pieces of veal generously with salt, pepper, and nutmeg. In a large, heavy frying pan or Dutch oven, heat butter and oil until foamy and brown veal lightly on all sides.

2. Sprinkle with tarragon, onion, and carrot. Pour on wine. Bring to a boil, cover, reduce heat, and simmer until veal is very tender (about 2 hours). Remove veal to a serving dish and keep warm.

3. To pan juices add cream and 3 tablespoons of the parsley; bring to a boil. Cook, stirring, until reduced and thickened (large, shiny bubbles will form). Pour sauce over veal. Sprinkle with remaining 1 tablespoon parsley, and serve.

Serves 4.

VEAL STEW WITH FRESH PEAS

Here is another delicate spring or summer stew, also made with veal. The tender veal chunks and bright green peas go well with butter-browned new potatoes. To complete the menu add a leafy green salad tossed with your favorite dressing, French bread and butter, and milk, or a dry white wine. For dessert, indulge in some of spring's first strawberries.

2 pounds cubed boneless
  veal shoulder
  Salt, white pepper, and
  paprika
2 tablespoons butter or
  margarine
1 tablespoon salad oil
1 small onion, finely chopped
1 medium tomato, peeled
  and chopped
1 large carrot, cut in
  ¼-inch slices
⅛ teaspoon dried tarragon
¾ cup dry white wine
½ cup shelled fresh peas,
  or thawed frozen peas
  Chopped parsley, for garnish

1. Sprinkle veal with salt, white pepper, and paprika. Heat butter with oil in a large heavy frying pan or Dutch oven and brown veal lightly on all sides. Add onion, tomato, carrot, tarragon, and wine. Bring to a boil, cover, reduce heat, and simmer until veal is very tender (about 1½ hours).

2. Mix in peas and cook, uncovered, 5 to 8 minutes longer, until they are just tender. Salt to taste. Sprinkle with parsley and serve.

Serves 6.

OVEN STEWS

Making a stew can be both time- and cost-efficient: When you cook a stew in the oven, you can use the same heat source to prepare accompaniments—potatoes or other vegetables, a baked dessert, a bread to warm. Covered ceramic or enameled metal casseroles are ideal for oven stews; many are handsome enough to bring directly to the dinner table.

LAMB SHANKS WITH HONEY AND SPICES

Inspired by the exotically flavored stews of Morocco, these lamb shanks are good accompanied by brown rice and a lettuce and tomato salad with a piquant oil-and-vinegar dressing.

> 1 tablespoon each *butter or margarine and olive oil or salad oil*
> 2 medium onions, thinly sliced
> 1 clove garlic, minced or pressed
> 1 teaspoon salt
> ½ teaspoon each *ground turmeric and ginger*
> ¼ teaspoon each *ground allspice and coriander*
> ¾ cup water
> ¼ cup honey
> 2 cinnamon sticks
> 4 to 5 pounds lamb shanks, cracked
> 1 lemon, thinly sliced
> Cooked brown rice

1. Preheat oven to 350° F. In a large frying pan heat together butter and oil. Sauté onions until limp but not browned. Add garlic, salt, turmeric, ginger, allspice, and coriander and stir to coat onions; simmer about 2 minutes. Mix in water, honey, and cinnamon sticks; bring to a boil, then remove from heat.

2. Arrange lamb shanks in a deep casserole just large enough to hold them in a single layer. Pour on onion mixture. Arrange lemon slices over lamb. Cover and bake until lamb is very tender (about 2 hours).

3. Remove lamb and lemons to a serving dish and keep warm. Skim fat from cooking liquid; boil liquid to reduce and thicken it slightly. Pour over lamb and serve with brown rice.

Serves 4 to 6.

Invite your friends over for Moroccan lamb shanks that are baked with honey, lemon, and exotic spices. This golden dish, served over brown rice, will allure taste buds to new and flavorful adventures.

Layers of beef, fresh mushrooms, herbs, and onion make an easy Oven Beef Stew.

OVEN BEEF STEW

This easy oven stew is ideal for a busy day—you can simmer it in the oven for hours, giving it no attention whatsoever. It is a big recipe, ideal for a company buffet served with a mixed green salad, noodles, green beans or broccoli, and, for dessert, your favorite apple pastry.

  4 *pounds boneless beef chuck, cut in 1½-inch cubes*
  1 *cup dry red wine*
  2 *tablespoons brandy (optional)*
  ⅓ *cup chopped parsley*
  2 *cloves garlic, mashed*
  ¼ *teaspoon each* dried thyme and rosemary
  1 *bay leaf*
  2 *medium onions, thinly sliced*
  ½ *cup flour*
  1 *teaspoon each* salt and paprika
  ¼ *teaspoon pepper*
  6 *carrots, cut in ½-inch slices*
  ½ *pound small whole mushrooms*

1. Trim any fat from meat cubes; place meat in large bowl. Add wine, brandy (if used), parsley, garlic, thyme, rosemary, bay leaf, and onions; mix lightly. Cover and refrigerate 8 to 24 hours; remove meat, saving marinade.

2. Preheat oven to 325° F. Pat meat dry with paper towels. In a shallow dish mix flour, salt, paprika, and pepper. Roll cubed meat in flour mixture to coat. Place about a third of the meat in a deep 4½- to 5-quart casserole. Top with half the carrots and mushrooms, another third of the meat, the remaining vegetables, and the last of the meat. Bring reserved marinade and onions to a boil; pour over meat.

3. Cover and bake until meat is very tender (about 4 hours). Discard bay leaf. Salt stew to taste. Garnish with chopped parsley.

Serves 8 to 10.

SAVORY OVEN PORK STEW

This stew is made in the manner of a French *daube*—the meat is seasoned and floured, then layered with vegetables and cooked in wine in a deep ceramic casserole. This one requires no marinating before baking, so it is fairly quick to assemble.

    5 pounds country-style
      spareribs, cut in serving pieces
      Salt, pepper, paprika,
      and flour
    1 medium onion, thinly sliced
      and separated into rings
    ½ pound small white boiling
      onions
    ½ cup slivered smoked pork
      shoulder picnic or ham
    2 cloves garlic, minced
      or pressed
    1 carrot, shredded
    ¼ pound mushrooms, quartered
    1 cup dry red wine
    2 tablespoons Beef Concentrate
      (see page 13) or 1 tablespoon
      powdered beef stock base
    ½ teaspoon each dried
      marjoram and rosemary
    ⅛ teaspoon ground allspice
    1 bay leaf
    2 tablespoons brandy
      (optional)
      Chopped parsley, for garnish

1. Preheat oven to 350° F. Sprinkle spareribs with salt, pepper, and paprika; coat with flour. In a medium bowl combine sliced and boiling onions, pork or ham strips, garlic, carrot, and mushrooms. Place about a third of the spareribs in a deep 5-quart casserole; cover with half of the vegetable mixture. Repeat with another layer of spareribs and remaining vegetables. Top with the last of the spareribs.

2. In a small saucepan heat together wine, Beef Concentrate, marjoram, rosemary, allspice, and bay leaf, stirring until the concentrate dissolves. Add brandy (if used); pour mixture over spareribs.

3. Cover and bake until meat is very tender (about 3 hours). With a slotted spoon, remove meat and onions to a heated serving dish; keep warm. Skim and discard fat from cooking liquid. Pour liquid into a saucepan and boil until reduced and slightly thickened; salt to taste. Pour over meat. Sprinkle with parsley.

Serves 8.

RICH RED SPARERIBS

Here is a delicious and easy way to bake spareribs in a covered casserole. Corn on the cob completes the meal.

    4 pounds meaty spareribs,
      cut in serving pieces
    ¼ cup each soy sauce, lemon
      juice, and honey
    ½ cup catsup
    ½ teaspoon ground ginger
    1 clove garlic, minced or pressed

1. Preheat oven to 350° F. Place spareribs in a large frying pan, Dutch oven, or electric skillet. Add water to cover. Bring to a boil, cover, reduce heat, and simmer 30 minutes. Drain well, patting spareribs dry with paper towels.

2. Arrange ribs in a broad 2- to 3-quart casserole. Mix soy sauce, lemon juice, honey, catsup, ginger, and garlic until smooth. Pour over spareribs, coating them well with sauce. Cover and bake, basting two or three times with sauce, until spareribs are tender and well browned, 1 to 1½ hours.

Serves 4 to 6.

ROUND STEAK AND KIDNEY BEANS

Cubed bottom round with red kidney beans makes a hearty casserole that's great for a potluck supper or a tailgate picnic.

    1 pound red kidney beans,
      rinsed and drained
    6 cups water
    ½ pound pork link sausages
    1 pound bottom round steak,
      trimmed of fat and cut in
      about ¾-inch cubes
    1 large onion, finely chopped
    1 clove garlic, minced or pressed
    1 teaspoon salt
    ½ teaspoon dried rosemary
    1 can (8 oz) tomato sauce

1. Put kidney beans and water in a large kettle and bring to a vigorous boil for 2 minutes. Cover, remove from heat, and let stand 1 hour.

2. Preheat oven to 350° F. In a large, deep frying pan or Dutch oven, brown the pork sausages well on all sides; as they brown, remove them from pan. Pour off all but 2 tablespoons of the drippings. In sausage drippings, brown round steak cubes very well on all sides. Add prepared beans and their liquid, onion, garlic, salt, rosemary, and tomato sauce. Bring to a boil, stirring occasionally.

3. Transfer meat and bean mixture to a deep 3- to 4-quart casserole. Arrange sausages on top. Cover and bake until beans and meat are tender (about 3 hours).

Serves 6.

SPICY ALSATIAN MEAT AND VEGETABLE STEW

In Alsace, the charming wine-growing region of eastern France, it is traditional to serve this stew at large family gatherings. Typically, this casserole, which is made with four different kinds of meat, is so enormous that it must be taken from the home and cooked in a baker's oven. But you can make it on a smaller scale in your own kitchen, and it will still serve 8 to 10 dinner guests bountifully.

- 1 pound veal shanks, sliced 1 inch thick
- 2 pounds cubed boneless beef chuck
- 1 lamb shank (about 1 lb)
- 1 pound boneless pork butt, cubed
- 1 cup dry white wine
- 2 large onions, thinly sliced
- 1 bay leaf
- 1 teaspoon whole white or black peppercorns
- ½ teaspoon each ground cinnamon and whole cloves
- ¼ teaspoon ground nutmeg
- 4 carrots, thinly sliced
- 2 leeks, thinly sliced (use part of tops)
- 4 medium boiling potatoes, thinly sliced

1. Place meats in a deep bowl; add wine, onions, bay leaf, and spices. Mix lightly. Cover and marinate in refrigerator 8 hours or overnight.

2. Preheat oven to 450° F. Place carrots and leeks in bottom of a deep 5-quart casserole. Then make layers of marinated meats, onions, and potatoes until all are used, ending with a layer of potatoes on top. Pour on marinade.

3. Cover tightly and bake for 30 minutes; reduce oven to 350° F and continue baking until meats are very tender (about 3 hours). Salt to taste.
Serves 8 to 10.

SINGAPORE CHICKEN

Colorful with pineapple, mandarin oranges, and sliced apples, this baked chicken is attractive served on a bed of white rice.

- 2 small whole chickens, about 2½ pounds each
- ½ teaspoon ground ginger
- 1 tablespoon curry powder
- 1 teaspoon salt
- 2 tablespoons butter or margarine
- 1 can (8 oz) sliced pineapple
- 1 can (11 oz) mandarin oranges
- 1 tart apple (unpeeled), cored and sliced
- ⅓ cup whipping cream
- 1 tablespoon lemon juice
  Sliced pimiento, for garnish

1. Preheat oven to 350° F. Cut chickens in quarters, reserving giblets for another use. Combine ginger, curry powder, and salt. Sprinkle chicken with seasonings. Melt butter in a large shallow baking dish (about 13 by 9 inches) in oven. Arrange chicken quarters, skin side down, in melted butter. Bake, uncovered, for 30 minutes.

2. Meanwhile, drain pineapple and oranges. Halve pineapple slices. Turn chicken; cover with pineapple slices, mandarin oranges, and apple slices. Pour on cream and lemon juice. Cover and continue baking until the chicken and apples are tender (about 40 minutes more).

3. Uncover, baste with pan drippings, and continue baking until chicken is well browned, about 15 minutes longer. Garnish with pimiento slices.
Serves 8.

GASCON BEANS AND CHICKEN GIZZARDS

If you have saved and frozen the gizzards from chickens purchased whole, here is a delicious way to cook them: a sort of simplified cassoulet. Even the lowly chicken gizzard becomes tender and flavorful when it bakes for several hours in a bean pot.

- 1 pound small white beans, rinsed and drained
- 6 cups water
- 6 slices bacon, cut in squares
- 1 pound chicken gizzards (15 to 20), cut in halves
- 3 medium onions, thinly sliced and separated into rings
- 2 cloves garlic, minced or pressed
- 1 bay leaf
- 1 teaspoon salt
- ½ teaspoon dried marjoram
- ⅛ teaspoon white pepper
- 1 pound Polish sausage
- 1 can (8 oz) tomato sauce

Buttery Bread Crumbs

- 1 tablespoon salad oil
- 2 tablespoons butter or margarine
- ½ cup soft French bread crumbs

1. Place beans in a large bowl, add the water, and let stand overnight. (Or, if you prefer, bring beans and water to a boil in a 4-quart kettle, boil briskly for 2 minutes, then remove from heat and let stand, covered, 1 hour.)

2. Preheat oven to 350° F. In a large frying pan, brown bacon; drain on paper towels. Pour off all but 2 tablespoons of the bacon drippings. Brown chicken gizzards slowly in reserved drippings, removing them as they brown. In the same pan, cook sliced onions until limp and beginning to brown.
Serves 6.

3. To soaked beans add bacon, gizzards, onions, garlic, bay leaf, salt, marjoram, and pepper. Transfer to a deep 4-quart casserole, cover, and bake until beans are tender (about 3 hours).

4. Cut sausage in 2-inch chunks, and pierce each piece in several places with a fork. To cooked beans add sausage and tomato sauce, mixing lightly. Top with bread crumbs. Return to oven and bake, uncovered, about 45 minutes longer, until crumbs are browned.

Serves 6 to 8.

Buttery Bread Crumbs In a frying pan heat together salad oil and butter or margarine until foamy. Stir in bread crumbs until coated.

COUNTRY CAPTAIN

This chicken dish, a southern favorite, probably had its origins in India. However it made its way to our shores, it is a good choice for a party buffet. Serve with green beans.

  2 *frying chickens, about*
    3 pounds each
    Salt and pepper
  2 *to 3 tablespoons butter*
    or margarine
  1 *large onion, finely chopped*
  1½ *cups long-grain rice*
  2 *green peppers, seeded*
    and chopped
  1 *large clove garlic, minced*
    or pressed
  ½ *cup raisins*
  2 *teaspoons curry powder*
  1 *can (1 lb) tomatoes, coarsely*
    chopped, liquid reserved
  1¼ *cups regular-strength chicken*
    broth (homemade or canned)
  ¾ *teaspoon dried thyme*
  ½ *cup slivered blanched*
    almonds

1. Preheat oven to 375° F. Cut chickens into serving pieces (see page 11), reserving back bones, breastbones, necks, and giblets for other uses.

Sprinkle lightly with salt and pepper. In a large frying pan, melt butter and brown chicken pieces, 4 or 5 at a time (do not crowd). Remove them from pan as they brown.

2. When all the chicken is browned, stir onion and rice in the same pan until onion is soft and lightly browned. Mix in green peppers, garlic, raisins, and curry powder; cook and stir for about 3 minutes. Add tomatoes and their liquid, broth, and thyme, stirring to mix in browned bits from pan. Transfer the rice mixture to a broad 4-quart casserole. Arrange chicken pieces over the rice, in a single layer if possible, pouring on any accumulated juices.

3. Cover and bake until chicken is tender (45 minutes). Remove chicken and stir rice well; replace chicken on rice. Sprinkle chicken with almonds and continue baking, uncovered, until chicken and almonds are golden (about 15 minutes longer).

Serves 8.

Spicy, curried Country Captain is delicious for a company buffet. The slow cooking time allows the flavors of curry, almonds, garlic, and spices to meld with the chicken. Serve with rice and green beans.

COUNTRY-STYLE SPARERIBS IN RATATOUILLE

Ratatouille (rah-tah-TOO-ye)—is a splendid melange of garlic-seasoned vegetables. Here, it sets off oven-roasted spareribs.

- 1 large eggplant (about 1½ lbs)
  Salt
- ½ cup olive oil or salad oil (approximately)
- 3 cloves garlic, minced or pressed
- 1 large onion, chopped
- 1 each red and green bell pepper, seeded and cut in strips
- ½ teaspoon each salt and dried basil
- ¼ teaspoon each dried thyme and rosemary
- ¼ cup chopped parsley
- 2 large tomatoes, peeled and coarsely chopped
- 4 to 5 pounds country-style spareribs, cut in serving pieces

1. Preheat oven to 350° F. Cut unpeeled eggplant into ¾-inch cubes. Spread in a single layer on several thicknesses of paper towels. Sprinkle liberally with salt; let stand 20 minutes. Then blot up surface moisture with paper towels. In a large frying pan over moderately high heat, heat about half of the oil with garlic. Add eggplant and brown lightly on all sides, stirring often and adding more oil as needed. As eggplant cubes brown, remove them from pan and transfer to a large, broad casserole (at least 4-quart size). Add onion to the oil remaining in the pan; cook until soft and lightly browned.

2. Mix cooked onions, red and green pepper, the ½ teaspoon salt, basil, thyme, rosemary, parsley, tomatoes, and browned eggplant in casserole. Cover and bake for 1 hour.

3. Meanwhile, arrange spareribs in a single layer in an open roasting pan; sprinkle with salt. Place in same oven with vegetable casserole. At the end of 1 hour, arrange spareribs over vegetables, cover, and continue baking for 45 minutes. Uncover; bake until ribs are tender and well browned (about 15 minutes more). Remove spareribs to a platter. Skim fat from ratatouille; spoon ratatouille over spareribs.

Serves 6.

YANKEE CLIPPER CHICKEN

This vegetable-baked chicken goes well with mashed potatoes and hot biscuits with honey.

- 1 frying chicken (3 to 3½ lbs), quartered (see page 11)
  Salt, white pepper, ground nutmeg, and flour
- 1 tablespoon each butter or margarine and salad oil
- 4 carrots, sliced about ⅜ inch thick
- 1 onion, thinly sliced
- ½ cup chopped celery
- ¼ cup each regular-strength chicken broth (homemade or canned) and dry vermouth

1. Preheat oven to 325° F. Sprinkle quartered chicken lightly on all sides with salt, pepper, and nutmeg; then coat with flour, shaking off excess. In a large frying pan heat together butter and oil; brown chicken well on all sides and place in a single layer, skin side up, in a 10-inch square casserole.

2. Pour off most of the drippings in the frying pan and sauté carrots, onion, and celery until onion is tender and beginning to brown. Add chicken broth and vermouth, stirring to loosen pan drippings. Pour vegetable mixture over chicken.

3. Cover and bake until chicken and vegetables are tender (about 1 hour). Uncover and bake 10 to 15 minutes longer. Spoon vegetables and sauce over chicken.

Serves 4.

SLOW-COOKER STEWS

Electric slow cookers offer many possibilities for making stews. Because they cook so gently and are tightly covered, there is little evaporation, thus keeping meats and poultry moist and juicy. (If you are adapting a favorite stew recipe to the slow cooker, cut back on cooking liquid.)

HAM AND LIMA BEAN POT

This generous pot of well-seasoned lima beans is simmered with large cubes of economical smoked pork shoulder or leftover ham. Crisp cole slaw and homemade corn muffins are favorite accompaniments.

- Fat trimmed from ham
- 2 medium onions, sliced
- 1 green pepper, seeded and chopped
- 2 to 3 cups cubed cooked smoked pork shoulder picnic or ham
- 1 pound dried baby lima beans, rinsed and drained
- 4½ cups water
- ¼ cup each catsup and dark molasses
- 1 tablespoon white vinegar
- ¼ teaspoon hot-pepper sauce
- 1 teaspoon dry mustard
- 2 tablespoons butter or margarine

1. In a 4- to 6-quart Dutch oven, fry fat trimmed from ham. Add onions and green pepper and cook until onions are lightly browned. Mix in ham, beans, water, catsup, molasses, vinegar, hot-pepper sauce, and dry mustard. Boil gently, uncovered, stirring occasionally, for 15 minutes.

2. Transfer mixture to an electric slow cooker preheated on High setting. Dot with butter. Cover and cook for 1 hour; reduce heat to Low and continue cooking until beans are tender, about 6 hours. Stir occasionally, during the last 2 hours. Taste and add salt, if needed.

Serves 6.

ROSEMARY ROUND STEAK

Layers of tomatoes, onions, beef, and seasonings all blend their flavors while slowly cooking.

- 2 pounds top round, about ¾ inch thick, cut in serving-sized pieces
  Salt, pepper, and flour
- 2 tablespoons butter or margarine
- 1 tablespoon salad oil
- ½ teaspoon dried rosemary
- ¼ teaspoon garlic powder
- 2 teaspoons Dijon mustard
- ½ cup regular-strength beef broth (homemade or canned)
- 3 large tomatoes, peeled and thinly sliced
- 1 medium onion, sliced and separated into rings
  Chopped parsley, for garnish

1. Trim fat from pieces of meat; sprinkle with salt and pepper, then coat with flour. In a large frying pan heat together butter and oil, and brown meat well on both sides. As pieces brown, remove them to an electric slow cooker, preheated to High. Sprinkle with rosemary and garlic powder.

2. After removing all the meat, pour off and discard fat. Add mustard and broth to pan drippings, stirring until smooth and well blended, loosening browned bits from pan; set pan aside.

3. Make layers of tomatoes over meat, then layers of onion rings. Pour on liquid mixture from frying pan. Cook at High setting 1 hour. Reduce heat to Low, and continue cooking until meat is very tender (6 to 8 hours longer). Stir occasionally, if possible, during the last 2 hours. Salt to taste. Sprinkle with parsley.
Serves 6.

PIEDMONTESE POT ROAST

This moistly tender, Italian-style pot roast has a rich, dark wine sauce. Serve the meat with butter-browned potato chunks and steamed Swiss chard or fresh spinach with lemon.

- 1 boneless rump roast (3½ to 4 lbs)
- 1 teaspoon salt
- ¼ teaspoon pepper
- ½ teaspoon dried rosemary
- 1 large onion, chopped
- 1 clove garlic, mashed
- 2 medium carrots, shredded
- 1 stalk celery, chopped
- 1 small bay leaf
- 10 whole cloves
- 1 cup dry red wine
- 1 tablespoon tomato paste
- ¼ cup rum or brandy

1. Preheat oven to 500° F. Rub roast with a mixture of salt, pepper, and rosemary. Brown roast, with fat side up, in an open roasting pan for 15 minutes; discard the fat.

2. Mix onion, garlic, carrots, celery, bay leaf, and cloves. Place about half of the vegetable mixture in electric slow cooker, preheated on High setting. Top with browned roast. Surround with remaining vegetable mixture. Mix wine and tomato paste; pour over meat and vegetables.

3. Cover and cook on High until meat is very tender (about 5 hours). Remove meat and keep it warm while preparing sauce. Discard bay leaf. Skim and discard fat from cooking liquid, then purée liquid and vegetables in blender until thick and smooth. Pour into a saucepan and reheat to serving temperature (boil several minutes to reduce, if sauce is too thin). Stir in rum or brandy and heat several minutes longer. Salt to taste. Slice beef, spoon sauce over, and serve.
Serves 6 to 8.

SLOW-COOKER CORNED BEEF AND LENTILS

If cooked on top of the range, corned beef may remain tenaciously tough; but when cooked in a slow cooker, it is transformed. Lentils absorb the good corned beef flavor deliciously.

- 1 corned beef brisket (3 to 3½ lbs)
- 8 cups water
- 2 cups lentils, rinsed and drained
- 1 stalk celery, shredded
- ½ pound small white boiling onions
- ¼ cup chopped parsley
- 1 tablespoon mixed pickling spice, tied in a square of cheesecloth
- 2 cups hot water
- ½ cup dry white wine
  Dijon mustard

1. Rinse corned beef in cold running water to remove as much salt as possible, then place it in a 4- to 6-quart Dutch oven. Cover with the 8 cups water and bring to a boil; drain and discard salty water. Add lentils, celery, onions, parsley, pickling spice, hot water, and wine; bring to a boil. Cover and boil gently for 15 minutes.

2. Transfer ingredients to an electric slow cooker preheated on High setting. Reduce heat to Low and cook, covered, for about 8 hours, until corned beef is very tender.

3. Discard cheesecloth with seasonings. Slice corned beef and arrange on a warm, deep platter. Remove lentils with a slotted spoon, place them around the meat and serve. Pass the mustard.
Serves 6 to 8.

Cooked with lentils and vegetables in a clay pot, a whole chicken is a generous meal for four. Slow-cooking the chicken in clay produces a moist, savory dish.

CLAY-POT STEWS

Dome-lidded terra-cotta cookers designed for baking chicken and meats are an attractive kitchen accessory. If you have used yours only for chicken, you may want to know about its considerable versatility.

If you have a new clay pot with an unglazed interior, season it before using it. This will dispel its earthy smell and also help temper and strengthen the pottery. Here is a good method: Rub the pot, inside and out (including the cover), with peeled garlic. (A large pot may require several cloves.) Then place the pot in a 350° F oven, fill it almost to the top with hot water, cover, and bake for 4 to 6 hours. Pour out any remaining water, wipe dry, and your pot is ready to be used.

Lining an *unglazed* pot with baking parchment will keep fats, oils, and other food flavors from being absorbed by the porous pottery and from mingling—perhaps unappetizingly—with subsequent foods cooked in it.

All of the following stews are designed to be baked in clay cookers. However, they can also be prepared as oven stews in any ceramic ovenware casserole of appropriate size and shape. If the interior is a smooth, shiny, or glazed surface, you don't need to use the parchment paper lining.

BEEF BAKED IN BEER

This oniony beef stew is a version of the notable Belgian dish *carbonnade*. Beer helps the beef cook to estimable tenderness, giving it a subtle, malty flavor.

> 3 pounds bottom round, cut in 1-inch cubes
>   Salt, pepper, and flour
> 5 large onions, thinly sliced
> 1 clove garlic, minced or pressed
> 1 small bay leaf
> ½ teaspoon dried rosemary
> 1 can (12 oz) beer
> 2 tablespoons red wine vinegar
> 1 teaspoon Dijon mustard
>   Chopped parsley, for garnish

1. Preheat oven to 350° F. Sprinkle cubed meat with salt and pepper, then coat lightly with flour. Mix onions, garlic, bay leaf, and rosemary. Line a 4- to 5-quart unglazed clay cooker with parchment paper, trimming paper about 2 inches above rim of baking dish.

2. Alternate layers of the onion mixture and the beef cubes in parchment-lined casserole, beginning and ending with onions. Pour on beer. Cover and bake until meat is very tender (4 to 4½ hours).

3. Mix in vinegar and mustard. Taste and add salt, if needed. Sprinkle with parsley and serve.
Serves 6 to 8.

CHICKEN AND LENTILS IN CLAY

In a clay cooker, chicken roasts to moist perfection, surrounded by a savory mixture of lentils and vegetables.

　　1 *frying chicken (3 to 3½ lbs)*
　　1 *cup lentils, rinsed and*
　　　drained
　　1 *large clove garlic, minced*
　　　or pressed
　　1 *medium onion, thinly sliced*
　　　and separated into rings
　　¼ *cup finely chopped celery*
　　½ *cup slivered smoked pork*
　　　shoulder picnic or ham
　　1 *medium carrot, shredded*
　　¼ *cup chopped parsley*
　　1 *small bay leaf*
　　½ *teaspoon salt*
　　⅛ *teaspoon pepper*
　　1 *cup regular-strength beef*
　　　broth (homemade or canned)
　　½ *cup dry red wine*
　　1 *teaspoon dry mustard*

1. Preheat oven to 375° F. Rinse chicken; pat dry. Coarsely chop liver and reserve. (Discard remaining giblets, or save them for another use.) Line a 3-quart unglazed clay cooker with parchment paper, trimming paper even with rim of baking dish. Place chicken, breast up, within parchment.

2. Place lentils around chicken. Combine garlic, onion, celery, ham, carrot, parsley, and chicken liver; place mixture and bay leaf atop lentils. Sprinkle with salt and pepper. Heat together beef broth, wine, and mustard; pour over chicken.

3. Cover and bake, stirring lentils occasionally, until chicken is browned and lentils are tender (about 3 hours). Carve chicken and serve with lentils.
Serves 4.

ITALIAN VEAL SHANKS IN TOMATO SAUCE

The marrow of *osso buco* (literally, "hollow bones") is prized and should be scooped out and enjoyed. The traditional accompaniment for this dish is a saffron-spiced risotto, but it is also good with green noodles.

　　6 *pounds meaty veal shanks,*
　　　cut in 2-inch lengths
　　　Salt, white pepper, and flour
　　1 *carrot, shredded*
　　3 *cloves garlic, minced*
　　　or pressed
　　1 *medium onion, finely chopped*
　　1 *can (1 lb) tomatoes, coarsely*
　　　chopped, liquid reserved
　　½ *cup dry red wine*
　　1 *tablespoon salt*
　　1 *teaspoon sugar*
　　½ *teaspoon dried rosemary*
　　¼ *teaspoon dried sage*
　　⅓ *cup finely chopped parsley*
　　1 *tablespoon grated lemon rind*

1. Preheat oven to 350° F. Sprinkle veal shanks with salt and pepper; coat lightly with flour. Line a 3½- to 5-quart unglazed clay cooker with parchment paper, trimming paper about 2 inches above rim of dish. Place half of the veal shanks within the parchment.

2. Mix carrot, about two thirds of the minced garlic (reserve a third for topping), and onion. Layer this mixture on top of veal shanks, then top with remaining veal shanks. Heat tomatoes and their liquid, wine, salt, sugar, rosemary, and sage. Pour over veal shanks. Cover. Bake until meat is very tender (2½ to 3 hours).

3. With a slotted spoon, remove veal shanks to a serving dish; keep warm. Pour cooking liquid into a saucepan; bring to a boil, and cook, stirring, until reduced and thickened. Salt, if needed. Mix remaining garlic with parsley and lemon rind; stir about half the mixture into the cooking liquid and simmer for 2 minutes. Pour over veal shanks. Sprinkle with remaining parsley mixture.
Serves 6.

CURRIED OXTAILS IN CLAY

Although you may think of oxtails strictly in connection with soup, they can also make a delicious stew. Serve this colorful dish with rice.

　　⅓ *cup flour*
　　1 *teaspoon salt*
　　1 *tablespoon each paprika*
　　　and curry powder
　　4 *to 4½ pounds meaty oxtails,*
　　　cut in segments
　　1 *large onion, chopped*
　　½ *pound mushrooms, sliced*
　　1 *red bell pepper, seeded*
　　　and cut in thin strips
　　1 *clove garlic, minced or pressed*
　　¾ *cup each dry sherry and*
　　　regular-strength beef broth
　　　(homemade or canned)
　　　Cucumber slices, for garnish

1. Preheat oven to 350° F. Mix flour, salt, paprika, and curry powder. Coat oxtails with flour mixture; reserve any remaining flour. Line a 2½- to 3-quart unglazed clay cooker with parchment paper, trimming paper about 2 inches above rim of dish. Place oxtails within paper.

2. Top with onion, mushrooms, red pepper, and garlic. Pour on sherry and broth. Cover. Bake, stirring once or twice, until oxtails are very tender (about 3½ hours).

3. With a slotted spoon, transfer meat and vegetables to a serving bowl and keep them warm. Skim fat from cooking liquid. Pour liquid into a saucepan. Mix 1 tablespoon of the reserved flour mixture with 2 tablespoons cold water until smooth; stir into liquid. Bring to a boil, stirring constantly, until thickened. Simmer 3 to 5 minutes. Pour sauce over meat. Garnish with cucumbers.
Serves 6.

This traditional chicken pie made with carrots, peas, mushrooms, and a creamy sauce is a dish everyone will surely enjoy (see page 116).

Make-Ahead Casseroles & Meat Pies

Nothing makes a cook
(whether experienced
or novice) feel quite so
relaxed and confident as having
a dinner main dish
all done long before serving time.
All the dishes and menu
ideas featured here can be made
in advance, so they're
ideal for entertaining friends or
family. They're also perfect
for the working person who often
doesn't have the time or
energy to prepare a nutritious
and satisfying meal
after work.

ADVANCE MENU PLANNING

When you make casseroles and meat pies in advance, you end up with elegance, economy, and convenience. Whether you plan to entertain friends or family, the dishes and menu ideas offered here will liberate you. Now you can be one of the gang, rather than behind the scenes. Enjoy potlucks and carry-in suppers, picnics in the park or at the beach, on-the-go weekends with the whole family, or company buffets on days so busy that guests may put in an appearance almost before you do!

All the following recipes clearly indicate how far to prepare, then refrigerate, the dish in advance. If you plan to transfer a container of food directly from the refrigerator to a hot oven, be sure to use the kind of baking dish or pan that will withstand such an abrupt temperature change without cracking.

Most made-in-advance casseroles will bake more satisfactorily if you let them stand at room temperature for up to an hour before baking, if your schedule permits. In warm weather, however, it is a wise safety precaution to keep any dish with eggs or a cream sauce cool until you are ready to put it in the oven.

Baking times for make-ahead dishes are approximations; they depend on the actual temperature of the food when it goes into the oven. To be sure that a dish is ready to serve, check the center by inserting a small sharp knife; if steam rises, the dish probably has baked enough. If the top or edges become too brown before the center heats through, cover with aluminum foil during the last 15 or 20 minutes.

EASY INDIVIDUAL PIZZAS

These shortcut pizzas made with English muffins are so speedy that you really don't even need to make them ahead—unless you want to leave them in the refrigerator for a simple do-it-yourself family supper on the cook's night out.

> 1 pound mild Italian sausages
> 1 can (8 oz) tomato sauce
> 1 can (4 oz) mushroom pieces and stems, well drained
> 1 clove garlic, minced or pressed
> 2 teaspoons Italian herb seasoning
> 4 English muffins, split
> ½ cup grated Parmesan cheese
> 2 cups shredded Monterey jack cheese

1. Preheat oven to 450° F. Remove sausage casings and crumble meat into a large frying pan. Cook, stirring, until browned; spoon off excess fat. Mix in tomato sauce, mushrooms, garlic, and Italian herb seasoning. Bring the mixture to a boil, reduce heat, and simmer, covered, 10 minutes.

2. Meanwhile, toast English muffins in broiler until cut sides are browned. Spread each toasted muffin half with sausage mixture. Then top each with 1 tablespoon Parmesan cheese and ¼ cup of the jack cheese. (At this point, pizzas can be covered and refrigerated for several hours until ready to bake.)

3. Place pizzas on a baking sheet and bake until cheese is melted and lightly browned (10 to 15 minutes). *Serves 4 (2 pizzas each).*

GARDEN FRESH SPAGHETTI SAUCE

Make this spaghetti sauce in the summer—when the tomatoes in your garden (or your neighbor's) ripen all at once—and freeze it for winter suppers.

> 2 tablespoons butter or margarine
> 1 carrot, shredded
> 1 clove garlic, minced or pressed
> 1 large onion, chopped
> 1 pound lean ground beef, crumbled
> ½ pound ground pork, crumbled (or use 1½ lbs ground beef instead of pork)
> 5 large tomatoes, peeled and coarsely chopped
> 1 can (8 oz) tomato sauce
> 1 teaspoon salt
> 1 tablespoon dried basil
> ½ teaspoon each sugar and oregano
> 1 cup dry red wine

1. Heat butter in a large frying pan or Dutch oven; in it cook carrot, garlic, and onion until soft but not browned. Add ground meats and cook, stirring frequently, until they lose all their red color.

2. Stir in tomatoes, tomato sauce, salt, basil, sugar, oregano, and wine. Bring to a boil, reduce heat, cover, and simmer 1 hour. Uncover and cook over moderate heat, stirring occasionally, until sauce is thick (about 1 hour longer).

3. Salt to taste. Refrigerate, then reheat. Or freeze; later, when you want to use it, thaw in refrigerator and reheat to serving temperature. *Makes about 6 cups, 8 to 10 servings.*

STUFFED PASTA WITH TOMATO SAUCE

1   package (7½ to 8 oz)
    manicotti
1   pound ground beef, crumbled
1   large onion, finely chopped
½   cup soft bread crumbs
2   cups shredded Monterey
    jack cheese
1   teaspoon salt
⅛   teaspoon pepper
1   clove garlic, minced or pressed
1   can (15 oz) tomato sauce with
    tomato bits
1   cup regular-strength beef
    broth (homemade or canned)
½   cup dry red wine
1   teaspoon dried basil
½   teaspoon dried oregano
½   cup grated Parmesan cheese

1. Preheat oven to 350° F. Cook manicotti in boiling salted water, according to package directions; undercook slightly. Drain, rinse with warm water, and drain again. Separate on paper towels; set aside.

2. In a large, heavy frying pan, cook ground beef in its own drippings with about half of the onion; stir until meat is well browned. Spoon off most of the fat. With a slotted spoon, remove meat and onions to a bowl; stir in bread crumbs, 1 cup of the jack cheese, salt, and pepper.

3. In the same frying pan, cook remaining onion until soft. Stir in garlic, tomato sauce, broth, wine, basil, and oregano. Bring to a boil and boil gently, uncovered, 5 minutes. Pour about half the sauce into a greased, shallow 3-quart baking dish.

4. Carefully fill the drained manicotti with the meat mixture. Arrange it in sauce in baking dish. Pour on remaining sauce. Sprinkle with remaining 1 cup jack cheese and Parmesan cheese. (At this point, casserole can be covered and refrigerated until ready to bake.)

5. Bake, uncovered, until pasta heats through, sauce bubbles, and cheese browns lightly (25 to 45 minutes).

Serves 5 to 6.

Manicotti, stuffed with a ground beef filling and crowned with Monterey jack cheese, makes for a special dish to bring to a potluck. This tasty meal can be prepared in advance and refrigerated until you are ready to pop it in the oven.

BEEF AND SAUERKRAUT BUNS

Who can forget the tempting smell of freshly baked bread, steamy and fragrant as it comes from the oven— so soft you know you should wait, but too good to resist? This main dish has just such appeal: wheaty pan rolls filled with ground beef and sauer-kraut. Made with a refrigerator dough that requires no kneading, the meat-filled buns are a good family supper served with milk or beer, crisp vegetables, and fresh apples and ginger cookies for dessert.

1 package active dry yeast
1 cup hot water
¼ cup sugar
¾ teaspoon salt
½ cup soft butter or margarine
3 cups unsifted all-purpose flour
1 egg
½ cup graham or whole wheat flour
2 tablespoons salad oil
Soft butter or margarine

Beef and Sauerkraut Filling

1 pound ground beef
1 small onion, finely chopped
1 teaspoon salt
¼ teaspoon pepper
1 can (1 lb) sauerkraut

1. In large bowl of electric mixer, sprinkle yeast over water; let stand about 5 minutes to soften. Stir in sugar, salt, and the ½ cup butter, mixing until the butter melts.

Add 2½ cups of the all-purpose flour. Mix to blend, then beat 5 minutes at medium speed. Beat in egg, then vigorously mix in remaining ½ cup all-purpose flour and all the graham flour until well combined.

2. Cover and let rise in a warm place until doubled in bulk (about 1 hour). Punch down, turn dough out on a generously floured board or pastry cloth, and roll to a 16-inch square. Cut dough into 4-inch squares. Place 2 to 3 generous table-spoons of filling in center of each square. Bring opposite corners togeth-er; pinch to seal.

3. Pour oil into a 9- by 13-inch baking pan. As each square of dough is filled, turn it in oil, placing buns side by side in pan, pinched sides down. (At this point, pan may be covered and refrigerated, 3 to 5 hours or overnight.)

4. Uncover pan, if necessary. Let rise until buns are puffy (45 minutes to 1 hour). Preheat oven to 400° F and bake until well browned (22 to 28 minutes). Brush tops of rolls with soft butter. Serve hot.

Makes 16 meat-filled buns, 4 to 6 servings.

Beef and Sauerkraut Filling

Crumble beef into a large frying pan. Cook in its own drippings, stirring, until browned. Spoon off excess fat. Mix in onion, salt, and pepper; cook 3 to 5 minutes longer. Remove from heat and mix in sauerkraut, well drained.

BAKED MEATBALLS IN RED WINE

Baking meatballs in a very hot oven is easier than browning and turning each one individually on top of the range. These baked meatballs, enriched with an elegant wine and mushroom sauce, go well with hot rice.

2 eggs
¾ cup soft bread crumbs
⅓ cup half-and-half
1½ teaspoons salt
⅛ teaspoon each *ground allspice and pepper*
1 small onion, chopped
2 pounds ground beef
2 tablespoons butter or margarine
1 can (4 oz) mushroom pieces and stems, drained
1 clove garlic, minced or pressed
1½ tablespoons flour
1 cup dry red wine
2 tablespoons Beef Concentrate (see page 13) or 2 teaspoons beef stock base
Chopped parsley, for garnish

1. Preheat oven to 500° F. In a large bowl beat eggs. Mix in bread crumbs, half-and-half, salt, allspice, pep-per, and half of the onion; then lightly mix in ground beef. Shape into golf-ball-sized meatballs. Arrange in a single layer in a shallow baking pan. Bake until browned (about 10 minutes).

2. In a 1½-quart saucepan, heat butter and cook remaining onion until lightly browned. Mix in mushrooms, garlic, and flour; cook until bubbly. Remove from heat and gradually stir in wine and Beef Concentrate. Return to heat and cook, stirring, until thickened and bubbling.

3. Transfer meatballs to a 2- to 3-quart casserole. Pour on sauce. (At this point you may refrigerate casserole, covered, for several hours or overnight.) Reduce oven to 350° F and bake until meatballs and sauce are heated through and flavors are blended (25 to 45 minutes). Salt to taste. Sprinkle with parsley and serve.

Serves 6 to 8.

STUFFED ZUCCHINI PROVENÇALE

Meat mixtures bake well inside scooped-out vegetables, too, as good cooks around the world have discovered. This recipe offers zucchini from the south of France.

> 6 *medium zucchini*
> 1 *pound ground beef, crumbled*
> 1 *medium onion, finely chopped*
> 1 *clove garlic, minced or pressed*
> 1 *can (1 lb) tomatoes, coarsely chopped, liquid reserved*
> ¼ *cup dry red wine*
> 1 *tablespoon tomato paste*
> 1 *teaspoon each salt and Italian herb seasoning mixture*
> ⅛ *teaspoon pepper*
> 1½ *cups shredded Monterey jack cheese*

1. Preheat oven to 425° F. Scrub zucchini; cut off stem and blossom ends. Drop into boiling water and cook until barely tender (about 5 minutes). Remove from cooking water and immerse in cold water; let stand until cool, then drain. Cut in halves lengthwise and scoop out pulp, leaving a ¼-inch-thick shell. Chop pulp coarsely and reserve, along with shells.

2. In a frying pan over moderately high heat, brown ground beef in its own drippings. Mix in onion and garlic, stirring over moderate heat until onion is soft. Spoon off fat, if necessary. Stir in tomatoes and their liquid, wine, tomato paste, salt, and Italian herb seasoning. Bring to a boil, reduce heat, and simmer, covered, 15 minutes. Uncover, add chopped zucchini, and cook uncovered, stirring occasionally until sauce is thick (15 to 20 minutes).

3. Arrange zucchini shells in a shallow, oiled baking dish just large enough to hold them, and heap meat mixture into shells. Sprinkle with cheese. (At this point casserole can be covered and refrigerated until ready to bake.)

4. Bake uncovered until zucchini is tender and cheese is browned (25 to 35 minutes).

Serves 6.

Stuffed zucchini makes a pleasant and unusual change from the standard seasoned ground beef dish. In addition their abundance during the summer season makes this dish affordable as well as nutritious.

107

A well-stocked kitchen is a good cook's secret for a repertoire of easy and delicious casseroles. Inexpensive meats can be enhanced by garden-fresh vegetables, tempting cheeses, and exotic seasonings, and combined with a diverse selection of noodles or rice.

GREEK GROUND BEEF AND MACARONI CASSEROLE

In Greece, this attractive casserole is known as *pastitsio*. Its ingredients are macaroni, an exotically spiced ground beef sauce, and a creamy topping.

> 2 *pounds ground beef, crumbled*
> 1 *large onion, finely chopped*
> 1 *clove garlic, minced or pressed*
> 1 *teaspoon salt*
> ½ *teaspoon ground cinnamon*
> ⅛ *teaspoon each ground cloves and allspice*
> 1 *can (15 oz) tomato sauce*
> ¼ *cup water*
> 1 *package (1 lb) elbow macaroni*
> 1¼ *cups shredded Parmesan cheese*

Custard Cream Sauce

> ¼ *cup butter or margarine*
> 3 *tablespoons flour*
> ¾ *teaspoon salt*
> ¼ *teaspoon ground nutmeg*
> *Dash white pepper*
> 2 *cups milk*
> 3 *eggs*

1. Preheat oven to 350° F. In a large, heavy frying pan or Dutch oven, brown ground beef in its own drippings, stirring frequently. Pour off most of the drippings. Mix in onion and cook, stirring occasionally, until soft. Mix in garlic, salt, cinnamon, cloves, allspice, tomato sauce, and water. Bring to a boil, cover, reduce heat, and simmer 20 minutes.

2. Cook macaroni in boiling salted water, according to package directions; undercook slightly. Drain, rinse, and drain again thoroughly.

3. Spread half the macaroni in a large buttered baking dish about 9 by 13 inches; sprinkle with ¼ cup of the cheese. Top with meat sauce; sprinkle with ¼ cup more cheese. Cover with remaining macaroni and sprinkle with ¼ cup more cheese. Pour on Custard Cream Sauce evenly; sprinkle with remaining ½ cup cheese. (At this point, casserole may be covered and refrigerated for several hours or overnight.)

4. Bake, uncovered, until center is hot and top is lightly browned (45 minutes to 1 hour). Cut in squares to serve.
Serves 8.

Custard Cream Sauce In a 2-quart saucepan, melt butter or margarine. Stir in flour, salt, nutmeg, and pepper; cook until bubbly. Remove from heat and gradually stir in milk. Return to heat and cook, stirring constantly, until thickened. Beat eggs in a mixing bowl; using a wire whisk, gradually mix in hot sauce, whisking until smooth and well blended (do not heat further).

Makes 2 cups.

STUFFED GREEN PEPPERS MEXICANA

These stuffed peppers have a sweetly spicy, south-of-the-border flavor.

> 6 medium-sized green peppers (about 2 lbs)
> 2 tablespoons butter or margarine
> ½ cup slivered almonds
> 1 pound ground beef, crumbled
> 1 large onion, finely chopped
> 1 clove garlic, mashed
> ⅓ cup raisins
> 1 tablespoon cider vinegar
> 1 teaspoon each sugar, salt, and ground cinnamon
> ¼ teaspoon each ground cumin and cloves
> 1 can (15 oz) tomato sauce

Rice

> 1 cup water
> ¼ teaspoon salt
> ½ cup short-grain or pearl rice

1. Preheat oven to 350° F. Cut a thin slice from stem end of each pepper; carefully cut out seeds. Cook peppers, uncovered, in boiling salted water to cover, for 5 minutes; turn upside down to drain.

2. Heat butter in a large frying pan; add almonds and cook until lightly browned. Remove from pan with a slotted spoon. In the same pan cook ground beef and onion until lightly browned. Mix in garlic, raisins, vinegar, sugar, ¾ teaspoon of the salt, the cinnamon, cumin, cloves, and half of the tomato sauce. Simmer, uncovered, about 10 minutes. Mix in cooked rice (see below) and almonds.

3. Fill peppers with ground beef mixture. Arrange in an ungreased, deep, covered baking dish just large enough to hold the 6 peppers. Pour on remaining tomato sauce. (At this point peppers can be covered and refrigerated for several hours or overnight.)

4. Bake, covered, for 45 minutes; uncover, spoon sauce over, and continue baking for 15 minutes.

Serves 6.

Rice To cook rice, in a small saucepan bring water and salt to a boil. Add rice, cover tightly, reduce heat, and simmer until water is absorbed (20 minutes).

BAKED STUFFED EGGPLANT

Remember the subtly colored pear-shaped eggplant; it's another perfect envelope for tasty stuffings. Here, the hearty Italian-style filling is made of meat and rice topped with a Parmesan cheese cream sauce. This is a complete meal all-in-one!

> 2 small eggplants, about 1 pound each
> Salt
> ¼ cup olive oil or salad oil
> 1 pound ground beef, crumbled
> ½ cup short-grain or pearl rice, uncooked
> 1 medium onion, finely chopped
> 1 clove garlic, minced or pressed
> ½ teaspoon dried oregano
> ¼ teaspoon ground cinnamon
> ¼ cup chopped parsley
> 1 can (8 oz) tomato sauce
> ¼ cup shredded Parmesan cheese

Cream Sauce

> 2 tablespoons butter or margarine
> 2 tablespoons flour
> ⅛ teaspoon ground nutmeg
> Dash cayenne pepper
> ½ cup each regular-strength chicken broth (homemade or canned) and half-and-half
> ¼ cup shredded Parmesan cheese

1. Preheat oven to 400° F. Remove stem ends of eggplants; cut in halves lengthwise. Score pulp, cutting to within ½ inch of skin. Sprinkle generously with salt; let stand 30 minutes. Use paper towels to blot moisture from cut surfaces.

2. Heat oil in a large frying pan. Place eggplant halves, cut sides down, in the oil; cover and cook slowly (about 5 minutes per side). Leaving the shells intact, cut out pulp with a curved knife and dice it. Reserve shells and diced eggplant.

3. In the same pan brown ground beef with rice and onion, stirring until onion is soft. Mix in garlic, oregano, cinnamon, parsley, and tomato sauce. Bring to a boil, cover, reduce heat, and simmer until rice is nearly tender (about 20 minutes). Mix in reserved diced eggplant.

4. Divide filling evenly into eggplant shells. Place shells in a shallow greased casserole just large enough to hold them. Spread Cream Sauce on top of each filled shell; sprinkle with the ¼ cup Parmesan cheese. (At this point, casserole can be covered and refrigerated for several hours or overnight, until you are ready to bake it.)

5. Bake uncovered until sauce is browned and filling is heated through (25 to 45 minutes). If you wish, cut eggplant halves lengthwise to serve.

Serves 4 to 6.

Cream Sauce In a 1½-quart saucepan melt butter or margarine; stir in flour, nutmeg, and cayenne. Cook until bubbly. Remove from heat and gradually stir in chicken broth and half-and-half. Return to heat and cook, stirring constantly, until thickened. Cook gently, stirring, for 3 to 5 minutes. Smoothly mix in Parmesan cheese. Sauce will spread more easily if it is warm.

THREE PIES FROM ENGLISH PUBS

Some of the most typical and enjoyable English foods can be found in pubs—"public houses"—especially at noontime. There you are likely to find well-prepared cold plates, fine cheeses, and exceptional meat pies.

Steak and kidney pie is the most formal; accompany it with a green vegetable and a crisp salad. Ham and cheese pie makes a nice brunch or family supper. And pork pie, the jauntiest of the trio, is delightful for picnic fare, served with a well-chilled English cider or ale.

TRADITIONAL ENGLISH PORK PIES

The best baking pans for these meaty little pies are straight-sided, deep, individual foil pans. Look for them at the grocery or hardware store, in packages of 8. Bake the pies on a rimmed cookie sheet to prevent drippings from spilling over in your oven.

   1 *large onion, finely chopped*
   2 *tablespoons butter or*
     margarine
   1 *clove garlic, minced or pressed*
   ¼ *cup brandy (optional)*
   2 *pounds lean boneless*
     pork butt
   2 *eggs*
   ¼ *cup finely chopped parsley*
   1½ *teaspoons salt*
   ½ *teaspoon dried thyme*
   ¼ *teaspoon ground allspice*
   ⅛ *teaspoon white pepper*
   1 *egg, beaten with 1 teaspoon*
     water

Pastry

   4 *cups unsifted flour*
   1 *teaspoon salt*
   ½ *cup each cold butter or*
     margarine and lard
   1 *egg*

1. Preheat oven to 375° F. Cook onion in butter until soft but not browned. Mix in garlic and brandy (if used); continue cooking until onion browns lightly and most of the liquid cooks away.

2. Using the fine blade of a food chopper or a food processor fitted with steel blade, grind pork (you should have at least 4 cups). Mix in onions, eggs, parsley, salt, thyme, allspice, and pepper. Beat until well combined.

3. On a floured board or pastry cloth, roll out the larger ball of pastry to about ⅛ inch thick. Cut into 5-inch circles and press them into 10 individual foil baking pans about 3 inches in diameter and 1½ inches deep. Divide pork filling into the pastry-lined pans. Roll out remaining pastry and cut it into 3½-inch circles. Cover pork filling with top crusts, moistening edges and pressing them together to seal. Cut a small round air vent in top of each. (At this point pies can be covered and refrigerated for several hours or overnight until ready to bake.)

4. Brush top crusts with egg mixture. Place pans on a baking sheet and bake until well browned (about 1 hour and 15 minutes). Cool slightly before serving.

Serves 10.

Pastry In a large bowl combine flour and salt. Cut in butter and lard, continuing until mixture is crumbly and forms coarse crumbs. Beat egg in a measuring cup; mix in cold water to make ⅔ cup. Add egg mixture to flour mixture, 1 or 2 tablespoons at a time, mixing lightly with a fork after each addition until the pastry clings together. Use your hands to shape the pastry into 2 balls, 1 twice as large as the other.

STEAK AND KIDNEY PIE

   6 *tablespoons flour*
   1½ *teaspoons salt*
   ¼ *teaspoon each pepper and*
     dried thyme, chervil, marjoram, and summer savory
   2 *pounds boneless top round*
     (see page 10), cut in ½-inch
     cubes
   ½ *pound beef or lamb kidneys,*
     sliced
   ½ *pound mushrooms, quartered*
   2 *tablespoons butter or*
     margarine
   ½ *cup dry red wine or*
     regular-strength beef broth
     (homemade or canned)
   6 *frozen patty shells*
     (1 10-oz pkg), thawed
   1 *egg, beaten with 1 teaspoon*
     water

1. Preheat oven to 325° F. In a large bowl mix flour, salt, pepper, thyme, chervil, marjoram, and savory. Mix in round steak cubes and kidney slices, coating well with flour mixture. Sauté mushrooms in butter until lightly browned.

2. Place half the beef and kidney mixture in a 2-quart, 2-inch-deep baking dish. Top with mushrooms, then with remaining meat. Pour on wine or broth.

3. Arrange the 6 patty shells, overlapping slightly, on a floured board or pastry cloth. Roll out pastry into a slightly larger shape than the top of the casserole.

4. Arrange pastry over steak and kidney mixture; trim and flute edge, sealing it to baking dish. Pierce or slit top in several places to allow steam to escape. Trim with pastry scraps cut into decorative shapes, if you wish. (At this point you may cover and refrigerate the pie for several hours or overnight until ready to bake.)

5. Brush pastry with egg mixture. Bake until meat is tender (insert a long wooden skewer to test) and pastry is well browned (1½ to 2 hours). Serve immediately.

Serves 6 to 8.

HAM AND CHEDDAR PIE

Excellent for brunch or supper, this pie goes well with a dessert of fresh fruit.

- 1 large boiling potato (about 12 oz)
- 1 medium onion, finely chopped
- 3 tablespoons butter or margarine
- ¼ cup milk
- 1 egg
- 1 teaspoon dry mustard
- ½ teaspoon salt
- ⅛ teaspoon ground cloves
- 4 cups ground, cooked, smoked pork shoulder picnic or leftover ham
- ½ cup shredded Cheddar cheese

Pastry

- 1¼ cups unsifted flour
- ¼ teaspoon salt
- ¼ cup cold butter or margarine
- 2 tablespoons lard
- 2 to 3 tablespoons cold water

Cheese Sauce

- 2 tablespoons butter or margarine
- 2 tablespoons flour
  Dash each white pepper, ground nutmeg, and cayenne pepper
- 1¼ cups milk
- 1 cup shredded Cheddar cheese
- 1 tablespoon dry sherry

1. Preheat oven to 450° F. Peel and quarter potato and cook in boiling salted water to cover, until tender (15 to 20 minutes). Meanwhile, cook onion in butter until soft and beginning to brown. Drain potato well. In a large bowl beat potato with milk until fluffy; then beat in onion mixture, egg, dry mustard, salt, and cloves. Lightly mix in ground ham.

2. Line a 10-inch pie pan or quiche dish with rolled-out pastry, trimming and fluting edge. Fill with ham mixture. Top with Cheese Sauce. Sprinkle with shredded cheese. (At this point pie may be covered and refrigerated for several hours or overnight.)

3. Bake on the lowest rack of oven for 10 minutes. Reduce heat to 350° F and continue baking until top browns and center is heated through (25 to 40 minutes longer). Let stand about 5 minutes before cutting. *Serves 8.*

Pastry Mix flour with salt. Cut in butter or margarine and lard until coarse crumbs form. Gradually mix in cold water, until pastry clings together. On a floured board or pastry cloth, roll pastry out to a circle a little larger than baking pan.

Cheese Sauce Melt butter or margarine in a 1½-quart saucepan. Stir in flour, pepper, nutmeg, and cayenne; cook until bubbly. Remove from heat and gradually stir in milk. Return to heat and cook, stirring, until thickened and bubbly. Stir in cheese until melted; then mix in sherry.

For traditional English lunch fare try these three favorite meat pies. The rich Ham and Cheddar Pie, savory English Pork Pies, and classic Steak and Kidney Pie can be complemented by hearty English beers and ales.

menu

A GREEK DINNER FOR SIX

Lemon and Rice Soup
(Avgolemono)

Moussaka

Greek Olive and Feta
Green Salad

Sesame-Seeded Bread

Baklava

Suggested wine: Retsina,
Zinfandel, or Gamay
Beaujolais

Sometimes it's fun to plan a menu around a special ethnic dish, selecting appropriate accompaniments from the cuisine of the same culture. Moussaka, an elegant layered lamb-and-eggplant casserole, suggests a glorious Greek evening.

MOUSSAKA

1 *large eggplant (about 1½ lbs)*
   Salt
1 *pound ground lamb, crumbled*
   About ⅓ cup olive oil or salad oil
1 *large onion, finely chopped*
1 *clove garlic, minced or pressed*
¼ *teaspoon ground cinnamon*
1 *teaspoon salt*
⅛ *teaspoon each ground nutmeg and white pepper*
¼ *teaspoon dried oregano*
¼ *cup chopped parsley*
2 *tablespoons tomato paste*
½ *cup dry red wine or beef broth*
½ *cup grated Parmesan cheese*

Cream Sauce

2 *tablespoons butter or margarine*
2 *tablespoons flour*
½ *teaspoon salt*
   Dash each ground nutmeg and white pepper
2 *cups milk*
2 *whole eggs*
1 *egg yolk*

1. Preheat oven to 350° F. Cut off stem end of eggplant; cut unpeeled eggplant in half lengthwise. Cut crosswise in ½-inch slices. Arrange in a single layer on paper towels; sprinkle with salt. Set aside.

2. In a large frying pan heat 1 tablespoon of the oil and cook lamb, stirring until browned. Spoon off excess fat. Mix in onion and cook, stirring occasionally, until onion is tender. Mix in garlic, cinnamon, salt, nutmeg, pepper, oregano, parsley, tomato paste, and wine or broth. Bring to a boil, reduce heat, and simmer, covered, 15 minutes; uncover and continue simmering until sauce is thick (about 5 minutes longer).

3. Blot up moisture from eggplant slices with paper towels. Arrange eggplant in a single layer in a large shallow pan. Brush with some of the remaining oil. Broil, about 4 inches from heat, until lightly browned

(about 5 minutes). Turn, brush second sides with oil, and broil until browned (about 5 minutes longer).

4. To assemble the dish, place half the eggplant in a single layer in an ungreased square or oval casserole (about 2-quart capacity). Top with meat sauce; sprinkle with 2 tablespoons of Parmesan cheese. Cover with remaining eggplant; sprinkle with 2 more tablespoons cheese. Pour on Cream Sauce; sprinkle with remaining cheese. (Casserole can be covered and refrigerated overnight.)

5. Bake until top is lightly browned (45 minutes to 1 hour).

Serves 6.

Cream Sauce Melt butter or margarine in a medium-sized saucepan; stir in flour, salt, nutmeg, and pepper. Remove from heat and gradually stir in milk. Return to heat and cook, stirring, until thickened. In a small bowl beat eggs and egg yolk. Mix in a little of the hot sauce. Over low heat, blend egg mixture gradually into sauce and mix well.

LEMON AND RICE SOUP
Avgolemono

5 *cups Golden Chicken Broth (see page 13), or 3 cans (13¾ oz each) regular-strength chicken broth*
3 *tablespoons uncooked long-grain rice*
5 *eggs*
¼ *cup fresh lemon juice*
   Thin lemon slices

1. In a medium saucepan simmer broth and rice, covered, until rice is tender (about 20 minutes).

2. In a bowl, beat eggs until foamy; gradually mix in lemon juice, beating until blended. Pour part of the soup slowly into egg mixture; then return mixture to remainder of soup, stirring constantly. Stir over low heat until hot, but do not boil. Serve at once, garnish with lemon slices.

Serves 6.

BAKLAVA

Look for the tissue-thin pastry called phyllo (also spelled filo), found in the refrigerated section of specialty food stores.

½ pound (half of a 1-lb package) phyllo dough
2 cups ground blanched almonds (whirl in blender until powdery)
¾ cup sugar
1 teaspoon grated lemon rind
¾ teaspoon ground cinnamon
½ pound unsalted butter, melted
  Sliced almonds, for garnish

Honey and Rose Water Syrup

¼ cup each sugar and water
1 cup honey
1 tablespoon rose water

1. Thaw phyllo, if frozen (remainder can be refrozen). Bring to room temperature; unfold sheets of dough so they lie flat. Cover with a damp towel, to prevent them from drying out.

2. Preheat oven to 325° F. In a medium bowl combine almonds, sugar, lemon rind, and cinnamon. Butter an 8- or 9-inch square pan generously.

3. Carefully fold 2 sheets of phyllo to fit pan; place in pan 1 at a time, brushing each with butter. Sprinkle about 3 tablespoons of the almond mixture over the top sheet of phyllo. Fold 1 sheet of phyllo to fit pan; brush with butter. Sprinkle evenly with 3 tablespoons more of the almond mixture.

4. Add more layers, using 1 folded sheet of phyllo, a generous brushing of butter, and 3 to 4 tablespoons of the almond mixture for each, until nut mixture is used up (you should have about 10 nut-filled layers).

5. Fold remaining 2 to 3 sheets of phyllo to fit pan. Place on top, brushing each with butter before adding the next. With a very sharp knife, carefully cut diagonally across the pan to make small diamond shapes—about 1½ inches on a side—cutting all the way to the bottom of the pan. Pour on any remaining butter.

6. Bake until golden brown (about 45 minutes). Pour warm Honey and Rose Water Syrup over the top. Decorate each piece with an almond slice. Cool before serving.

Makes about 2 dozen pastries.

Honey and Rose Water Syrup
Combine sugar and water in a 1½-quart saucepan; bring to a boil, stirring. Mix in honey and cook until syrup boils again. Remove from heat; mix in rose water.

This splendid Greek dinner features a green salad with feta cheese and greek olives, a tart and creamy lemon soup, and lamb and eggplant Moussaka. For dessert, serve the honey and almond filled pastry, Baklava.

Green chiles add a spicy touch to hot chicken salad. Serve this bold salad with fresh raw vegetables and a cold drink for a refreshing meal on a hot summer night.

HOT CHICKEN AND GREEN CHILE SALAD

For a light meal, try this Mexican-accented hot chicken salad. Accompany it with crisp raw vegetables and beer or iced tea.

 1 *frying chicken (3 to 3½ lbs)*
 ½ *cup mayonnaise*
 2 *teaspoons lemon juice*
 1 *teaspoon white wine vinegar*
 ½ *teaspoon dry mustard*
 ¼ *teaspoon each garlic salt and ground cumin*
 1 *stalk celery, finely chopped*
 4 *green onions, thinly sliced (use part of tops)*
 2 *canned green chiles, seeded and chopped*
 ½ *cup each shredded Monterey jack and Cheddar cheese*
 1 *cup crushed corn chips*

1. Prepare chicken as directed in recipe for Chicken Tetrazzini (page 119). Divide cooked chicken into bite-sized chunks. Reserve broth for other uses.

2. Preheat oven to 400° F. To make dressing, in a small bowl mix mayonnaise, lemon juice, vinegar, mustard, garlic salt, and cumin until smooth.

3. Lightly combine dressing, prepared chicken, celery, green onions, green chiles, and cheeses. Divide the chicken mixture into 4 to 6 buttered shallow individual baking dishes. Top with crushed corn chips. (At this point the salad can be covered and refrigerated for several hours.)

4. Bake, uncovered, until salad is bubbly and heated through (15 to 25 minutes).

Serves 4 to 6.

114

LAMB AND EGGPLANT CASSEROLE

A generous, crusty Swiss cheese topping gives this vegetable-rich ground lamb casserole an extravagant finishing touch.

    1 large eggplant (about 1½ lbs)
      Salt
    ½ cup olive oil or salad
      oil (approximately)
    1 pound ground lamb,
      crumbled
    1 large onion, finely chopped
    2 cloves garlic, minced
      or pressed
    1 small red or green bell pepper,
      seeded and cut in strips
    ¾ teaspoon each salt and
      dried basil
    ¼ teaspoon dried oregano
    ⅛ teaspoon dried thyme
    ¼ cup chopped parsley
    2 large ripe tomatoes, peeled
      and coarsely chopped
    2 cups shredded Swiss cheese

1. Preheat oven to 425° F. Cut unpeeled eggplant into ¾-inch cubes. Spread in a single layer on several thicknesses of paper towels. Sprinkle liberally with salt; let stand for 20 minutes. Then blot up surface moisture. Heat about half the oil in a large frying pan over moderately high heat. Add eggplant, about half at a time, and brown on all sides, removing and reserving it as it browns. Add more oil as needed.

2. When all the eggplant is browned, add ground lamb and cook in its own drippings, stirring until browned. Spoon off excess fat, if necessary. Mix in onion, garlic, and red or green pepper, cooking until onion is soft. Mix in salt, basil, oregano, thyme, parsley, and tomatoes. Cover and simmer 15 minutes. Uncover and continue cooking until thick (8 to 10 minutes). Mix in eggplant. Cover and simmer until eggplant becomes tender (8 to 10 minutes longer).

3. Transfer lamb and eggplant mixture to an ungreased shallow 2-quart baking dish; sprinkle with cheese. (At this point casserole can be covered and refrigerated.)

4. Bake uncovered until cheese is crusty and well browned (25 to 35 minutes).

Serves 6.

BAKED FRANKFURTERS AND LENTILS

The lentils make this dish a pleasant change from the usual beans-and-franks combination. Accompany with sharp mustard and rye bread.

    2 cups lentils
    1 can (1 lb) tomatoes, coarsely
      chopped, liquid reserved
    1 can (13¾ oz) regular-
      strength beef broth
    6 slices bacon, cut in squares
    ½ cup catsup
    1 medium onion, finely chopped
    1 bay leaf
    ¼ cup brown sugar
    1 tablespoon prepared mustard
    2 tablespoons molasses
    1 pound frankfurters

1. Preheat oven to 350° F. Rinse and drain lentils. In a 2- to 3-quart casserole, mix lentils, tomatoes and liquid, broth, uncooked bacon, catsup, onion, bay leaf, brown sugar, mustard, and molasses.

2. Cover and bake until lentils are tender (about 2 hours). Stir 2 or 3 times; add up to 1 cup water if mixture seems dry. (You can do this much ahead, then refrigerate the lentils for several hours or overnight.)

3. Using a cooking fork, pierce frankfurters in several places to prevent bursting. Add to lentils, pressing them down into lentil mixture. Cover and continue baking until frankfurters are heated through (15 to 20 minutes longer, or up to 1 hour and 15 minutes, if lentils were refrigerated). Remove the bay leaf.

Serves 5 to 6.

PIZZA LOAF IN FRENCH BREAD

This makes a good picnic main dish with an antipasto assortment, a red jug wine, and pears and sugar cookies for dessert. If you make it at home to take along, first wrap the hot, filled loaf tightly in aluminum foil, then insulate it well with layers of newspaper. It will stay warm for several hours.

    1 long loaf (1 lb) French bread
    1 small onion, coarsely chopped
    1 clove garlic, minced or pressed
    2 tablespoons olive oil or
      salad oil
    ½ cup grated Parmesan cheese
    1 can (8 oz) tomato sauce
    1 can (4 oz) sliced mushrooms,
      drained
    ¾ teaspoon salt
    ½ teaspoon dried oregano
    ⅛ teaspoon pepper
    1 pound lean ground beef
    1 egg, slightly beaten
      Soft butter or margarine
    ½ cup mozzarella cheese, cut
      in strips

1. Preheat oven to 375° F. Cut a slice about ½ inch deep from the top of the loaf of French bread. Scoop out most of the bread; tear into small pieces to make 1½ cups; reserve. (Freeze any extra bread crumbs for other uses, such as in meatballs or meat loaves, or to top casseroles.)

2. Brown onion and garlic in oil. Mix in reserved bread crumbs, Parmesan cheese, tomato sauce, mushrooms, salt, oregano, and pepper. Add ground beef and egg; mix lightly. Spoon into hollowed-out bread shell. Lightly butter outside of loaf. Wrap securely in foil. (At this point, loaf can be refrigerated for several hours or overnight.)

3. Bake about 1 hour and 20 minutes. Fold back foil; arrange cheese strips over top. Return loaf to oven and bake until cheese is melted and bubbly (about 5 minutes).

Serves 6.

OLD-FASHIONED DEEP-DISH CHICKEN PIE

¼ cup butter or margarine
1 small onion, finely chopped
¼ cup finely chopped celery
3 tablespoons flour
   Dash each white pepper and ground nutmeg
½ cup thawed frozen peas
1 can (4 oz) mushroom pieces and stems, drained

Simmered Chicken and Broth

2 whole frying chickens (about 3 lbs each)
1 medium onion (chopped)
3 medium carrots (cut in ½-inch slices)
2 sprigs parsley
1 bay leaf
1 stalk celery (coarsely chopped)
1 tablespoon salt
¼ teaspoon dried thyme
4 cups water

Flaky Pastry

1¼ cups unsifted flour
¼ teaspoon salt
3 tablespoons each firm butter or margarine and lard
1 egg yolk (reserve egg white to glaze pastry)
2 tablespoons cold water

1. Prepare Simmered Chicken and Broth as directed.

2. Preheat oven to 425° F. In a 3-quart saucepan melt butter over medium heat. In it cook onion and celery until onion is soft but not browned. Stir in flour, pepper, and nutmeg, cooking until bubbly. Remove from heat and gradually stir in the 2 cups of reserved chicken broth. Return to heat and cook, stirring, until mixture is thickened.

3. Mix in chicken pieces, carrots reserved from cooking chicken, peas, and mushrooms. Salt to taste. Spread chicken mixture in a straight-sided round baking dish about 9½ inches in diameter and 2 inches deep. Place pastry over chicken mixture; trim and flute edge, and cut slits in top for steam to escape. (At this point pie can be refrigerated and baked several hours later or the following day.)

4. Beat egg white reserved from pastry with 1 teaspoon water. Brush over top of crust. Bake until pastry is golden and filling is bubbly (30 to 40 minutes).

Serves 8.

Simmered Chicken and Broth

1. Cut chickens into serving pieces (see page 11). In a 5½- to 6-quart kettle or Dutch oven, combine chicken pieces, onion, carrots, parsley, bay leaf, celery, salt, thyme, and water. Bring to a boil, reduce heat, cover, and simmer for about 1½ hours, until chicken is very tender.

2. Strain and reserve broth; measure 2 cups of the broth for pie and freeze remainder for another use.

3. Remove chicken from bones, discarding skin and bones; divide it into generous bite-sized pieces (about 6 cups). Reserve carrots; discard remaining vegetables.

Flaky Pastry Mix flour with salt. Cut in butter or margarine and lard until mixture forms coarse crumbs. Beat egg yolk with cold water (reserve egg white to glaze pastry); add to flour mixture and stir with a fork until pastry begins to cling together. Shape with your hands into a smooth ball. Roll out on a floured board or pastry cloth to a circle about 12 inches in diameter.

HAM AND CHEESE CRÊPES

Crêpes make a versatile (as well as delectable) entrée. These are baked in a delicate cheese sauce, complemented by a moist ham filling. (Crêpes can be made ahead and frozen, too.)

4 cups ground smoked pork shoulder picnic or ham
1 cup sour cream
3 green onions, thinly sliced (use part of tops)
2 teaspoons Dijon mustard
2 tablespoons each butter or margarine and flour
   Dash each white pepper and cayenne pepper
1 cup milk
½ cup regular-strength chicken broth (homemade or canned)
1 cup shredded Cheddar cheese
1 tablespoon dry sherry
½ cup shredded Parmesan cheese

Crêpes

1 cup unsifted flour
¾ cup water
⅔ cup milk
3 eggs
2 tablespoons salad oil
¼ teaspoon salt

1. If crêpes were made ahead and frozen, thaw them.

2. Preheat oven to 400° F. Mix ham, sour cream, onions, and mustard. Fill crêpes with ham mixture and roll up. Place them side by side, seam side down, in a buttered baking dish, about 9 by 13 inches.

3. For sauce, melt butter in a 1½-quart saucepan. Stir in flour, white pepper and cayenne; cook until bubbly. Remove from heat and gradually mix in milk and chicken broth. Return to heat and cook, stirring, until thickened and bubbly. Stir in Cheddar cheese until melted; mix in sherry.

4. Pour cheese sauce over crêpes; sprinkle with Parmesan cheese. (At this point casserole can be covered and refrigerated for several hours or overnight.)

5. Bake, uncovered, until crêpes are heated through and cheese sauce is lightly browned (20 to 30 minutes).

Serves 6 to 8.

Crêpes In blender container combine flour, water, milk, eggs, salad oil, and salt. Whirl about 1 minute at high speed; scrape down any flour clinging to sides, then whirl again briefly. Cover and refrigerate at least 1 hour. Heat a 6- to 8-inch pan, grease lightly, and pour in a small amount of batter, tilting to spread it evenly over the bottom. When brown, flip and lightly brown the other side.

BAKED CHICKEN SAVOYARD

Few French dishes lend themselves as well to advance preparation as this elegant chicken. Serve with asparagus.

> 1 *frying chicken (3 lbs), cut up (see page 11)*
> *Salt, white pepper, and ground nutmeg*
> 3 *tablespoons butter or margarine*
> 2 *teaspoons flour*
> ½ *cup each dry white wine and half-and-half*
> 1 *egg yolk*
> 1 *tablespoon lemon juice*
> ½ *cup each shredded Swiss cheese and soft French bread crumbs*
> 1 *tablespoon chopped parsley*

1. Preheat oven to 375° F. Sprinkle chicken pieces with salt, pepper, and nutmeg. In a large frying pan, brown chicken in 2 tablespoons of the butter. Remove to a shallow baking dish and arrange pieces in a single layer.

2. Stir flour into pan drippings until bubbly. Remove from heat and add wine and half-and-half, stirring to mix in browned drippings.

Return to low heat and cook, stirring, until sauce thickens slightly and boils. Meanwhile, beat egg yolk with lemon juice. Gradually stir in a little of the hot sauce. Return egg mixture to sauce; stir in cheese. Cook over very low heat until cheese melts (do not boil). Pour sauce over chicken.

3. In a small skillet melt remaining 1 tablespoon butter; add bread crumbs and parsley, and mix together. Sprinkle over chicken. (At this point, casserole can be covered and refrigerated for several hours or overnight.)

4. Bake, uncovered, until chicken is done in thickest part (test with a small knife) and topping is well browned (30 to 45 minutes). Serve immediately.

Serves 4 to 5.

Rolling out the pastry for the top crust of Old-Fashioned Deep-Dish Chicken Pie is fun for the whole family. Chicken, simmered until tender, shares the spotlight with tasty vegetables and a flaky pastry shell.

This large platter is brimming with Chicken Tetrazzini, a sturdy entrée that satisfies even the most hearty appetite. Complement this classic San Francisco dish with a full-bodied white wine such as a California Chardonnay or a French Chablis.

BAKED VEAL MEATBALLS WITH MUSHROOM SAUCE

The secret ingredient of these meatballs is—surprise!—veal. In the same oven, you might bake sweet potatoes or yams. You could even bake a dessert at the same time; apples are just right—core them, then stuff them with raisins and brown sugar.

        2   *eggs*
        1   *cup soft bread crumbs*
        1   *teaspoon poultry seasoning*
     1½   *pounds ground veal*
        1   *medium onion, very*
            finely chopped
        2   *tablespoons butter or*
            margarine
        1   *can (10¼ oz) condensed*
            cream of mushroom soup
       ⅓   *cup dry white wine or water*
        4   *to 6 medium-sized sweet*
            potatoes or yams (see Note)

1. Preheat oven to 350° F. Beat eggs; mix in bread crumbs and poultry seasoning, then lightly stir in veal and chopped onion. Shape into 1½-inch meatballs.

2. In a large frying pan, melt butter and brown meatballs on all sides. As they brown, transfer them to a 2- to 3-quart casserole. Pour off the fat. To the same pan add mushroom soup; gradually mix in wine or water, stirring until smooth. Pour sauce over meatballs. (At this point casserole can be covered and refrigerated for several hours or overnight.)

3. Bake, covered, until meatballs are browned and bubbling (about 1 hour).

Serves 4 to 6.

<u>Note</u> To prepare sweet potatoes, scrub with a stiff brush, pierce in several places with a fork, and rub lightly with butter or margarine. Arrange on oven rack around casserole to bake.

118

TURKEY ENCHILADAS

This meaty main dish makes an attractive choice for a summer-evening buffet—especially when served with gazpacho, baked red beans, and a dessert of sherbet frozen in fresh pineapple halves.

> 1 half turkey breast (2½ to 3 lbs), thawed if frozen
> 1 can (1 lb) tomatoes, coarsely chopped, liquid reserved
> 1 medium onion, finely chopped
> 1 clove garlic, minced or pressed
> 1½ teaspoons salt
> ¼ teaspoon each ground cumin and coriander
> 1 can (4 oz) diced green chiles
> 1 cup whipping cream
> 12 corn tortillas
> 1½ cups each shredded Monterey jack and Cheddar cheese
> ½ cup sour cream, mixed with 2 tablespoons milk until smooth
> Sliced ripe olives and green onions, for garnish

1. Preheat oven to 375° F. Place turkey breast in a deep frying pan or Dutch oven. Top with tomatoes and their liquid, onion, garlic, salt, cumin, and coriander. Bring to a boil, cover, reduce heat, and simmer for about 2 hours, until turkey is tender. When cool, remove bones and skin; shred turkey into bite-sized pieces (about 4 cups).

2. Bring cooking liquid to a boil; cook, uncovered, stirring occasionally, until reduced to about 2 cups; stir in green chiles. Spread sauce in an ungreased, large, shallow baking dish (about 9 by 13 inches).

3. In a small frying pan heat cream. Dip tortillas, one at a time, in hot cream until they become limp.

Fill tortillas with turkey, using about ⅓ cup for each. Roll tortillas, and place side by side in sauce in baking dish. Pour on any remaining cream. Sprinkle with a mixture of cheeses. (At this point enchiladas can be covered and refrigerated for several hours.)

4. Bake, uncovered, until enchiladas in center of dish are heated through and cheese is browned (25 to 45 minutes). Spoon sour cream over the enchiladas; sprinkle with olives and green onions, and serve.

Serves 6.

CHICKEN TETRAZZINI

Created by a legendary San Francisco chef, this combination of poultry and pasta takes many forms. It is at its best when you start with a whole chicken, simmer it in its own broth, then use the broth in the creamy sauce. Chicken Tetrazzini is a reliable dish to make ahead and refrigerate for a buffet.

> ⅓ cup butter or margarine
> 1 cup sliced mushrooms
> ⅓ cup flour
> ¾ teaspoon salt
> ⅛ teaspoon each ground nutmeg, white pepper, and paprika
> 1 cup each milk and half-and-half
> ½ cup cooked smoked pork shoulder picnic or leftover ham, cut in julienne strips
> ¼ cup dry sherry
> ½ pound spaghetti or vermicelli
> 1 cup grated Parmesan cheese

Chicken and Broth

> 1 frying chicken (3 lbs)
> 1 small onion, coarsely chopped
> 1 sprig parsley
> 1½ teaspoons salt
> ⅛ teaspoon dried thyme
> 2 cups water

1. Prepare chicken as directed below, reserving broth.

2. Preheat oven to 375° F. In a 3-quart saucepan heat butter and cook mushrooms until lightly browned. Remove with a slotted spoon and reserve. To the butter in the pan add flour, salt, nutmeg, pepper, and paprika; cook until bubbly. Remove from heat and gradually stir in 1½ cups of the reserved strained chicken broth; then mix in milk and half-and-half. Return to heat and cook, stirring constantly, until thickened and bubbly. Mix in chicken, ham, sherry, and reserved mushrooms.

3. Cook spaghetti in boiling salted water according to package directions, undercooking slightly. Drain, rinse with hot water, and drain again. Mix spaghetti with chicken and sauce. Place in a buttered 3-quart casserole; sprinkle with cheese. (At this point casserole can be covered and refrigerated for several hours or overnight.)

4. Bake, uncovered, until casserole is heated through and top browns (30 minutes to 1 hour).

Serves 6 to 8.

Chicken and Broth Cut a 3-pound frying chicken into serving pieces (see page 11). In a large frying pan or Dutch oven, combine with onion, parsley, salt, thyme, and water. Bring to a boil, reduce heat, cover, and simmer for about 1½ hours, until chicken is very tender. Strain and reserve broth. Remove chicken from bones in large pieces, discarding bones and skin.

GROUND TURKEY LASAGNE

2 pounds ground turkey,
crumbled

¼ cup butter or margarine

1 large onion, finely chopped

1 clove garlic, minced or pressed

1 can (6 oz) tomato paste

1 can (28 oz) tomatoes,
coarsely chopped, liquid
reserved

¾ cup dry white wine

2 teaspoons salt

1 teaspoon dried basil

½ teaspoon dried oregano

¼ teaspoon each ground nutmeg
and dried thyme

½ cup chopped parsley

8 ounces lasagne noodles

2 cups (1 lb) ricotta cheese

3 cups shredded Monterey
jack cheese

½ cup grated Parmesan cheese

1. Preheat oven to 350° F. In a large, deep frying pan or Dutch oven, brown turkey in heated butter. Mix in onion; continue cooking until soft. Stir in garlic, tomato paste, tomatoes and their liquid, wine, salt, basil, oregano, nutmeg, and thyme. Bring to a boil, cover, reduce heat, and simmer 20 minutes. Uncover and continue cooking, stirring occasionally, until liquid is reduced by about half (20 to 30 minutes). Remove from heat. Add parsley.

2. While sauce is cooking, cook lasagne in boiling salted water according to package directions until just tender, stirring occasionally. Drain, rinse with cold water, and drain again.

3. Grease a large, shallow baking dish about 9 by 13 inches. Spread about one third of the meat sauce into the dish; top with one third of the lasagne, then ⅔ cup ricotta cheese and 1 cup jack cheese. Repeat layers twice, ending with cheeses. Sprinkle Parmesan cheese over top. (At this point casserole may be covered and refrigerated.)

4. Bake, uncovered, until center is heated through and top is browned (35 to 45 minutes).

Serves 8 to 10.

BOHEMIAN CABBAGE ROLLS

Plump cabbage-wrapped packets of ground ham and pork are steamy and delicious. Serve with fluffy white rice.

1 egg

⅓ cup whipping cream

¼ cup soft bread crumbs

¼ teaspoon salt

⅛ teaspoon each ground
allspice, dillweed, and white
pepper

2 cups ground smoked
pork shoulder picnic or
leftover ham

½ pound ground pork

1 large green cabbage
Paprika and flour

2 tablespoons butter or
margarine

1 medium carrot, thinly sliced

1 medium tomato, peeled
and chopped

1 medium onion, finely chopped

½ cup each dry white wine
and tomato juice
Sour cream and chopped
parsley, for garnish

1. Preheat oven to 375° F. To prepare filling, beat egg with cream; mix in bread crumbs, salt, allspice, dillweed, and pepper, then lightly combine with ground meats. Set aside.

2. To prepare cabbage, cut out core and carefully separate outer 6 leaves (reserve the remainder for salad or other uses). Cut out thickest part at base of each leaf. Place leaves loosely in a large, deep frying pan; add just enough water to cover the bottom. Cover and steam just until leaves are wilted and bright green (2 to 3 minutes). Remove from pan; drain.

3. Divide filling among the 6 prepared cabbage leaves. For each cabbage bundle, fold in sides, roll up loosely, and fasten with a wooden toothpick. Sprinkle cabbage rolls lightly with paprika, then coat with flour.

4. Pour out water from pan in which cabbage was steamed. In this pan heat butter. Brown the cabbage rolls lightly on all sides, transferring them to a 2- to 3-quart casserole as they brown. Surround with carrot and tomato.

5. In pan in which cabbage was browned, cook chopped onion until it begins to brown. Mix in wine and tomato juice. Bring to a boil and cook, stirring, for 3 minutes. Pour over cabbage rolls. (At this point casserole may be covered and refrigerated overnight.)

6. Bake, uncovered, for 1 hour. Uncover and continue cooking for 15 minutes longer. To serve, spoon vegetables and sauce over cabbage rolls, and top with a dollop of sour cream and a sprinkling of parsley.

Serves 6.

Fill steamed cabbage leaves with ham mixture; fold in the sides and roll up.

Sprinkle carrot and tomato around cabbage rolls.

Cabbage rolls filled with ground ham and pork are delicious served with their sauce spooned over a bed of white rice. Top with a dollop of sour cream.

CRÊPES CANNELLONI

Crêpes can be used in place of pasta to make cannelloni—a delicate northern Italian casserole with a subtle veal and ham filling and a mild tomato-cream sauce.

- 1 mild Italian sausage (about ¼ lb)
- 1 medium onion, chopped
- ¼ cup chopped parsley
- 1 carrot, shredded
- 1 jar (2 oz) sliced pimientos
- 1 can (1 lb) tomatoes
- 1 cup regular-strength chicken broth (homemade or canned)
- 1 teaspoon dried basil
  Salt
  Crêpes (see page 117)
- 2 cups shredded Monterey jack cheese

Cream Sauce

- ¼ cup butter or margarine
- 1 small onion, finely chopped
- 3 tablespoons flour
- ¼ teaspoon ground nutmeg
- ¾ cup regular-strength chicken broth (homemade or canned)
- 1 cup milk

Veal and Ham Filling

- 1 pound ground veal or turkey, crumbled
- 1 large onion, finely chopped
- ¼ cup butter or margarine
- 1 clove garlic, minced
- 1 cup diced, cooked, smoked pork shoulder picnic or leftover ham
- 1 cup (½ lb) ricotta cheese
- ½ cup grated Parmesan cheese
- 1 egg
- ½ teaspoon salt
- ⅛ teaspoon ground nutmeg

1. Preheat oven to 400° F. Remove casing from sausage and crumble the meat. In a large frying pan, cook sausage with onion in the sausage drippings until onion is soft.

Mix in parsley, carrot, and pimientos; cook about 5 minutes longer. Add tomatoes and their liquid, chicken broth, and basil. Bring to a boil; then cook, uncovered and stirring occasionally, at a gentle boil until sauce is thick (about 30 minutes). Cool slightly.

2. Mix tomato sauce with Cream Sauce; salt to taste. Spread in an ungreased, large shallow baking dish about 9 by 13 inches.

3. Fill crêpes, using about ¼ cup of the filling for each. Roll up and place, seam side down, side by side in sauce in baking dish. Sprinkle with cheese. (At this point casserole can be covered and refrigerated for several hours or overnight.)

4. Bake until crêpes are heated through and cheese browns lightly (30 to 45 minutes).

Serves 8.

Cream Sauce Heat butter or margarine in a 1½-quart saucepan. Add onion and cook until soft but not browned. Mix in flour and nutmeg; cook until bubbly. Remove from heat and gradually stir in chicken broth and milk. Return to medium heat and cook, stirring, until thick.

Veal and Ham Filling In a large frying pan cook veal or turkey and onion in butter until onion is soft and meat loses its pink color; mix in garlic. Remove from heat. Using the fine blade of a food chopper or in food processor fitted with steel blade, grind pork shoulder picnic or leftover ham. Mix ground ham with veal mixture, then mix in ricotta cheese, Parmesan cheese, egg, salt, and nutmeg. Cover the filling and chill until ready to use.

MOROCCAN PASTILLA

Moroccan restaurants serve small portions of this as a first course, but it also makes a substantial main dish. The pastry is phyllo, the same thin dough as used in the *baklava* in the Greek dinner on page 113.

- 1 frying chicken (3 to 3½ lbs)
- 1 cup finely chopped blanched almonds
- ¼ cup granulated sugar
- 2 teaspoons ground cinnamon
- ½ teaspoon ground ginger
- ¼ teaspoon each ground nutmeg and cardamom
- 1 small onion, finely chopped
- 1 cup butter or margarine
- 6 eggs
- 2 cloves garlic, minced or pressed
- 1 teaspoon salt
- ¼ teaspoon pepper
- ¼ cup finely chopped parsley
- ½ pound (half a 1-lb package) phyllo dough, thawed if frozen
- ¼ cup confectioners' sugar
  Ground cinnamon, for garnish

1. Simmer the chicken, preparing it and broth as in recipe for Chicken Tetrazzini (page 119). Reserve broth for another use.

2. Preheat oven to 350° F. Place almonds in a shallow baking pan; bake, stirring occasionally, until golden brown (10 to 15 minutes). Cool. In a small bowl mix granulated sugar, the 2 teaspoons cinnamon, ginger, nutmeg, and cardamom.

3. In a large frying pan, cook onion in 3 tablespoons of the butter until limp but not browned. Meanwhile, in a medium bowl beat eggs with garlic, salt, pepper, and parsley. Add to onion mixture and cook over low heat, stirring occasionally, until eggs are softly set. Remove from heat.

4. Melt remaining butter. Use it to brush a 9-inch springform pan generously. Unfold sheets of phyllo dough so they lie flat. Cover with waxed paper, then a damp towel, to prevent them from drying out. Line pan with 1 sheet of dough, allowing dough to extend over edge of pan; brush generously with butter. Top with a second sheet of dough and brush with butter. Fold 6 more sheets of dough to fit pan and stack them one atop the other, brushing each with butter, within the pan.

5. For filling, arrange a layer of prepared chicken, egg mixture, and then toasted almonds. Sprinkle sugar-and-spice mixture over almonds.

6. Fold remaining sheets of phyllo dough to fit pan. Reserve 2 of them for topping; stack phyllo over almonds, brushing each with butter. Fold edges of phyllo that extend beyond the pan in toward the center. Top with the last 2 sheets, folded to fit pan; tuck any protruding edges down inside pan rim. Brush with remaining butter. Using a razor blade or small sharp knife, cut through top layers of dough down to the almonds to mark pie in 8 wedge shapes. (At this point, you can cover and refrigerate the pie for several hours or until you are ready to bake it.)

7. Bake until well browned and heated through (45 minutes to 1 hour). Remove pan sides. Sift confectioners' sugar over pie, then about ½ teaspoon cinnamon. Serve immediately; cut in the marked wedges.

Serves 8.

Made with delicate phyllo dough, a common ingredient for many Middle Eastern cuisines, Moroccan Pastilla makes for an exotic Sunday brunch. This dish combines the light flavor of chicken with a nutty mixture of almonds, cinnamon, ginger, nutmeg, and cardamom in a crisp shell.

INDEX

Note: Page numbers in italics refer to illustrations separated from recipe text.

A

Appetizer, Eggplant Caviar, 78, *79*
Avgolemono (Lemon and Rice Soup), 112, *113*

B

Bacon, 6
  Canadian-style, timetable, 18
  in Gascon Beans and Chicken Gizzards, 96-97
  Skewered Swiss-Style Liver and, 32
Baked Chicken Savoyard, 117
Baked Frankfurters and Lentils, 115
Baked Meatballs in Red Wine, 106-7
Baked Stuffed Eggplant, 109
Baked Veal Meatballs with Mushroom Sauce, 118
Baklava, 113
Barbecued Chicken Picnic, 36, *37*
Barbecued Pork Buns, 35
Barbecuing, 35-41
  as dry-heat cooking, 6
  Barbecued Pork Buns, 35
  Lemon-Barbecued Lamb Shoulder Chops, 41
  marinades for, 41
  Mexican Barbecued Top Round, *38*, 39
  Mustard-Barbecued Chicken Legs, 36, *37*
  sauces for, 20, 41
  Skewered Pork and Red Pepper, 40
Barbecue Sauce, 20
  Tomato, 41
Barley
  Dilled Lamb and Barley Soup, 66
  Ruth's Barley and White Bean Soup, 65
  Turkey and Barley Soup, 77
Beans
  See also Lentils; Peas
  Chili Bean Soup, 65
  Gascon Beans and Chicken Gizzards, 96-97
  Ham and Lima Bean Pot, 98
  Joyce's New Orleans Red Beans and Rice, 91
  Refried Beans with Cheese, *38*, 39
  Rolled Lamb Shoulder with White Beans, 23
  Round Steak and Kidney Beans, 95
  Ruth's Barley and White Bean Soup, 65
  Slow-Cooker Corned Beef and Lentils, 99
  Spanish Garbanzo and Spinach Soup, 71
Beef
  See also Meats
  bottom round, 8, 10
    Beef Baked in Beer, 100
    Round Steak and Kidney Beans, 10, 95
    Sauerbraten-Style Steak Strips, 10, 84
  brisket, 6, 8

Corned Beef and Cabbage Soup, 64
Pot au Feu, 86, *87*
Slow-Cooker Corned Beef and Lentils, 99
broiled, 32, 34-35
Broth or Concentrate, 13
buying, 6-10, 13
chuck, 6, 8, 9
  Beef Stroganoff, 42
  Burgundy Beef Stew, 9, 83
  Caraway Beef Paprika, 84
  Chuck Roast Marinated in Beer, 19
  Gypsy-Style Steak, 9, 43
  Herb-Crusted Cross Rib Roast, 16
  Italian-Style Roast Beef with Baked Vegetables, 17
  Milanese Vegetable-Beef Soup, 62-63
  Mustard and Pepper Steak, 9, 45
  Oven Beef Stew, 94
  Spicy Alsatian Meat and Vegetable Stew, 96
  Steak and Onions for Two, 42
  Steak with Tangy Herb Butter, 44
concentrate, 13
  in Baked Meatballs in Red Wine, 106-7
  in Chicken, Hunter's Style, 91
  in Savory Oven Pork Stew, 95
cuts of, 6, 8, 9-10
eye of round, 8, 9, 10
  Braised Eye of Round Steaks, 9, 86
  Elegant Eye of Round Steaks, 9, 45
flank, 6, 8
  Gingered Flank Steak with Snow Peas, 56-57
foreshank. *See* shanks
gravy, 28
ground
  Baked Meatballs in Red Wine, 106-7
  Baked Stuffed Eggplant, 109
  Beef and Sauerkraut Buns, 106
  Easy Eggplant Soup, 69
  Garden Fresh Spaghetti Sauce, 104
  Giant Stuffed Hamburger Steaks with Tangy Sauce, 32
  Greek Ground Beef and Macaroni Casserole, 108
  Ground Beef and Spinach Stuffing, 24
  Hamburgers au Poivre, 46
  Joe's Special, 42
  Meatball and Ravioli Soup, 62
  Mediterranean Parslied Meat-balls, 46
  Mushroom-Stuffed Meat Loaf, 18
  Pizza Loaf in French Bread, 115
  Scandinavian Meatballs, 47
  Stuffed Green Peppers Mexicana, 109
  Stuffed Pasta with Tomato Sauce, 105
  Stuffed Zucchini Provençale, 107
kidneys, in Steak and Kidney Pie, 110, *111*
liver
  Alpine Liver Strips in Wine Cream Sauce, 46

Quick Liver and Mushrooms, 45
Swiss-Style Skewered Liver and Bacon, 32
oxtails, 6
  Curried Oxtails in Clay, 101
  Sherried Oxtail Soup, 68
roast, 15-16, 18, 21
  Roast Beef Hash with Fried Eggs, 21
rump roast, 6, 8, 18
  Piedmontese Pot Roast, 99
  Soy and Sesame Roast, 16
servings per pound, 6
shanks, 6, 8
  Beef and Sauerkraut Soup, 60
  Beefy French Onion Soup, 60, *61*
  in Kentucky Burgoo, 84-85
  Savory Braised, 82
short ribs, 6, 8
  Baked Short Ribs with Poppy Seed Noodles, 20
  Hungarian Goulash Soup, *74*, 75
  Mexican Short Ribs, 89
  Short Ribs and Celery Root Soup, 67
sirloin tip, 6, 8
  Sirloin Tip Roast with Oven-Browned Potatoes and Stuffed Mushroom Caps, 21
skillet dishes, 42-45, 46-47
stews
  Beef and Eggplant Sauté, 85
  Beef Baked in Beer, 100
  Beef Rolls Provençale, 88
  Braised Eye of Round Steaks, 9, 86
  Burgundy Beef Stew, 9, 82
  Caraway Beef Paprika, 84
  Curried Oxtails in Clay, 101
  Kentucky Burgoo, 84-85
  Mexican Short Ribs, 89
  Oven Beef Stew, 94
  Piedmontese Pot Roast, 99
  Pot au Feu, 86, *87*
  Rosemary Round Steak, 99
  Sauerbraten-Style Steak Strips, 84
  Savory Braised Beef Shanks, 82
  Spicy Alsatian Meat and Vegetable Stew, 96
  Slow-Cooker Corned Beef and Lentils, 99
Swiss steak, 10
top round, 8, 10
  Beef and Eggplant Sauté, 85
  Beef Fondue, 48
  Broiled Steak Satay with Pineapple, 34
  Marinated London Broil, 35
  Mexican Barbecued Top Round, *38*, 39
  Rosemary Round Steak, 99
  Shish Kebab Sauté, 10, 52
  Steak and Kidney Pie, 110, *111*
Beef Baked in Beer, 100
Beef broth, 9, 13
Beef concentrate, 13
  in Baked Meatballs in Red Wine, 106-7
  in Chicken, Hunter's Style, 91
  in Savory Oven Pork Stew, 95

Beef and Eggplant Sauté, 85
Beef Fondue, 10, 48
Beef Rolls Provençale, 88
Beef and Sauerkraut Buns, 106
Beef and Sauerkraut Soup, 60
Beef Stroganoff, 9, 42
Beefy French Onion Soup, 60, *61*
Beer
  Beef Baked in, 100
  Chuck Roast Marinated in, 18
Beets
  Beet and Herring Salad, 68
  Lamb-Bone Borsch, 78
Beverage, Easy Sangria, 39
Bohemian Cabbage Rolls, 120, *121*
Boiled dinner, Pot au Feu, 86, *87*
Boning
  chicken breasts, 11
  lamb shoulder roast, 23
  picnic shoulder, 26
  turkey breast, 55
Borsch, Lamb-Bone, 79
Braised Eye of Round Steaks, 9, 86
Braising, 6, 82
Breads
  Beef and Sauerkraut Buns, 106
  Buttermilk Rye Bread, 68-69
Broiling, 6, 32-35
  Broiled Steak Satay with Pineapple, 34
  Marinated London Broil, 35
  Russian Marinated Lamb on Skewers, *30*, 33
Brown gravy, 28
Brownies, Date and Walnut, 76
Burgundy Beef Stew, 9, 83
Burrito filling, Mexican Pork with Green Chiles, 86-87
Butter, Herb, 44
Buttermilk Rye Bread, 68-69
Buying meats, 6-10, 13
Buying poultry, 10

C

Cabbage Rolls, Bohemian, 120, *121*
Cakes. *See* Desserts
Canadian-style bacon, roasting timetable, 18
Cannelloni, Crêpes, 122
Caraway Beef Paprika, 84
Carbonnade, 100
Caviar, Eggplant, 78, *79*
Celery Root and Short Ribs Soup, 67
Cheese, Refried Beans with, *38*, 39
Cheese sauces
  for Ham and Cheddar Pie, 111
  Parmesan, 109
Cherry Streusel Pie, 78
Chicken
  See also Poultry
  Arlésienne, 88
  Baked, Savoyard, 117
  breasts
    boning, 11
    Chicken Breasts and Broth, 72
    Chicken Breasts with Grapes, 54-55

Chicken Breasts with Mushrooms, Swiss Cheese, and White Wine, 53
Fruited Chicken en Brochette, 35
Hungarian Chicken Breasts, 53
Szechwan Chicken and Peanuts, 57
Velvety Chicken and Mushroom Soup, 72
Broth, 13
and Broth, 119
buying, 10
Country Captain, 97
cutting up, 10, 11
Gizzards, Gascon Beans and, 96-97
gravy, 28
Honey-Glazed Baked Chicken Quarters, 26, *27*
Hot Chicken and Green Chile Salad, 114
Hunter's Style, 91
    in Kentucky Burgoo, 84-85
legs
    Hunter's Style, 91
    Mustard-Barbecued, 36, *37*
    and Lentils in Clay, *100*, 101
Livers, Spaghetti with, 55
Moroccan Pastilla, 122-23
Pie, Old-Fashioned Deep-Dish, *102*, 116, *117*
Piquant Roast Chicken Halves, 28
roasting, 16, 18, 26-28
Sausage-Stuffed Roast, 28
Singapore, 96
skillet dishes, 53-55
soups
    Chicken and Escarole Soup, *58*, 72
    Flemish Chicken Soup, 73
    Velvety Chicken and Mushroom Soup, 72
stews
    Chicken and Lentils in Clay, *100*, 101
    Chicken Arlésienne, 88
    Chicken, Hunter's Style, 91
    Country Captain, 97
    Gascon Beans and Chicken Gizzards, 96-97
    Kentucky Burgoo, 84-85
    Singapore Chicken, 96
    Yankee Clipper Chicken, 98
Tetrazzini, *118*, 119
Wings, Sweet-and-Sour, 53
Yankee Clipper, 98
Chili Bean Soup, 65
Choice meats, 7, 9
Chowder, Fresh Corn and Polish Sausage, 65
Chuck Roast Marinated in Beer, 19
Cider-Glazed Spareribs Flamed in Bourbon, *14*, 25
Clay-pot stews, 100-101
    Beef Baked in Beer, 100
    Chicken and Lentils in Clay, *100*, 101
    Curried Oxtails in Clay, 101
    Italian Veal Shanks in Tomato Sauce, 101
Cornbread Dressing, 29
Corned beef
    Corned Beef and Cabbage Soup, 64
    Slow-Cooker Corned Beef and Lentils, 99
Cornish Hens, Flaming, on a Spit, 29
Corn and Polish Sausage Chowder, 65
Country Captain, 97
Country-Style Spareribs in Ratatouille, 98
Cream sauces
    for Baked Stuffed Eggplant, 109
    for Crêpes Cannelloni, 122

Custard, for Greek Ground Beef and Macaroni Casserole, 108
    for Moussaka, 112
    Parmesan cheese, 109
Creamy Pork and Apple Sauté, 49
Crêpes, 117
    Cannelloni, 122
    Ham and Cheese, 116-17
Cross rib roast
    Herb-Crusted, 16
    Italian-Style Roast Beef with Baked Vegetables, 17
Crumbled Cornbread Dressing, 29
Curried Oxtails in Clay, 101
Curries
    Country Captain, 97
    Fruited Lamb, *90*, 91
Custard Cream Sauce, for Greek Ground Beef and Macaroni Casserole, 108

D
Date and Walnut Brownies, 76
Daube, 95
Desserts
    Baklava, 113
    Cherry Streusel Pie, 78
    Date and Walnut Brownies, 76
    Fresh Lemon Bars, 75
    Orange Chiffon Cake with Strawberries and Cream, 36
    Orange-Lemon Pound Cake, 51
Diamond Jim roast, 16
Dressings. *See* Stuffings
Dry-heat cooking, 6

E
Easy Eggplant Soup, 69
Easy Individual Pizzas, 104
Easy Sangria, 39
Eggplant
    Baked Stuffed, 109
    Beef and Eggplant Sauté, 85
    Caviar, 78, *79*
    in Country-Style Spareribs in Ratatouille, 98
    Lamb and Eggplant Casserole, 115
    Moussaka, 112, *113*
    Soup, Easy, 69
Elegant Eye of Round Steaks, 9, 45
Enchiladas, Turkey, 119
English pub pies, 110-11
Escarole and Chicken Soup, 72

F
Fillings
    Ham, in Beef Rolls Provençale, 88
    Veal and Ham, for Crêpes Cannelloni, 122
Flaming Cornish Hens on a Spit, 29
Flemish Chicken Soup, 73
Frankfurters, Baked with Lentils, 115
Freezing
    meat and poultry, 12
    soups, 71
French Onion Soup, Beefy, 60, *61*
Fresh Corn and Polish Sausage Chowder, 65
Fresh Lemon Bars, 75
Fricassees, 82
Fruited Chicken en Brochette, 35
Fruited Lamb Curry, *90*, 91
Frying, as dry-heat cooking, 6

G
Garbanzo and Spinach Soup, 71
Garden Fresh Spaghetti Sauce, 104
Garden Potato Salad, 36
Garlic Mayonnaise, 48
Gascon Beans and Chicken Gizzards, 96-97
Giant Stuffed Hamburger Steaks with Tangy Sauce, 32
Gingered Flank Steak with Snow Peas, 56-57
Glazed Fresh Picnic Shoulder Roast, 26
Golden Chicken Broth, 13
Golden Turkey Breast Parmigiana, 55
Goodbye-to-the-Thanksgiving-Turkey Soup, 71
Good meats, 7, 9
Gravy, 13, 28
Greek Dinner for Six, 112-13
Greek Ground Beef and Macaroni Casserole, 108
Greek Meatball and Zucchini Soup, 70
Green Peppers Mexicana, 109
Green Split Pea Soup with Ham Hocks, 66
Grilling, as dry-heat cooking, 6
Ground meats. *See specific meats*
Gypsy-Style Steak, 9, 43

H
Ham, 6
    in Bohemian Cabbage Rolls, 120
    in Burgundy Beef Stew, 83
    and Cheddar Pie, 111
    and Cheese Crêpes, 116-17
    in Chicken Tetrazzini, 119
    in Crêpes Cannelloni, 122
    filling, in Beef Rolls Provençale, 88
    in Green Split Pea Soup with Ham Hocks, 66
    in Joyce's New Orleans Red Beans and Rice, 91
    and Lima Bean Pot, 98
    roasting timetable, 18
    in Spanish Garbanzo and Spinach Soup, 71
    in Swedish Yellow Split Pea Soup, 66
Hamburgers au Poivre, 46
Hash, Roast Beef, with Fried Eggs, 21
Herb Butter, 44
Herb-Crusted Cross Rib Roast, 16
Honey and Rose Water Syrup, for Baklava, 113
Honey-Glazed Baked Chicken Quarters, 26, *27*
Horseradish Sauce, 16
Hot Chicken and Green Chile Salad, 114
Hungarian Chicken Breasts, 53
Hungarian Goulash Soup Supper, *74*, 75

I
Italian sausage
    in Crêpes Cannelloni, 122
    on Easy Individual Pizzas, 104
Italian Veal Sauté, 49
Italian Veal Shanks in Tomato Sauce, 101

J
Joe's Special, 42
Joyce's New Orleans Red Beans and Rice, 91

K
Kentucky Burgoo, 84-85
Kidney Beans, Round Steak and, 95
Kidneys
    Steak and Kidney Pie, 110, *111*
    Veal, in Sherry and Mustard Sauce, 49

L
Lamb
    See also Meats
    -Bone Borsch, 79
    boning, 23
    breast of, 6
    broiled, *30*, 33
    cuts of, 6
    ground
        Greek Meatball and Zucchini Soup, 70
        Ground Lamb in Pita Bread, 50
        Lamb and Eggplant Casserole, 115
        Moussaka, 112, *113*
    kidneys, in Steak and Kidney Pie, 110
    leg of, 6
    roasting, 16, 18
    servings per pound, 6
    shanks
        Dilled Lamb and Barley Soup, 66
        with Honey and Spices, 93
        in Kentucky Burgoo, 84-85
        servings per pound, 6
        in Spicy Alsatian Meat and Vegetable Stew, 96
    shoulder chops, Lemon-Barbecued, 41
    shoulder roast
        boning, 23
        Fruited Lamb Curry, *90*, 91
        Lamb with Five-Spice and Green Onions, 56
        Rolled Lamb Shoulder with White Beans, 23
        Russian Marinated Lamb on Skewers, *30*, 33
        Sautéed Lamb with Spring Vegetables, 92
        Stuffed Lamb Shoulder Provençale, 22
    stews, 84-85, *90*, 91, 92, 93, 96
        Fruited Lamb Curry, *90*, 91
        Kentucky Burgoo, 84-85
        Lamb Shanks with Honey and Spices, 93
        Sautéed Lamb with Spring Vegetables, 92
        Spicy Alsatian Meat and Vegetable Stew, 96
Lamb-Bone Borsch, 79
Lamb Borsch Supper, 78-79
Lasagne, Ground Turkey, 120
Lemon-Barbecued Lamb Shoulder Chops, 41
Lemon Bars, Fresh, 75
Lemon Mayonnaise, 50
Lemon and Rice Soup (*Avgolemono*), 112, *113*
Lentils
    Baked Frankfurters and Lentils, 115
    Chicken and Lentils in Clay, *100*, 101
    Slow-Cooker Corned Beef and Lentils, 99

Lima beans, in Ham and Lima Bean Pot, 98
Liver, beef
  Alpine Liver Strips in Wine Cream Sauce, 46
  Quick Liver and Mushrooms, 45
  Swiss-Style Skewered Liver and Bacon, 32
Livers, Chicken, Spaghetti with, 55
London broil, 6
  Marinated, 35

M

Macaroni, in Greek Ground Beef and Macaroni Casserole, 108
Make-ahead dishes, 103-23
  Baked Chicken Savoyard, 117
  Baked Frankfurters and Lentils, 115
  Baked Meatballs in Red Wine, 106-7
  Baked Stuffed Eggplant, 109
  Baked Veal Meatballs with Mushroom Sauce, 118
  Beef and Eggplant Sauté, 85
  Beef and Sauerkraut Buns, 106
  Bohemian Cabbage Rolls, 120, *121*
  Chicken Tetrazzini, *118*, 119
  cooking time and temperature, 104
  Crêpes Cannelloni, 122
  Easy Individual Pizzas, 104
  English pub pies, 110-11
  Garden Fresh Spaghetti Sauce, 104
  Greek Ground Beef and Macaroni Casserole, 108
  Ground Turkey Lasagne, 120
  Ham and Cheddar Pie, 111
  Ham and Cheese Crêpes, 116-17
  Hot Chicken and Green Chile Salad, 114
  Lamb and Eggplant Casserole, 115
  menu planning, 104
  Moroccan Pastilla, 122-23
  Moussaka, 112, *113*
  Old-Fashioned Deep-Dish Chicken Pie, *102*, 116
  Pizza Loaf in French Bread, 115
  Steak and Kidney Pie, 110, *111*
  Stuffed Green Peppers Mexicana, 109
  Stuffed Pasta with Tomato Sauce, 105
  Stuffed Zucchini Provençale, 107
  Traditional English Pork Pies, 110, *111*
  Turkey Enchiladas, 119
  Velvety Chicken and Mushroom Soup, 72
Manicotti, Stuffed, with Tomato Sauce, 105
Marbling, 9
Marinades
  Mustard and Herb, 41
  Red Wine, 52
  Teriyaki, 41
  Tomato Barbecue Sauce, 41
Marinated meats or poultry
  Barbecued Pork Buns, 35
  Beef Fondue, 10
  Broiled Steak Satay with Pineapple, 34
  Chuck Roast Marinated in Beer, 19
  Fruited Chicken en Brochette, 35
  Lemon-Barbecued Lamb Shoulder Chops, 41

Marinated London Broil, 35
Mexican Barbecued Top Round, *38*, 39
Russian Marinated Lamb on Skewers, *30*, 33
Shish Kebab Sauté, 10, 52
Skewered Pork and Red Pepper, 40
Soy and Sesame Roast, 16
Tangy Marinated Roast Pork Butt, 24
Mayonnaise
  Lemon, 50
  Spicy Garlic, 48
Meatballs
  Baked in Red Wine, 106-7
  Baked Veal Meatballs with Mushroom Sauce, 118
  Greek Meatball and Zucchini Soup, 70
  Meatball and Ravioli Soup, 62
  Mediterranean Parslied, 46
  Scandinavian, 47
Meat loaf
  Harvest Veal or Turkey, 21
  Mushroom-Stuffed, 18
Meats
  See also specific meats
  basic cooking methods, 6
  color, 9
  cuts of, 6-8
  fat cover, 9
  freezing, 12
  grades, 7, 9
  inspection marks, 7
  labels, 7, 9
  marbling, 9
  roasting timetable, 18
  servings per pound, 6
  storing, 12, 13
  tenderizing, 6, 88
  thawing, 12-13
  toughness, 6
  wrapping, 12
Meat thermometer, 16
Mediterranean Parslied Meatballs, 46
Menus
  advance planning, 104
  Barbecued Chicken Picnic, 36, *37*
  Greek Dinner for Six, 112-13
  Hungarian Goulash Soup Supper, *74*, 75
  Lamb Borsch Supper, 78-79
  Mexican Steak Barbecue, *38*, 39
  Oxtail Soup Supper, 68-69
  Pita Bread Sandwich Party, 50-51
  Turkey and Barley Soup Supper, 76-77
Mexican Pork with Green Chiles, 86-87
Mexican Short Ribs, 89
Mexican soup, 65
Mexican Steak Barbecue, *38*, 39
Mexican Stuffed Green Peppers, 109
Milanese Vegetable-Beef Soup, 62-63
Minestrone, 62
Moist-heat cooking, 6
Moroccan Lamb Shanks with Honey and Spices, 93
Moroccan Pastilla, 122-23

Moussaka, 112, *113*
Muffins, Spicy Pumpkin, 76, 77
Mushrooms
  Mushroom-Stuffed Meat Loaf, 18
  Stuffed Mushroom Caps, 21
  Velvety Chicken and Mushroom Soup, 72
Mustard and Herb Marinade, 41
Mustard and Pepper Steak, 9, 45
Mustard-Barbecued Chicken Legs, 36, *37*

N

National Livestock and Meat Board, 9
New York steak, 6

O

Onion Soup, Beefy French, 60, *61*
Orange Chiffon Cake with Strawberries and Cream, 36
Orange-Lemon Pound Cake, 51
Osso buco, 101
Oven stews, 93-99
  Country Captain, 97
  Country-Style Spareribs in Ratatouille, 98
  Gascon Beans and Chicken Gizzards, 96-97
  Lamb Shanks with Honey and Spices, 93
  Oven Beef Stew, 94
  Rich Red Spareribs, 95
  Round Steak and Kidney Beans, 95
  Savory Oven Pork Stew, 95
  Singapore Chicken, 96
  Spicy Alsatian Meat and Vegetable Stew, 96
  Yankee Clipper Chicken, 98
Oxtails
  Curried Oxtails in Clay, 101
  Oxtail Soup Supper, 68-69

P

Pan-broiling, 6, 42
Pan-frying, 42
Pasta
  Chicken Tetrazzini, *118*, 119
  Garden Fresh Spaghetti Sauce for, 104
  Greek Ground Beef and Macaroni Casserole, 108
  Ground Turkey Lasagne, 120
  Meatball and Ravioli Soup, 62
  Spaghetti with Chicken Livers, Stuffed, with Tomato Sauce, 105
Pastilla, Moroccan, 122-23
Pastitsio, 108
Pastries. *See* Pies and pastries
Peas
  Fresh, Veal Stew with, *80*, 92
  Green Split Pea Soup with Ham Hocks, 66
  Swedish Yellow Split Pea Soup, 66
Phyllo dough
  in Baklava, 113
  in Moroccan Pastilla, 122-23
Picnic shoulder. *See* Pork, picnic shoulder
Piedmontese Pot Roast, 99
Pies and pastries
  Baklava, 113
  Cherry Streusel, 78
  Ham and Cheddar, 111
  Old-Fashioned Deep-Dish Chicken, *102*, 116
  Steak and Kidney, 110, *111*
  Traditional English Pork, 110, *111*
Piquant Roast Chicken Halves, 28
Pita Bread, Ground Lamb in, 50

Pita Bread Sandwich party, 50-51
Pizza Loaf in French Bread, 115
Pizzas, Easy Individual, 104
Polish sausage
  Fresh Corn and Polish Sausage Chowder, 65
  in Gascon Beans and Chicken Gizzards, 96-97
Pork
  See also Bacon; Ham; Meats; Sausage
  butt, 6
    Barbecued Pork Buns, 35
    Creamy Pork and Apple Sauté, 49
    Mexican Pork with Green Chiles, 86-87
    Pork with Tofu, 56
    Roast Pork with Mustard Potatoes, 26
    Skewered Pork and Red Pepper, 40
    in Spicy Alsatian Meat and Vegetable Stew, 96
    Tangy Marinated Roast Pork Butt, 24
    Traditional English Pork Pies, 110, *111*
  buying, 6, 8, 9, 10
  cuts of, 6, 8, 10
  fresh hocks, in Kentucky Burgoo, 84-85
  gravy, 28
  ground
    Bohemian Cabbage Rolls, 120, *121*
    in Garden Fresh Spaghetti Sauce, 104
    in Scandinavian Meatballs, 47
  leg, 6
    cutting up, 10
  picnic shoulder (fresh), 6
    boning, 26
    cutting up, 10
    Glazed Fresh Picnic Shoulder Roast, 26
    roasting timetable, 18
  shoulder picnic (smoked), 26
    in Beef Rolls Provençale, 88
    in Bohemian Cabbage Rolls, 120
    in Burgundy Beef Stew, 83
    in Chicken Tetrazzini, 119
    in Crêpes Cannelloni, 122
    Ham and Lima Bean Pot, 98
    roasting timetable, 18
    in Spanish Garbanzo and Spinach Soup, 71
  roasting, 16, 18
  servings per pound, 6
  spareribs, 6
    Cider-Glazed Spareribs Flamed in Bourbon, *14*, 25
    Country-Style Spareribs in Ratatouille, 98
    Rich Red Spareribs, 95
    Roast Country-Style Spareribs with Sauerkraut, 25
    Savory Oven Pork Stew, 95
  stews
    Country-Style Spareribs in Ratatouille, 98
    Kentucky Burgoo, 84-85
    Mexican Pork with Green Chiles, 86-87
    Rich Red Spareribs, 95
    Savory Oven Pork, 95
    Spicy Alsatian Meat and Vegetable Stew, 96

Porterhouse steak, 6, 8
Potato Salad, Garden, 36
Pot au Feu, 86, *87*
Pot Roast, Piedmontese, 99
Poultry, 10-13
   See also Chicken; Turkey
   Flaming Cornish Hens on a Spit, 29
   freezing, 12
   roasting, 16, 18, 26-29
   servings per pound, 6
      storing, 12, 13
   thawing, 12-13
Pounding, 6, 88
Prime meats, 7

Q

Quick-cooking dishes. *See* Skillet dishes
Quick-cooking soups
   Easy Eggplant Soup, 69
   Fresh Corn and Polish Sausage
      Chowder, 65
   Quick Italian Sausage and Bean Soup,
      62
Quick Liver and Mushrooms, 45

R

Ratatouille, Country-Style Spareribs in, 98
Ravioli and Meatball Soup, 62
Red beans. *See* Beans
Red Wine Marinade, 52
Refried Beans with Cheese, *38*, 39
Rice
   Golden Rice Salad, 50
   Joyce's New Orleans Red Beans and Rice,
      91
   Lemon and Rice Soup (*Avgolemono*),
      112, *113*
   Tomato-Rice Casserole, *38*, 39
Rich Beef Broth or Concentrate, 13
Rich Red Spareribs, 95
Roast chicken
   Honey-Glazed Baked Chicken Quarters,
      26, *27*
   Piquant Roast Chicken Halves, 28
   Sausage-Stuffed, 28
Roast Country-Style Spareribs with
   Sauerkraut, 25
Roasting, 15-16
   See also specific meats
   as dry-heat cooking, 6
   gravy for, 28
   timetable, 18
Roast Pork with Mustard Potatoes, 26
Roast Rock Cornish game hens, 29
Roast Turkey with Cornbread Dressing, 29
Rolled Lamb Shoulder with White Beans,
   23
Rosemary Round Steak, 99
Round Steak and Kidney Beans, 10, 95
Russian Marinated Lamb on Skewers, *30*,
   33
Ruth's Barley and White Bean Soup, 65
Rye Bread, Buttermilk, 68-69

S

Salads
   Beet and Herring, 68
   Garden Potato, 36
   Golden Rice, 50
   Hot Chicken and Green Chile, 114
Sangria, Easy, 39

Sauces
   Barbecue, 20, 41
   Cheese
      for Ham and Cheddar Pie, 111
      Parmesan, 109
   Cream
      for Baked Stuffed Eggplant, 109
      for Crêpes Cannelloni, 122
      for Moussaka, 112
   Custard Cream, for Greek Ground Beef
      and Macaroni Casserole, 108
   Garden Fresh Spaghetti, 104
   Horseradish, 16
   Lemon Mayonnaise, 50
   Spicy Garlic Mayonnaise, 48
   stocks for, 13
   Tangy, 32
   Tomato, Stuffed Pasta with, 105
   Tomato Barbecue, 41
Sauerbraten-Style Steak Strips, 10, 84
Sauerkraut, in Beef and Sauerkraut Buns,
   106
Sausage
   Italian
      in Crêpes Cannelloni, 122
      on Easy Individual Pizzas, 104
      Quick Italian Sausage and Bean Soup,
         62
   Polish
      Fresh Corn and Polish Sausage
         Chowder, 65
      in Gascon Beans and Chicken
         Gizzards, 96-97
      in Round Steak and Kidney Beans, 95
Sausage-Stuffed Roast Chicken, 28
Sautéed Lamb with Spring Vegetables, 92
Sautéing, defined, 42
Savory Braised Beef Shanks, 82
Savory Oven Pork Stew, 95
Scandinavian Meatballs, 47
Sesame seeds, toasting and grinding, 34
Sherried Oxtail Soup, 68
Shish Kebab Sauté, 10, 52
Short ribs
   Baked, with Poppy Seed Noodles, 20
   and Celery Root Soup, 67
   Hungarian Goulash Soup, *74*, 75
   Mexican, 89
Simmering, as moist-heat cooking, 6
Singapore Chicken, 96
Skewered Pork and Red Pepper, 39
Skillet dishes
   Beef Stroganoff, 42
   Chicken Breasts with Grapes, 54-55
   Chicken Breasts with Mushrooms, Swiss
      Cheese, and White Wine, 53
   Creamy Pork and Apple Sauté, 49
   Elegant Eye of Round Steaks, 45
   Golden Turkey Breast Parmigiana, 55
   Ground Lamb in Pita Bread, 50
   Gypsy-Style Steak, 43
   Hamburgers au Poivre, 46
   Hungarian Chicken Breasts, 53
   Italian Veal Sauté, 49
   Joe's Special, 42
   Mediterranean Parslied Meatballs, 46
   Mustard and Pepper Steak, 45
   Quick Liver and Mushrooms, 45
   Scandinavian Meatballs, 47
   Shish Kebab Sauté, 10, 52
   Spaghetti with Chicken Livers, 55
   Steak and Onions for Two, 42
   Steak with Tangy Herb Butter, 44
   Sweet-and-Sour Chicken Wings, 53
   Veal Kidneys in Sherry and Mustard
      Sauce, 49

Slow-cooker stews, 98-99
   Corned Beef and Lentils, 99
   Ham and Lima Bean Pot, 98
   Piedmontese Pot Roast, 99
   Rosemary Round Steak, 99
Soups, 59-79
   Beef and Sauerkraut, 60
   Beefy French Onion, 60, *61*
   Chicken and Escarole, *58*, 72
   Chili Bean, 65
   Corned Beef and Cabbage, 64
   Dilled Lamb and Barley, 66
   Easy Eggplant, 69
   Flemish Chicken, 73
   freezing, 71
   Fresh Corn and Polish Sausage
      Chowder, 65
   Goodbye-to-the-Thanksgiving-Turkey,
      71
   Greek Meatball and Zucchini, 70
   Green Split Pea, with Ham Hocks, 66
   Hungarian Goulash, *74*, 75
   Lamb-Bone Borsch, 79
   Lemon and Rice (*Avgolemono*), 112,
      113
   Meatball and Ravioli, 62
   Milanese Vegetable-Beef, 62-63
   Quick Italian Sausage and Bean, 62
   Ruth's Barley and White Bean, 65
   Sherried Oxtail, 68
   Short Ribs and Celery Root, 67
   Spanish Garbanzo and Spinach, 71
   Swedish Yellow Split Pea, 66
   Turkey and Barley, 77
   Velvety Chicken and Mushroom, 72
Soup stocks, 9, 13
Soy and Sesame Roast, 16
Spaghetti
   with Chicken Livers, 55
   Chicken Tetrazzini, *118*, 119
   Garden Fresh Sauce for, 104
Spanish Garbanzo and Spinach Soup, 71
Spareribs, 6
   Cider-Glazed, Flamed in Bourbon, *14*,
      25
   Country-Style, in Ratatouille, 98
   Rich Red, 95
   Roast Country-Style, with Sauerkraut, 25
   roasting, 18
   Savory Oven Pork Stew, 95
   servings per pound, 6
   Spicy Alsatian Meat and Vegetable Stew,
      96
Spicy Garlic Mayonnaise, 48
Spicy Pumpkin Muffins, 76, 77
Spinach
   in Joe's Special, 42
   Spanish Garbanzo and Spinach Soup,
      70
   Spinach-Stuffed Breast of Veal, 24
Split peas
   Green Split Pea Soup with Ham Hocks,
      66
   Swedish Yellow Split Pea Soup, 66
Steak, 9
   Braised Eye of Round, 9, 86
   Broiled Steak Satay with Pineapple, 34
   Elegant Eye of Round, 9, 45
   Gingered Flank Steak with Snow Peas,
      56-57
   Gypsy-Style, 9, 43
   and Kidney Pie, 110, *111*

Marinated London Broil, 35
Mexican Barbecued Top Round, *38*, 39
Mustard and Pepper, 9, 45
and Onions for Two, 9, 42
Round Steak and Kidney Beans, 10, 95
Sauerbraten-Style Steak Strips, 10, 84
with Tangy Herb Butter, 9, 44
Stewing, 82
   in clay pots, 100
   as moist-heat cooking, 6
   in the oven, 93
   in slow cookers, 98
Stews
   beef
      Beef and Eggplant Sauté, 85
      Beef Baked in Beer, 100
      Beef Rolls Provençale, 88
      Braised Eye of Round Steaks, 9, 86
      Burgundy Beef, 9, 82
      Caraway Beef Paprika, 84
      Curried Oxtails in Clay, 101
      Kentucky Burgoo, 84-85
      Mexican Short Ribs, 89
      Oven Beef, 94
      Piedmontese Pot Roast, 99
      Pot au Feu, 86, *87*
      Rosemary Round Steak, 99
      Sauerbraten-Style Steak Strips, 84
      Savory Braised Beef Shanks, 82
      Slow-Cooker Corned Beef and Lentils,
         99
      Spicy Alsatian Meat and Vegetable, 96
   chicken
      Chicken and Lentils in Clay, *100*, 101
      Chicken Arlésienne, 88
      Chicken, Hunter's Style, 91
      Country Captain, 97
      Gascon Beans and Chicken Gizzards,
         96-97
      Kentucky Burgoo, 84-85
      Singapore Chicken, 96
      Yankee Clipper Chicken, 98
   lamb
      Fruited Lamb Curry, *90*, 91
      Kentucky Burgoo, 84-85
      Lamb Shanks with Honey and Spices,
         93
      Sautéed Lamb with Spring Vegetables,
         92
      Spicy Alsatian Meat and Vegetable, 96
   pork
      Country-Style Spareribs in Ratatouille,
         98
      Kentucky Burgoo, 84-85
      Mexican Pork with Green Chiles,
         86-87
      Rich Red Spareribs, 95
      Savory Oven Pork, 95
      Spicy Alsatian Meat and Vegetable, 96
   veal
      Italian Veal Shanks in Tomato Sauce,
         101
      Kentucky Burgoo, 84-85
      Spicy Alsatian Meat and Vegetable
         Stew, 96
      Veal Breast Braised with Tarragon, 92

Veal Stew with Fresh Peas, *80*, 92
Stir-frying, 42, 56–57
Gingered Flank Steak with Snow Peas, 56–57
Lamb with Five-Spice and Green Onions, 56
Pork with Tofu, 56
Szechwan Chicken and Peanuts, 57
Stock, 9, 13
Storing frozen soups, 71
Storing meat and poultry, 12, 13
Stroganoff, Beef, 9
Stuffed Green Peppers Mexicana, 109
Stuffed Lamb Shoulder Provençale, 22
Stuffed Mushroom Caps, 21
Stuffed Pasta with Tomato Sauce, 105
Stuffed Zucchini Provençale, 107
Stuffings
Cornbread, for Roast Turkey, 29
Ground Beef and Spinach, for veal, 24
ham, pork, and olive, for lamb, 22
Sausage, for Roast Chicken, 28
Swedish Yellow Split Pea Soup, 66
Sweet-and-Sour Chicken Wings, 53
Swiss steak cuts, 10
Swiss-Style Skewered Liver and Bacon, 32
Syrup, Honey and Rose Water, for Baklava, 113
Szechwan Chicken and Peanuts, 57

T
Tangy Marinated Roast Pork Butt, 24
Tangy Sauce, 32
T-bone steak, 6, 8
Tenderizing meat, 6
marinades for, 19
by pounding, 88
by stewing, 82
Teriyaki Marinade, 41
Thawing meats and poultry, 12–13
Tofu, Pork with, 56
Tomato Barbecue Sauce, 41
with Barbecued Pork Buns, 35
Tomato-Rice Casserole, 39
Tomato Sauce
Garden Fresh Spaghetti Sauce, 104
Stuffed Pasta with, 105
Top-of-the-range cooking. *See* Skillet dishes; Stir-frying; Top-of-the-range stews
Top-of-the-range stews, 82–92
Beef and Eggplant Sauté, 85
Beef Rolls Provençale, 88
Braised Eye of Round Steaks, 9, 86
Burgundy Beef Stew, 83
Caraway Beef Paprika, 84
Chicken Arlésienne, 88
Chicken, Hunter's Style, 91
Fruited Lamb Curry, *90*, 91
Joyce's New Orleans Red Beans and Rice, 91
Kentucky Burgoo, 84–85
Mexican Pork with Green Chiles, 86–87
Mexican Short Ribs, 89
Pot au Feu, 86, *87*
Sauerbraten-Style Steak Strips, 10, 84
Sautéed Lamb with Spring Vegetables, 92
Savory Braised Beef Shanks, 82
Veal Breast Braised with Tarragon, 92
Veal Stew with Fresh Peas, *80*, 92
Tortillas
corn, in Turkey Enchiladas, 119
flour, warming, 86
Traditional English Pork Pies, 110, *111*
Turkey
See also Poultry
breast
boning, 55
Golden Turkey Breast Parmigiana, 55
Turkey Enchiladas, 119
cutting up, 10
Goodbye-to-the-Thanksgiving-Turkey Soup, 71
gravy, 28
ground
in Crêpes Cannelloni, 122
Ground Turkey Lasagne, 120
Harvest Turkey Loaf, 21
legs, in Turkey and Barley Soup, 77
roast, 18, 29
thawing, 10
Turkey and Barley Soup Supper, 76–77

U
United States Department of Agriculture (USDA) meat grades, 7, 9

V
Veal
See also Meats
buying, 6, 8
boneless roast
Italian Veal Sauté, 49
Veal Stew with Fresh Peas, *80*, 92
breast of, 6
Braised with Tarragon, 92
Spinach-Stuffed, 24
ground
Baked Veal Meatballs with Mushroom Sauce, 118
in Crêpes Cannelloni, 122
Harvest Veal Loaf, 21
kidneys, in Sherry and Mustard Sauce, 49
roasting, 16, 18
shanks
Italian Veal Shanks in Tomato Sauce, 101
in Kentucky Burgoo, 84–85
in Spicy Alsatian Meat and Vegetable Stew, 96
stews
Italian Veal Shanks in Tomato Sauce, 101
Kentucky Burgoo, 84–85
Spicy Alsatian Meat and Vegetable Stew, 96
Veal Breast Braised with Tarragon, 92
Veal Stew with Fresh Peas, *80*, 92
Vegetable-Beef Soup, Milanese, 62–63
Velvety Chicken and Mushroom Soup, 72

W
White beans. *See* Beans
Wine, Easy Sangria, 39
Wrapping techniques, 12

Y
Yankee Clipper Chicken, 98

Z
Zucchini
Greek Meatball and Zucchini Soup, 70
marinated and barbecued, 40
Stuffed, Provençale, 107

U.S. Measure and Metric Measure Conversion Chart

		Formulas for Exact Measures			Rounded Measures for Quick Reference		
	Symbol	**When you know:**	**Multiply by**	**To find:**			
Mass (Weight)	oz	ounces	28.35	grams	1 oz		= 30 g
	lb	pounds	0.45	kilograms	4 oz		= 115 g
	g	grams	0.035	ounces	8 oz		= 225 g
	kg	kilograms	2.2	pounds	16 oz	= 1 lb	= 450 g
					32 oz	= 2 lb	= 900 g
					36 oz	= 2¼ lb	= 1,000 g (1 kg)
Volume	tsp	teaspoons	5.0	milliliters	¼ tsp	= 1/24 oz	= 1 ml
	tbsp	tablespoons	15.0	milliliters	½ tsp	= 1/12 oz	= 2 ml
	fl oz	fluid ounces	29.57	milliliters	1 tsp	= ⅙ oz	= 5 ml
	c	cups	0.24	liters	1 tbsp	= ½ oz	= 15 ml
	pt	pints	0.47	liters	1 c	= 8 oz	= 250 ml
	qt	quarts	0.95	liters	2 c (1 pt)	= 16 oz	= 500 ml
	gal	gallons	3.785	liters	4 c (1 qt)	= 32 oz	= 1 l.
	ml	milliliters	0.034	fluid ounces	4 qt (1 gal)	= 128 oz	= 3¾ l.
Length	in.	inches	2.54	centimeters	⅜ in.	= 1 cm	
	ft	feet	30.48	centimeters	1 in.	= 2.5 cm	
	yd	yards	0.9144	meters	2 in.	= 5 cm	
	mi	miles	1.609	kilometers	2½ in.	= 6.5 cm	
	km	kilometers	0.621	miles	12 in. (1 ft)	= 30 cm	
	m	meters	1.094	yards	1 yd	= 90 cm	
	cm	centimeters	0.39	inches	100 ft	= 30 m	
					1 mi	= 1.6 km	
Temperature	° F	Fahrenheit	5/9 (after subtracting 32)	Celsius	32° F	= 0° C	
					68 °F	= 20° C	
	° C	Celsius	9/5 (then add 32)	Fahrenheit	212° F	= 100° C	
Area	in.^{2}	square inches	6.452	square centimeters	1 in.^{2}	= 6.5 cm^2	
	ft^2	square feet	929.0	square centimeters	1 ft^2	= 930 cm^2	
	yd^2	square yards	8,361.0	square centimeters	1 yd^2	= 8,360 cm^2	
	a	acres	0.4047	hectares	1 a	= 4,050 m^2	